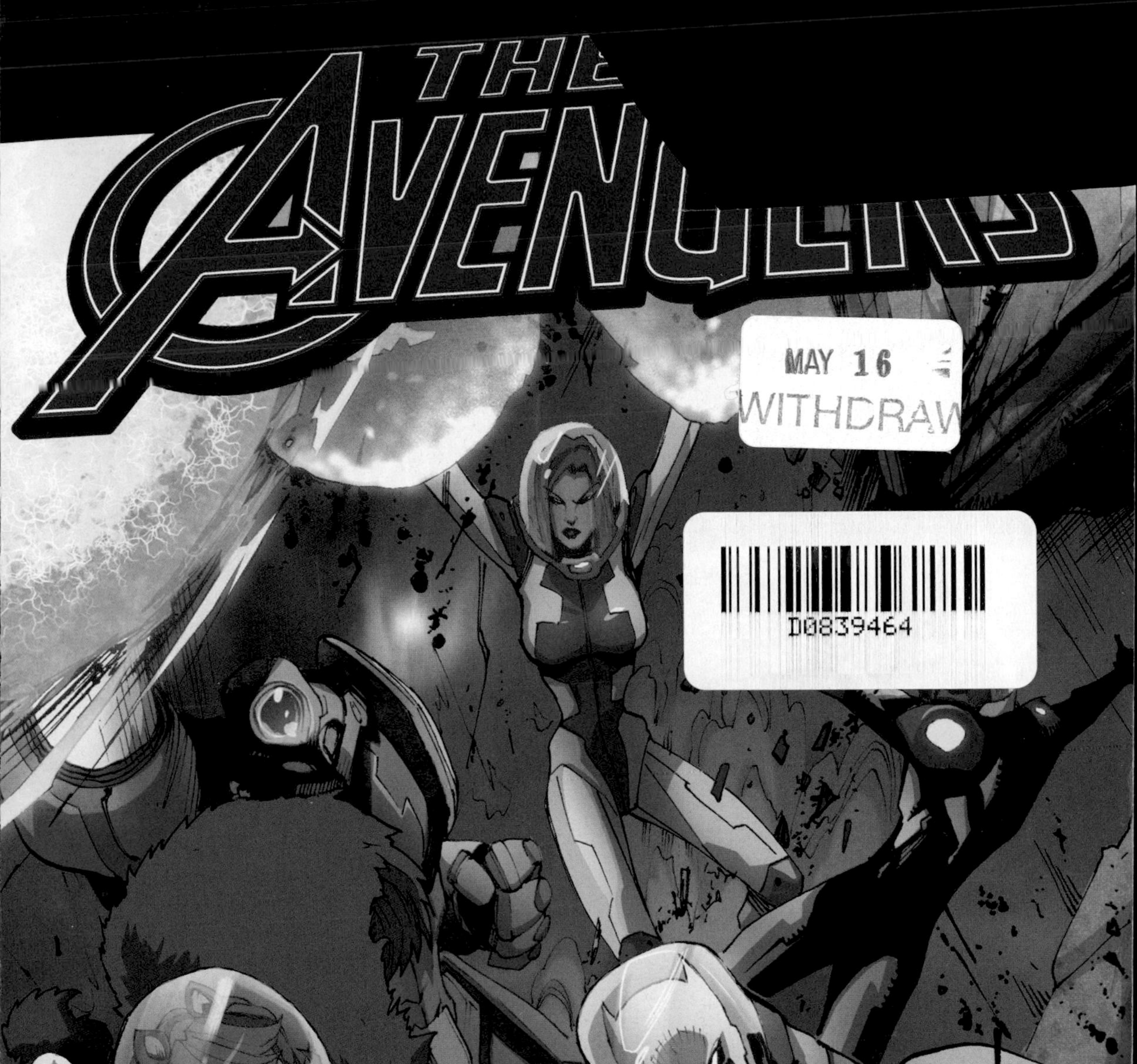
THE AVENGERS

Grafx New Ewing. A. Vol. 1

EVERYTHING IS **NEW**

WRITER: AL EWING

"EVERYTHING IS NEW"
(FROM *AVENGERS #0*)

ARTIST: GERARDO SANDOVAL

COLOR ARTIST: DONO SANCHEZ ALMARA

LETTERER: VC'S JOE CARAMAGNA

NEW AVENGERS #6

ARTIST: GERARDO SANDOVAL
COLOR ARTIST: DONO SANCHEZ ALAMARA

ART & COLOR, PP. 12-15: PHIL NOTO

PENCILER, PP. 19-20: MARK BAGLEY
INKER, PP. 19-20: SCOTT HANNA

LETTERER: VC'S JOE CARAMAGNA

COVER ART: MATT RHODES

NEW AVENGERS #1-5

ARTIST: GERARDO SANDOVAL

COLOR ARTIST: DONO SANCHEZ ALMARA

LETTERERS: VC'S JOE CARAMAGNA (#1-2, #4),
CLAYTON COWLES (#3)
& CHRIS ELIOPOULOS (#5)

COVER ART: GERARDO SANDOVAL (#1-4)
WITH MATTHEW WILSON (#1),
DAVID CURIEL (#2-3) & DONO SANCHEZ ALMARA (#4)
AND OSCAR JIMENEZ (#5)

ASSISTANT EDITOR: ALANNA SMITH

EDITORS: TOM BREVOORT WITH WIL MOSS

AVENGERS CREATED BY **STAN LEE** & **JACK KIRBY**

COLLECTION EDITOR: **JENNIFER GRÜNWALD**
ASSOCIATE EDITOR: **SARAH BRUNSTAD**
ASSOCIATE MANAGING EDITOR: **ALEX STARBUCK**
EDITOR, SPECIAL PROJECTS: **MARK D. BEAZLEY**
VP, PRODUCTION & SPECIAL PROJECTS: **JEFF YOUNGQUIST**
SVP PRINT, SALES & MARKETING: **DAVID GABRIEL**
BOOK DESIGN: **JAY BOWEN**

EDITOR IN CHIEF: **AXEL ALONSO**
CHIEF CREATIVE OFFICER: **JOE QUESADA**
PUBLISHER: **DAN BUCKLEY**
EXECUTIVE PRODUCER: **ALAN FINE**

NEW AVENGERS: A.I.M. VOL. 1 — EVERYTHING IS NEW. Contains material originally published in magazine form as NEW AVENGERS #1-6 and AVENGERS #0. First printing 2016. ISBN# 978-0-7851-9648-8. Published by MARVEL WORLDWIDE, INC., a subsidiary of MARVEL ENTERTAINMENT, LLC. OFFICE OF PUBLICATION: 135 West 50th Street, New York, NY 10020. Copyright © 2016 MARVEL No similarity between any of the names, characters, persons, and/o institutions in this magazine with those of any living or dead person or institution is intended, and any such similarity which may exist is purely coincidental. **Printed in the U.S.A.** ALAN FINE, President, Marvel Entertainment; DAN BUCKLEY President, TV, Publishing & Brand Management; JOE QUESADA, Chief Creative Officer; TOM BREVOORT, SVP of Publishing; DAVID BOGART, SVP of Business Affairs & Operations, Publishing & Partnership; C.B. CEBULSKI, VP of Brand Management & Development, Asia; DAVID GABRIEL, SVP of Sales & Marketing, Publishing; JEFF YOUNGQUIST, VP of Production & Special Projects; DAN CARR, Executive Director of Publishing Technology; ALEX MORALES, Director of Publishing Operations SUSAN CRESPI, Production Manager; STAN LEE, Chairman Emeritus. For information regarding advertising in Marvel Comics or on Marvel.com, please contact Vit DeBellis, Integrated Sales Manager, at vdebellis@marvel.com. For Marvel subscription inquiries, please call 888-511-5480. **Manufactured between 2/26/2016 and 4/4/2016 by R.R. DONNELLEY, INC., SALEM, VA, USA.**

10 9 8 7 6 5 4 3 2 1

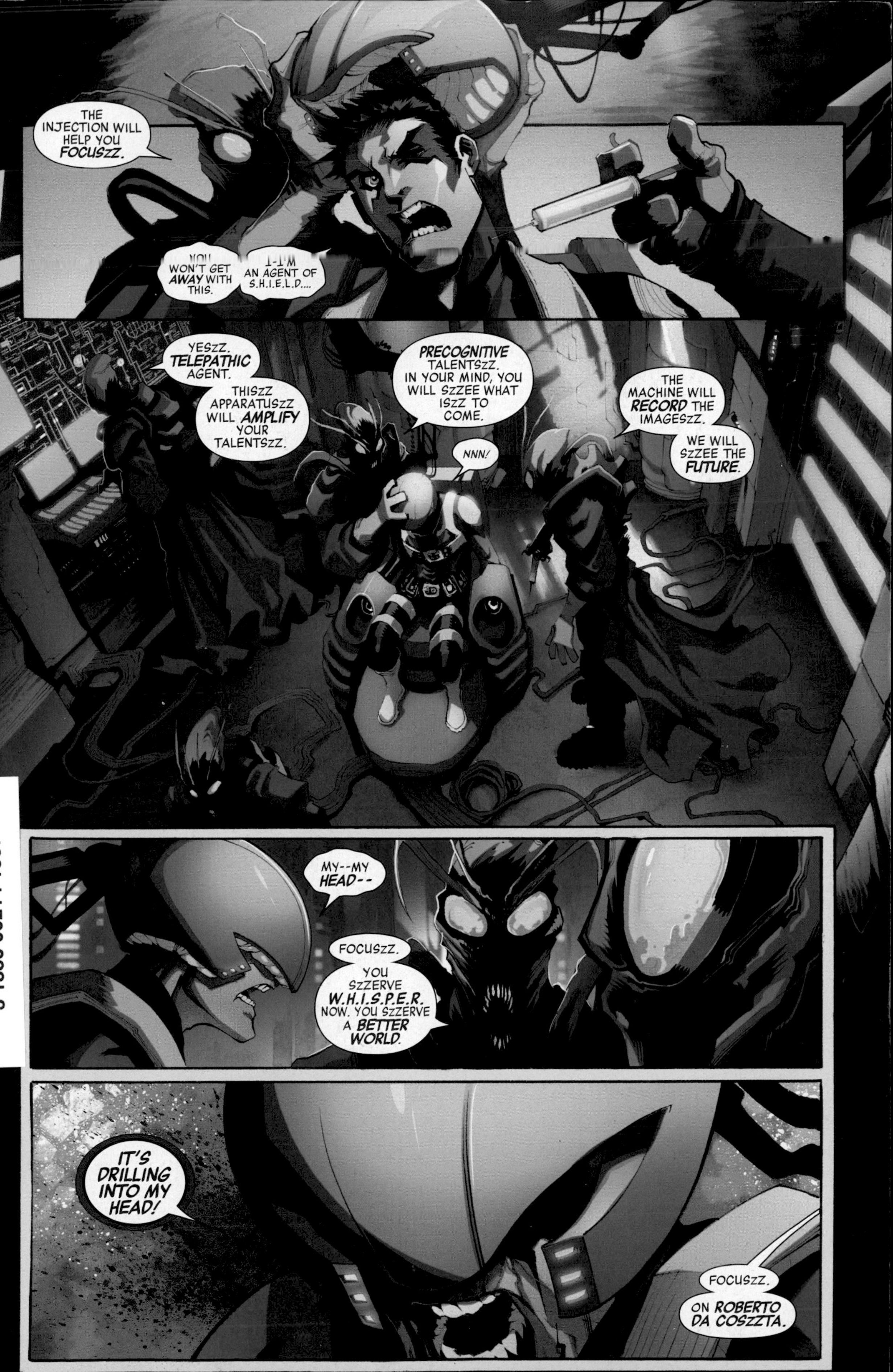
THE INJECTION WILL HELP YOU FOCUSzz.
YOU WON'T GET AWAY WITH THIS.
I-I'M AN AGENT OF S.H.I.E.L.D....
YESzz. TELEPATHIC AGENT.
THISzz APPARATUSzz WILL AMPLIFY YOUR TALENTSzz.
PRECOGNITIVE TALENTSzz. IN YOUR MIND, YOU WILL SzZEE WHAT ISzz TO COME.
NNN!
THE MACHINE WILL RECORD THE IMAGESzz.
WE WILL SzZEE THE FUTURE.
MY--MY HEAD--
FOCUSzz.
YOU SzZERVE W.H.I.S.P.E.R. NOW. YOU SzZERVE A BETTER WORLD.
IT'S DRILLING INTO MY HEAD!
FOCUSzz.
ON ROBERTO DA COSzZTA.

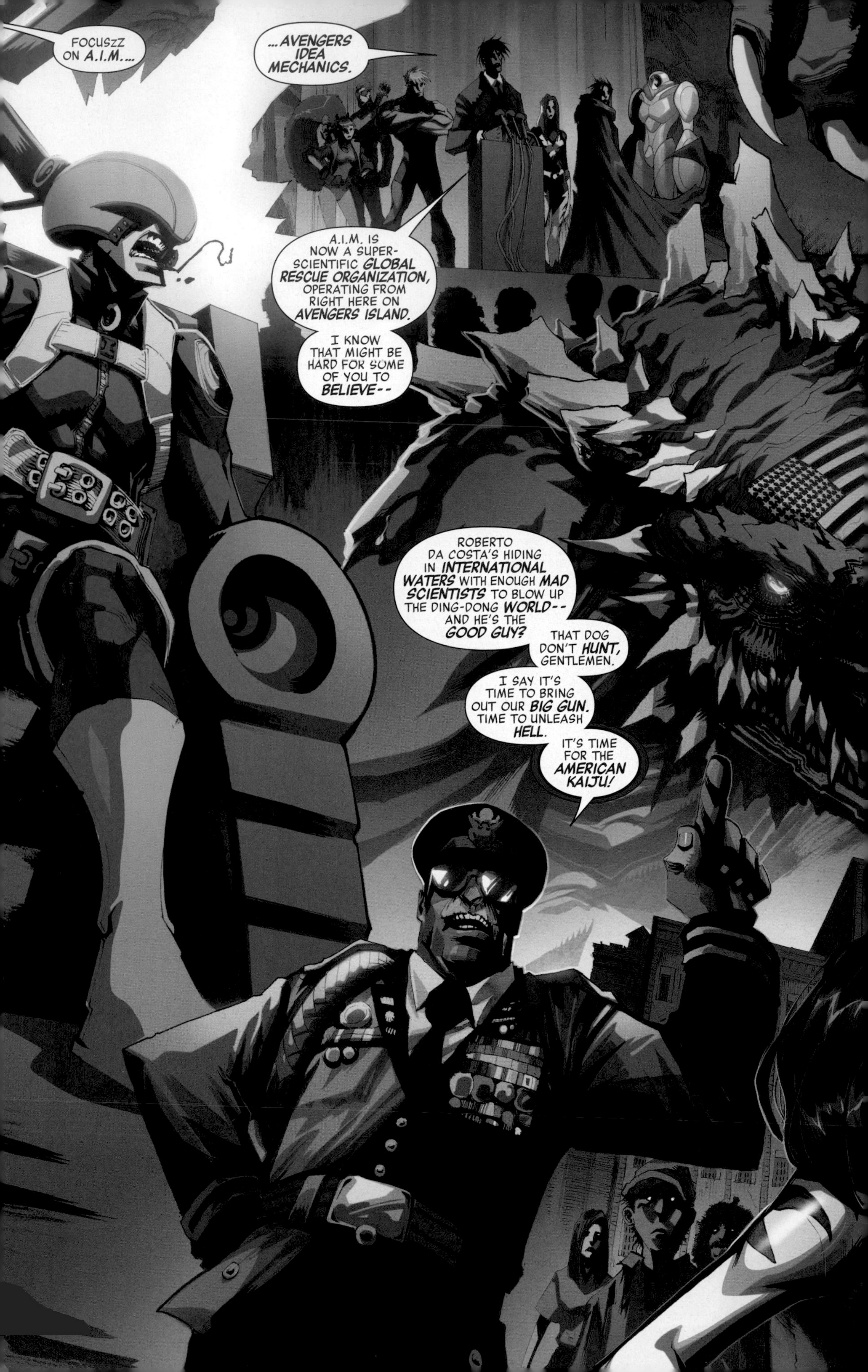
FOCUSZZ ON A.I.M....
...AVENGERS IDEA MECHANICS.
A.I.M. IS NOW A SUPER-SCIENTIFIC GLOBAL RESCUE ORGANIZATION, OPERATING FROM RIGHT HERE ON AVENGERS ISLAND.
I KNOW THAT MIGHT BE HARD FOR SOME OF YOU TO BELIEVE--
ROBERTO DA COSTA'S HIDING IN INTERNATIONAL WATERS WITH ENOUGH MAD SCIENTISTS TO BLOW UP THE DING-DONG WORLD--AND HE'S THE GOOD GUY?
THAT DOG DON'T HUNT, GENTLEMEN.
I SAY IT'S TIME TO BRING OUT OUR BIG GUN. TIME TO UNLEASH HELL.
IT'S TIME FOR THE AMERICAN KAIJU!

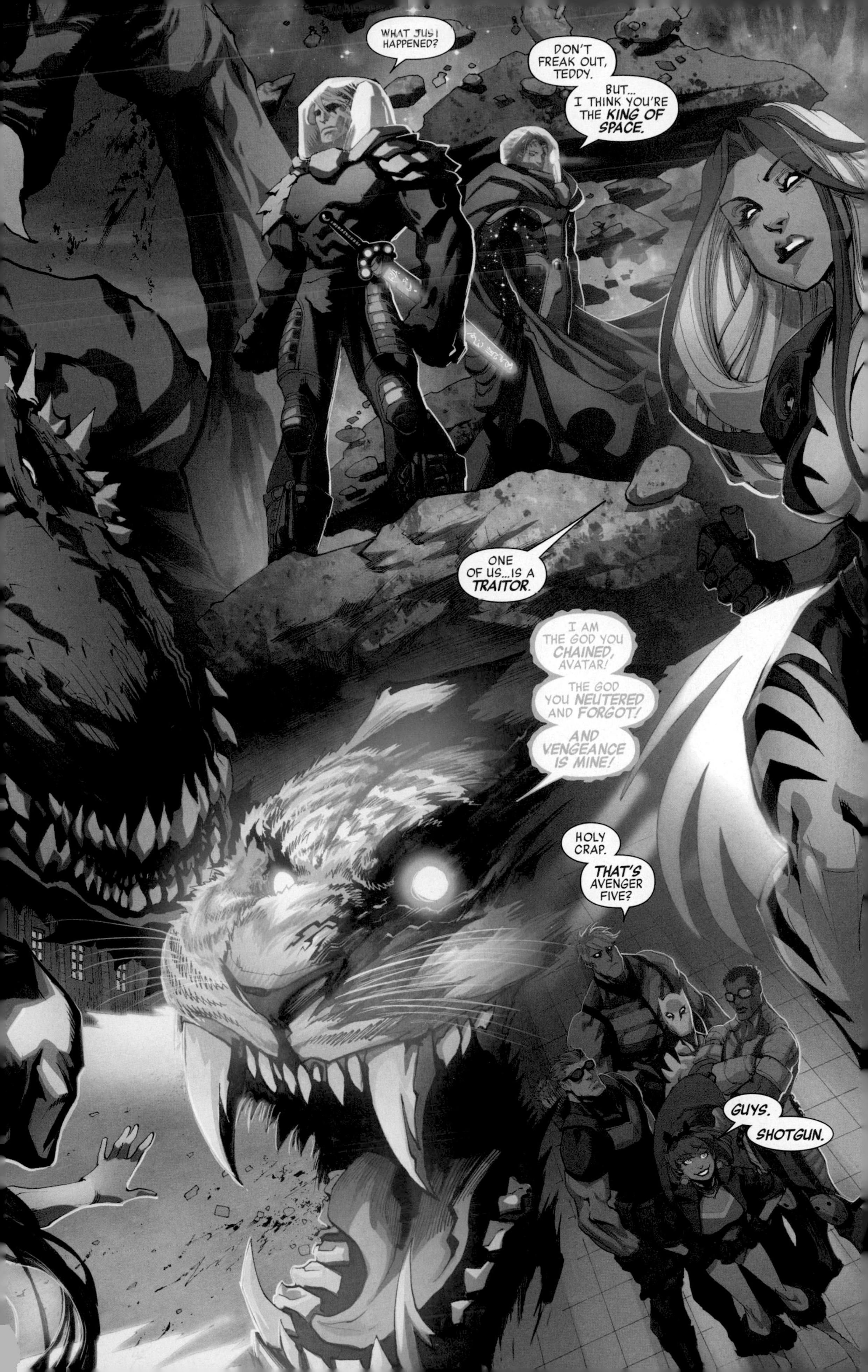
WHAT JUST HAPPENED?
DON'T FREAK OUT, TEDDY.
BUT... I THINK YOU'RE THE KING OF SPACE.
ONE OF US...IS A TRAITOR.
I AM THE GOD YOU CHAINED, AVATAR!
THE GOD YOU NEUTERED AND FORGOT!
AND VENGEANCE IS MINE!
HOLY CRAP.
THAT'S AVENGER FIVE?
GUYS.
SHOTGUN.

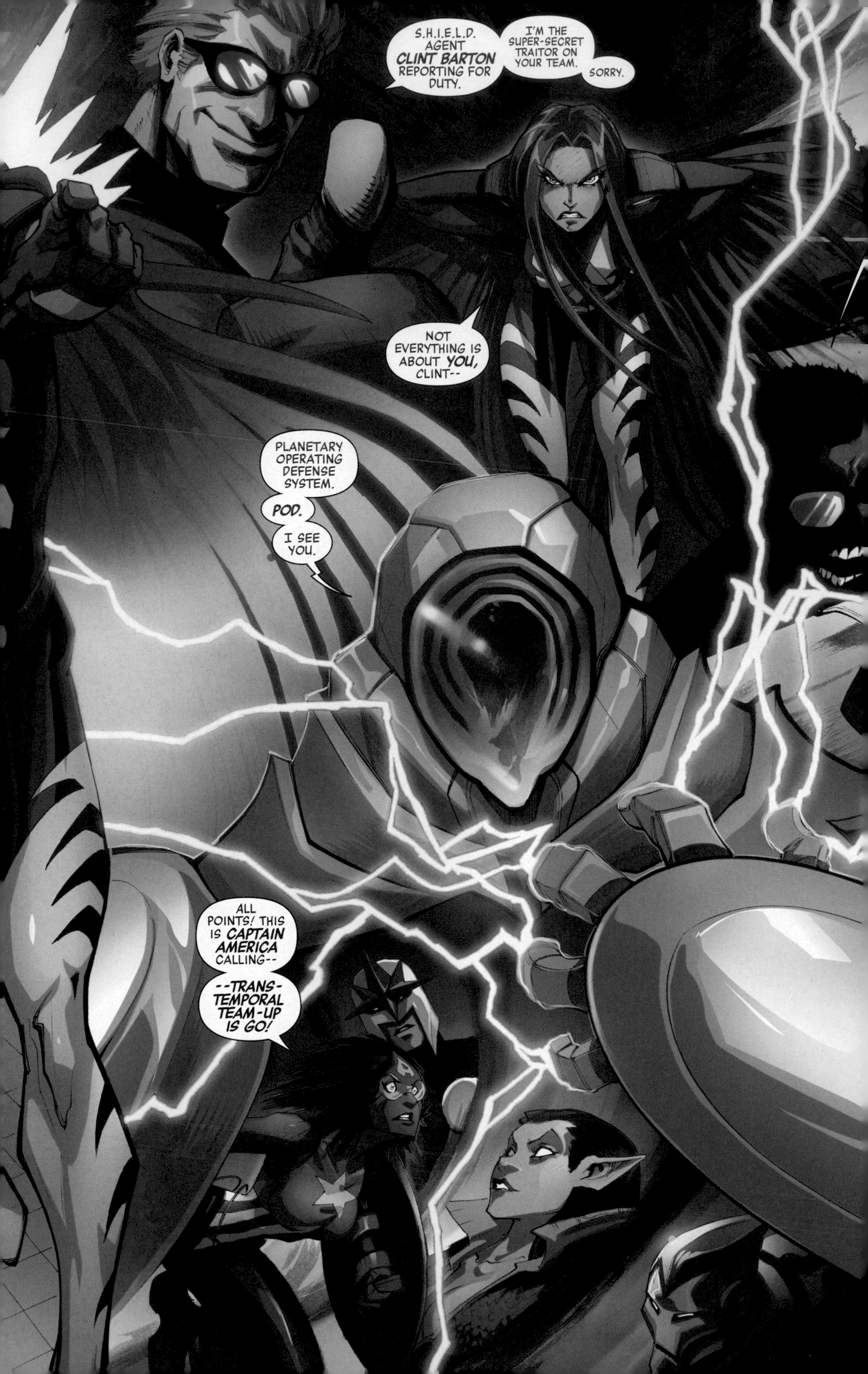
S.H.I.E.L.D. AGENT CLINT BARTON REPORTING FOR DUTY.
I'M THE SUPER-SECRET TRAITOR ON YOUR TEAM.
SORRY.
NOT EVERYTHING IS ABOUT YOU, CLINT--
PLANETARY OPERATING DEFENSE SYSTEM.
POD.
I SEE YOU.
ALL POINTS! THIS IS CAPTAIN AMERICA CALLING--
--TRANS-TEMPORAL TEAM-UP IS GO!

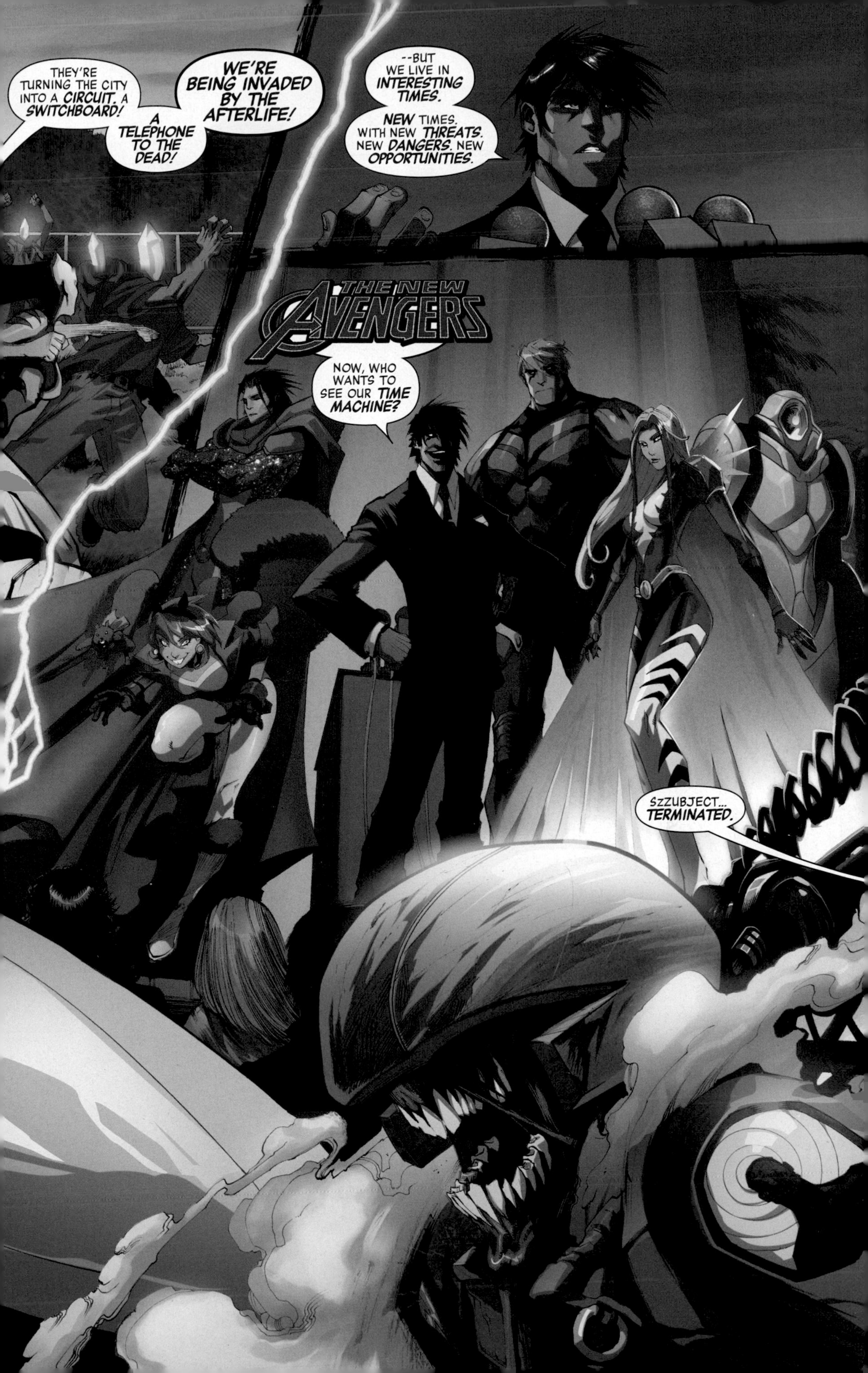
THEY'RE TURNING THE CITY INTO A CIRCUIT. A SWITCHBOARD!
A TELEPHONE TO THE DEAD!
WE'RE BEING INVADED BY THE AFTERLIFE!
--BUT WE LIVE IN INTERESTING TIMES.
NEW TIMES. WITH NEW THREATS. NEW DANGERS. NEW OPPORTUNITIES.
THE NEW AVENGERS
NOW, WHO WANTS TO SEE OUR TIME MACHINE?
SZZUBJECT... TERMINATED.

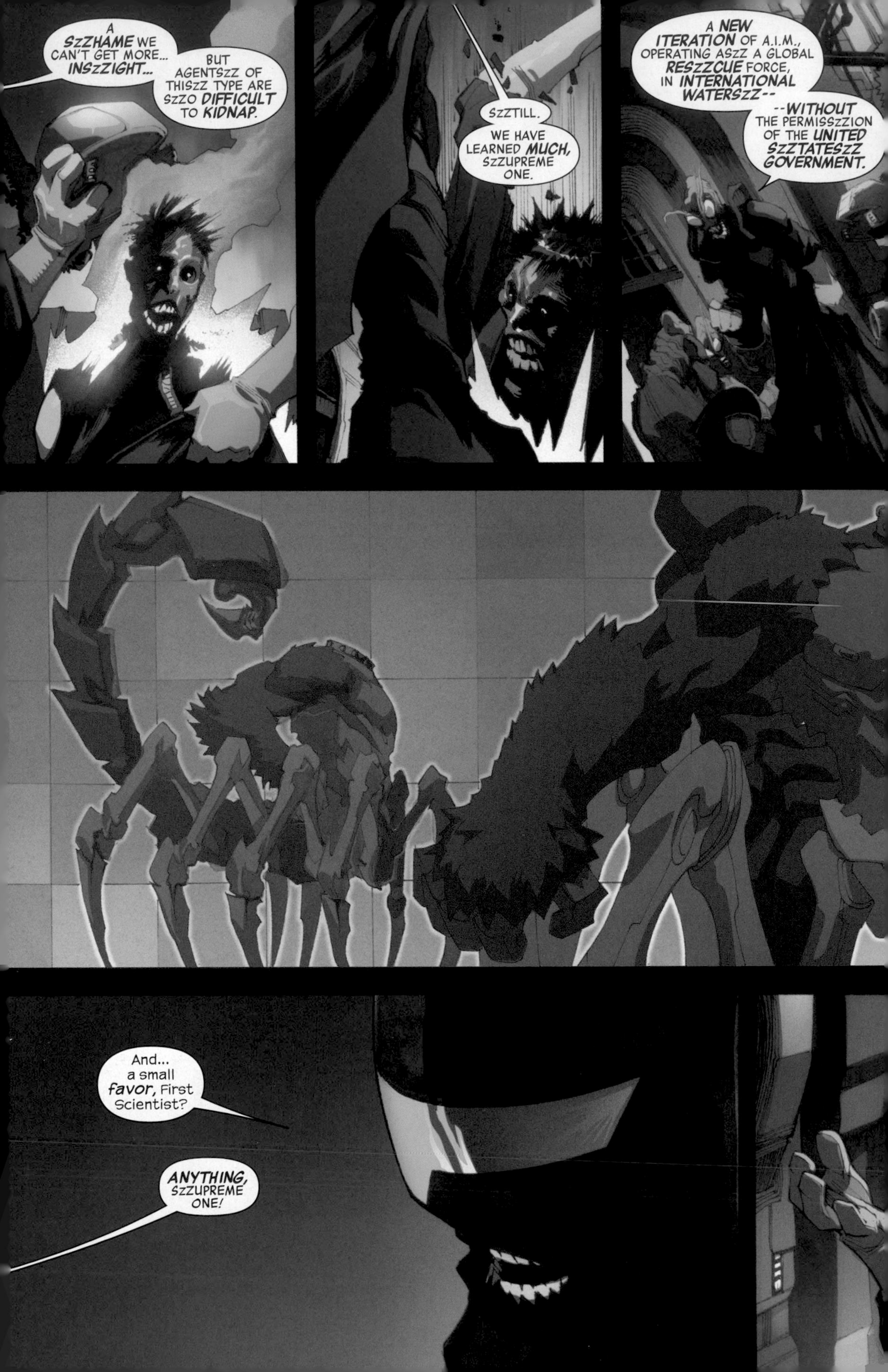
A SzZHAME WE CAN'T GET MORE... INSzZIGHT...
BUT AGENTSzZ OF THISzZ TYPE ARE SzZO DIFFICULT TO KIDNAP.
SzZTILL.
WE HAVE LEARNED MUCH, SzZUPREME ONE.
A NEW ITERATION OF A.I.M., OPERATING ASzZ A GLOBAL RESzZCUE FORCE, IN INTERNATIONAL WATERSzZ--
--WITHOUT THE PERMISSZZION OF THE UNITED SzZTATESzZ GOVERNMENT.
And... a small favor, First Scientist?
ANYTHING, SzZUPREME ONE!

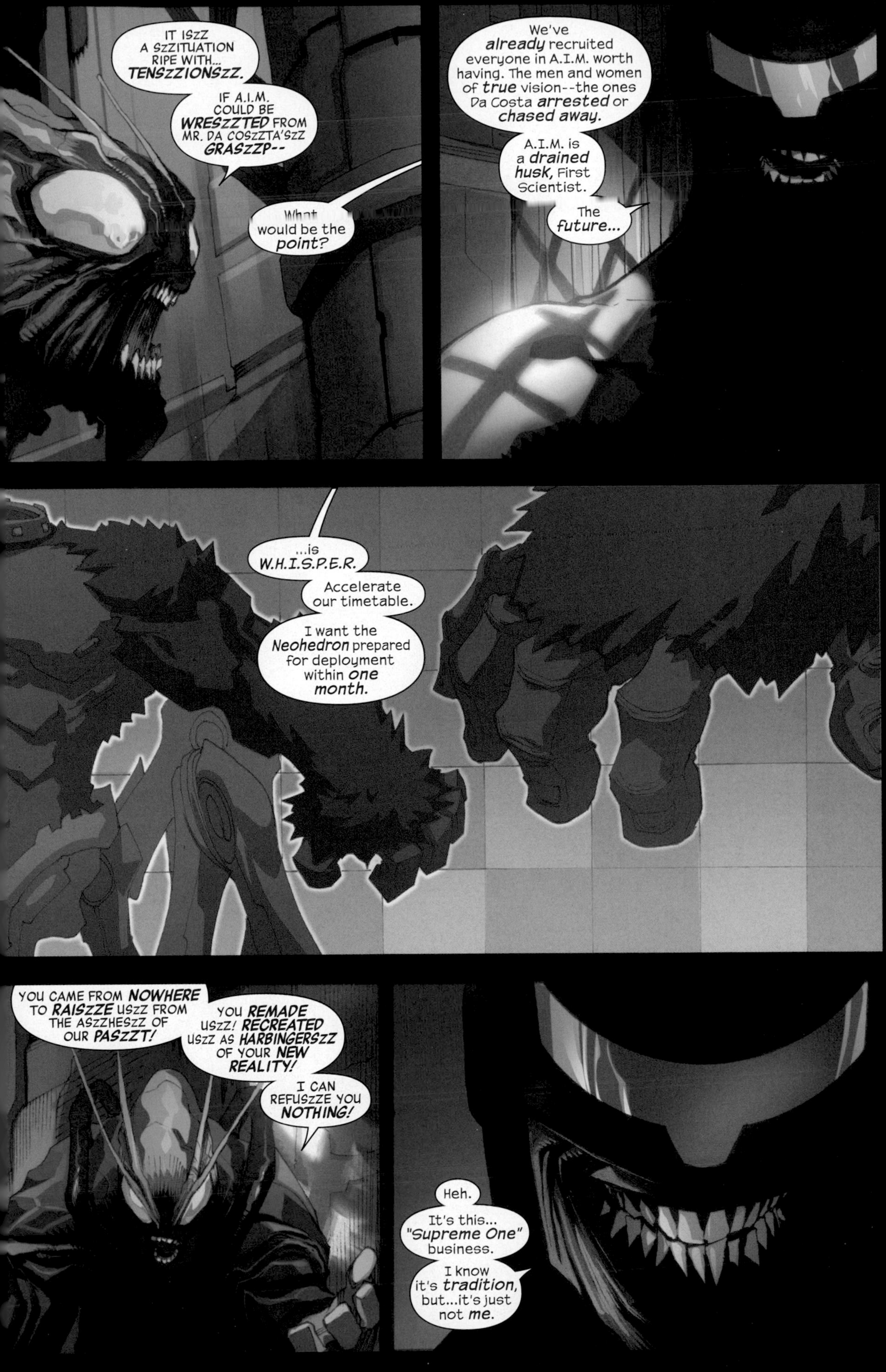
IT ISzZ A SzZITUATION RIPE WITH... TENSzZIONSzZ.
IF A.I.M. COULD BE WRESzZTED FROM MR. DA COSzZTA'SzZ GRASzZP--
What would be the point?
We've already recruited everyone in A.I.M. worth having. The men and women of true vision--the ones Da Costa arrested or chased away.
A.I.M. is a drained husk, First Scientist.
The future...
...is W.H.I.S.P.E.R.
Accelerate our timetable.
I want the Neohedron prepared for deployment within one month.
YOU CAME FROM NOWHERE TO RAISzZE USzZ FROM THE ASzZHESzZ OF OUR PASzZT!
YOU REMADE USzZ! RECREATED USzZ AS HARBINGERSzZ OF YOUR NEW REALITY!
I CAN REFUSzZE YOU NOTHING!
Heh.
It's this... "Supreme One" business.
I know it's tradition, but...it's just not me.

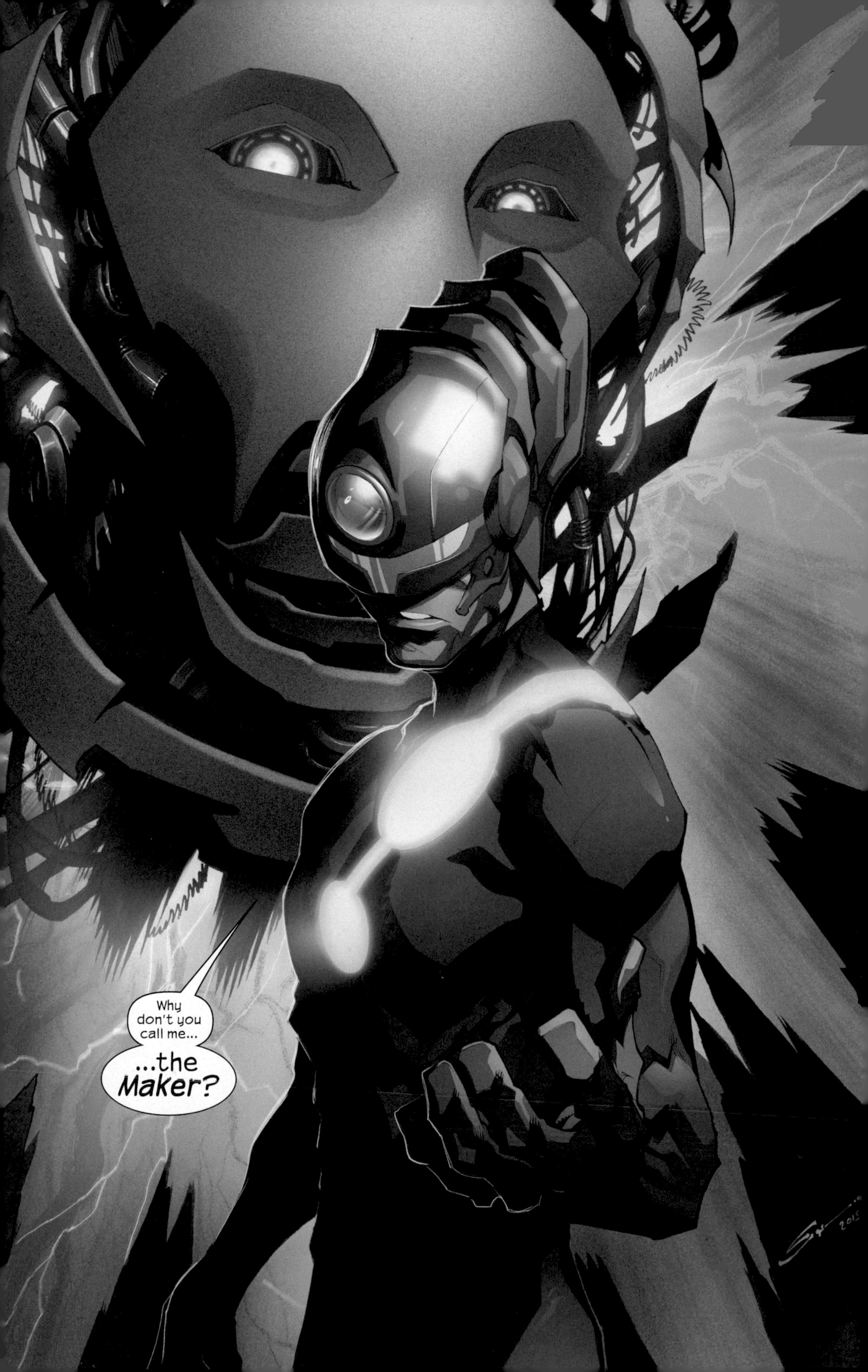
Why don't you call me...
...the Maker?

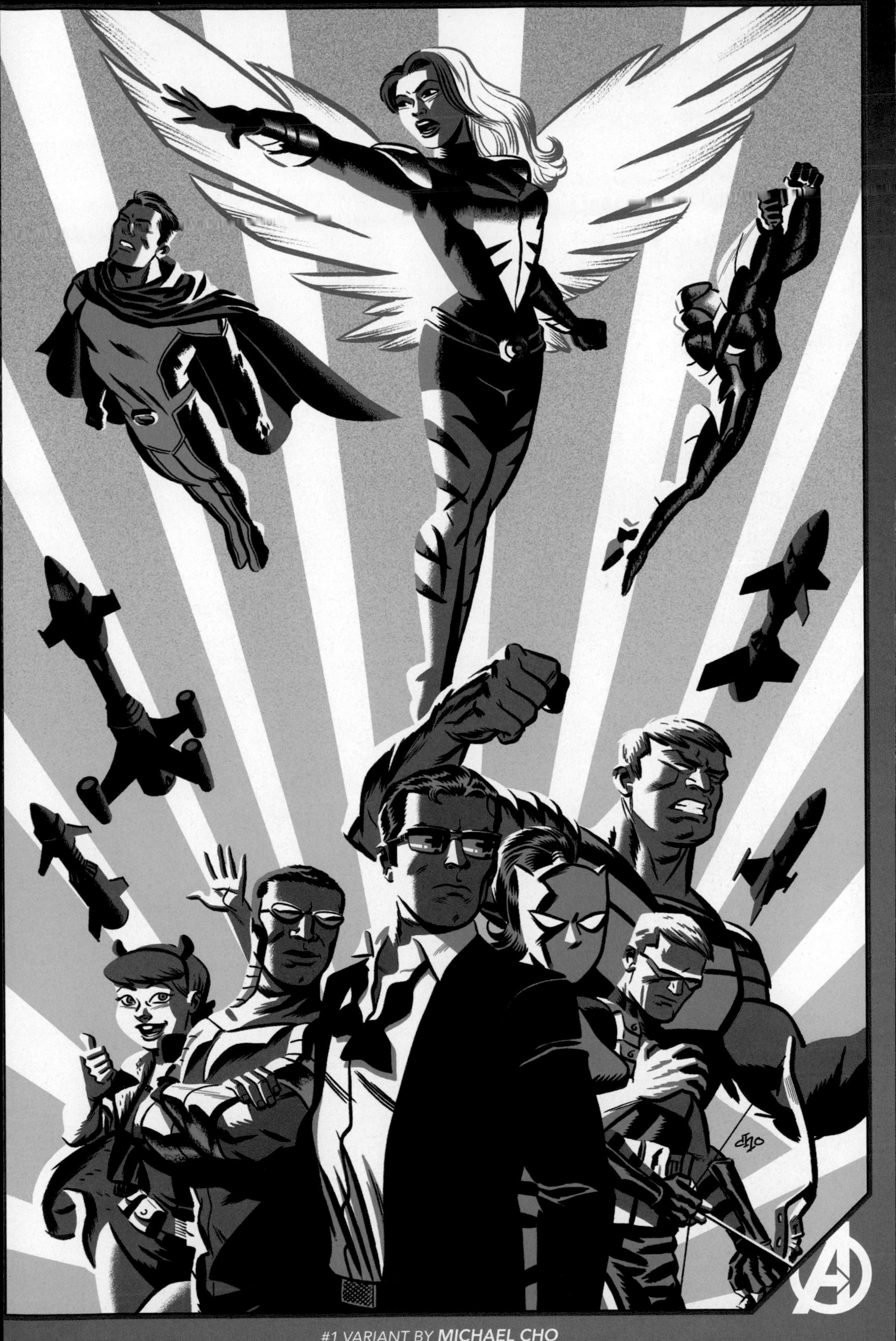
cho

#1 VARIANT BY **MICHAEL CHO**

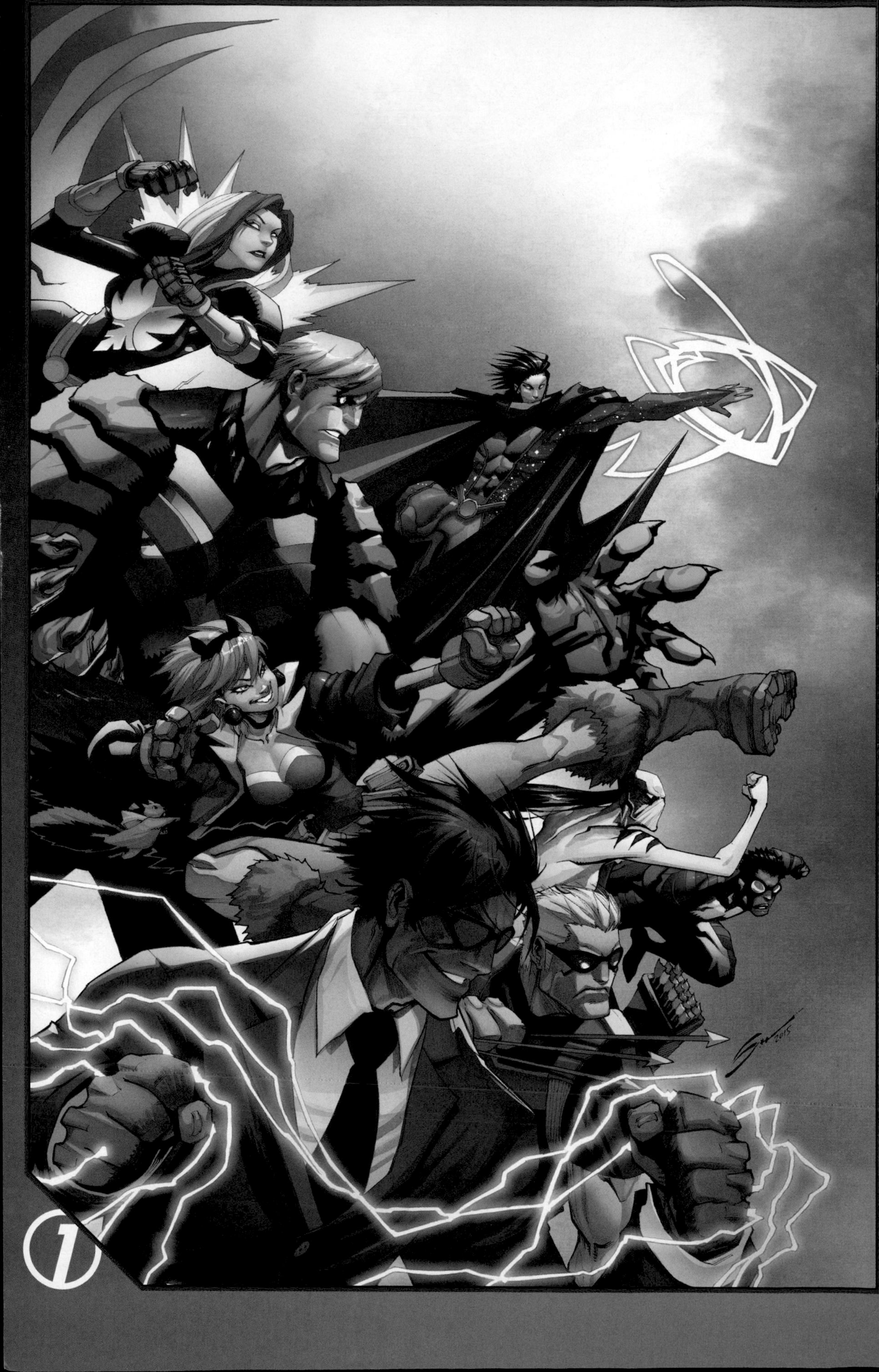

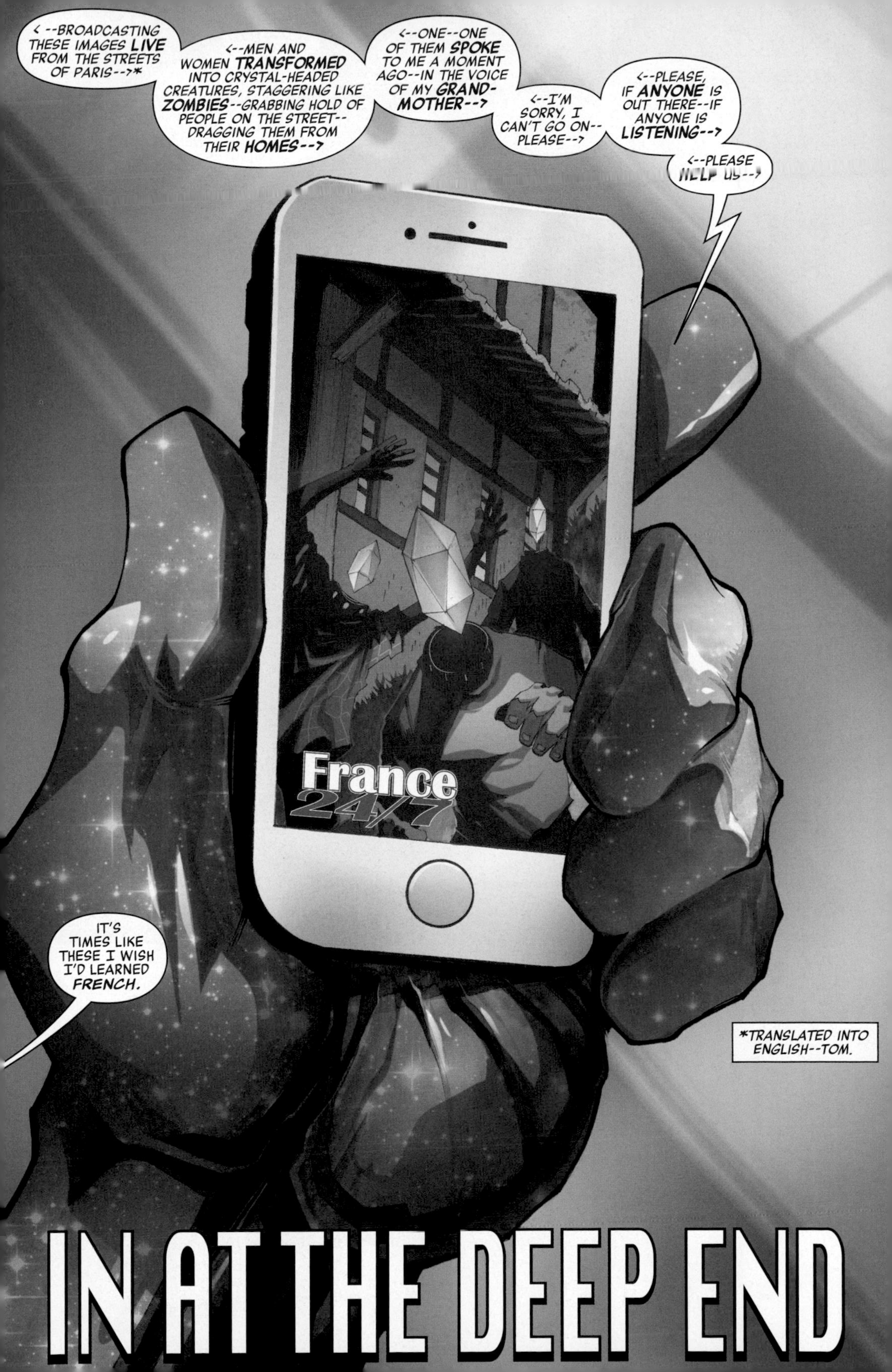

<--BROADCASTING THESE IMAGES LIVE FROM THE STREETS OF PARIS-->*
<--MEN AND WOMEN TRANSFORMED INTO CRYSTAL-HEADED CREATURES, STAGGERING LIKE ZOMBIES--GRABBING HOLD OF PEOPLE ON THE STREET--DRAGGING THEM FROM THEIR HOMES-->
<--ONE--ONE OF THEM SPOKE TO ME A MOMENT AGO--IN THE VOICE OF MY GRAND-MOTHER-->
<--I'M SORRY, I CAN'T GO ON--PLEASE-->
<--PLEASE, IF ANYONE IS OUT THERE--IF ANYONE IS LISTENING-->
<--PLEASE HELP US-->
France 24/7
IT'S TIMES LIKE THESE I WISH I'D LEARNED FRENCH.
*TRANSLATED INTO ENGLISH--TOM.
IN AT THE DEEP END

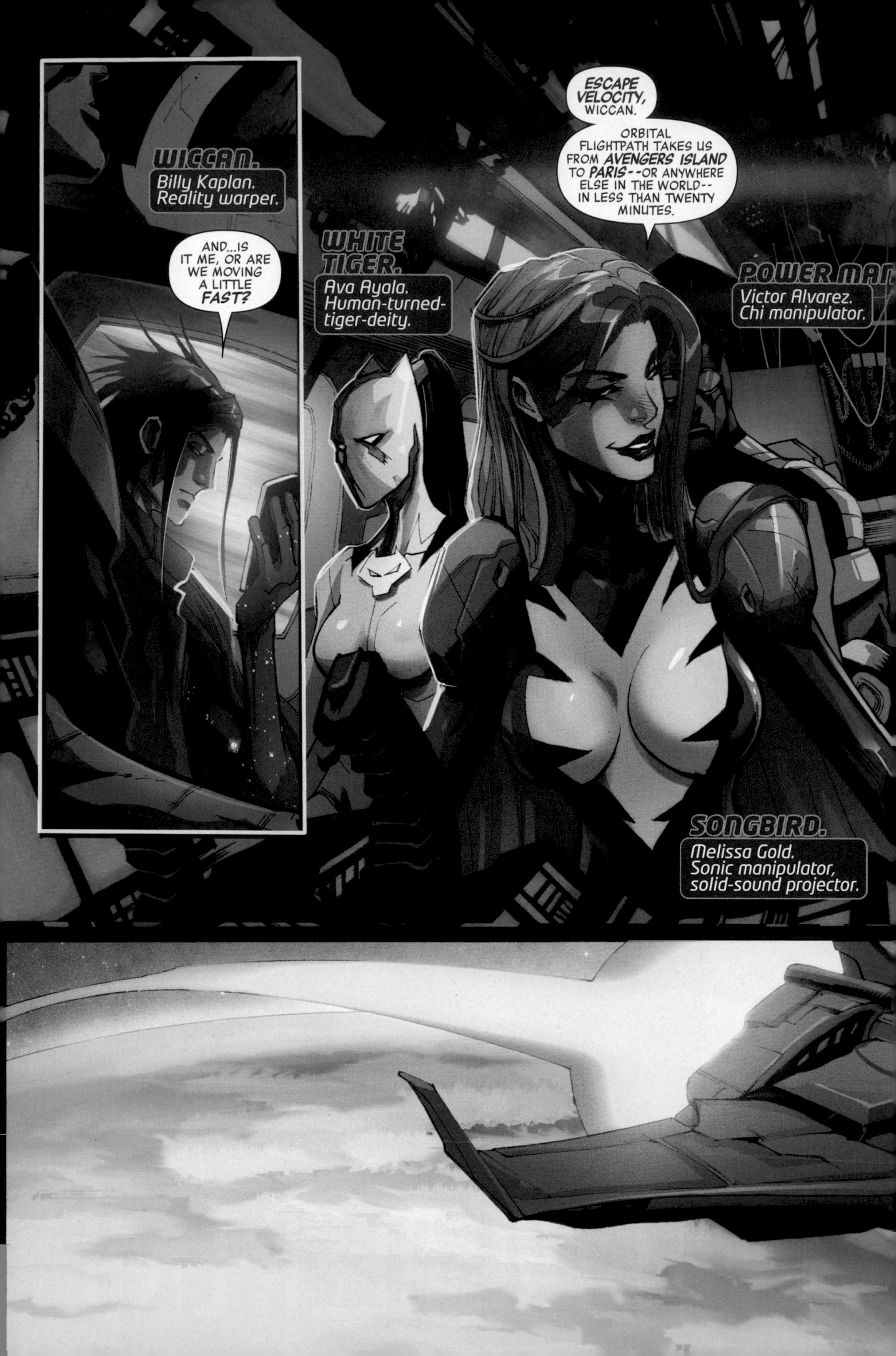
WICCAN.
Billy Kaplan. Reality warper.
AND...IS IT ME, OR ARE WE MOVING A LITTLE FAST?
WHITE TIGER.
Ava Ayala. Human-turned-tiger-deity.
ESCAPE VELOCITY, WICCAN.
ORBITAL FLIGHTPATH TAKES US FROM AVENGERS ISLAND TO PARIS--OR ANYWHERE ELSE IN THE WORLD--IN LESS THAN TWENTY MINUTES.
POWER MAN
Victor Alvarez. Chi manipulator.
SONGBIRD.
Melissa Gold. Sonic manipulator, solid-sound projector.

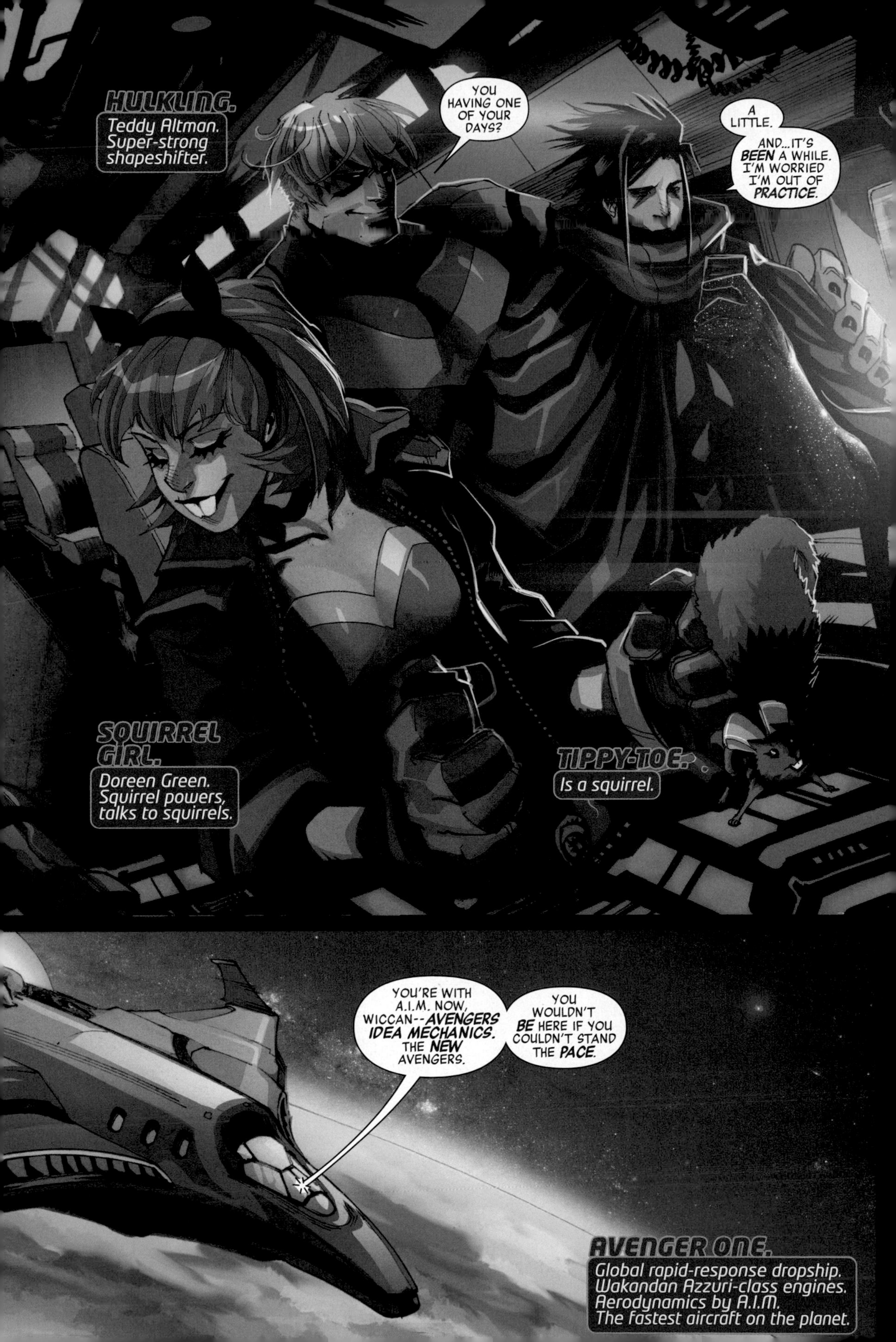
HULKLING.
Teddy Altman. Super-strong shapeshifter.
YOU HAVING ONE OF YOUR DAYS?
A LITTLE.
AND...IT'S BEEN A WHILE. I'M WORRIED I'M OUT OF PRACTICE.
SQUIRREL GIRL.
Doreen Green. Squirrel powers, talks to squirrels.
TIPPY-TOE.
Is a squirrel.
YOU'RE WITH A.I.M. NOW, WICCAN--AVENGERS IDEA MECHANICS. THE NEW AVENGERS.
YOU WOULDN'T BE HERE IF YOU COULDN'T STAND THE PACE.
AVENGER ONE.
Global rapid-response dropship. Wakandan Azzuri-class engines. Aerodynamics by A.I.M. The fastest aircraft on the planet.

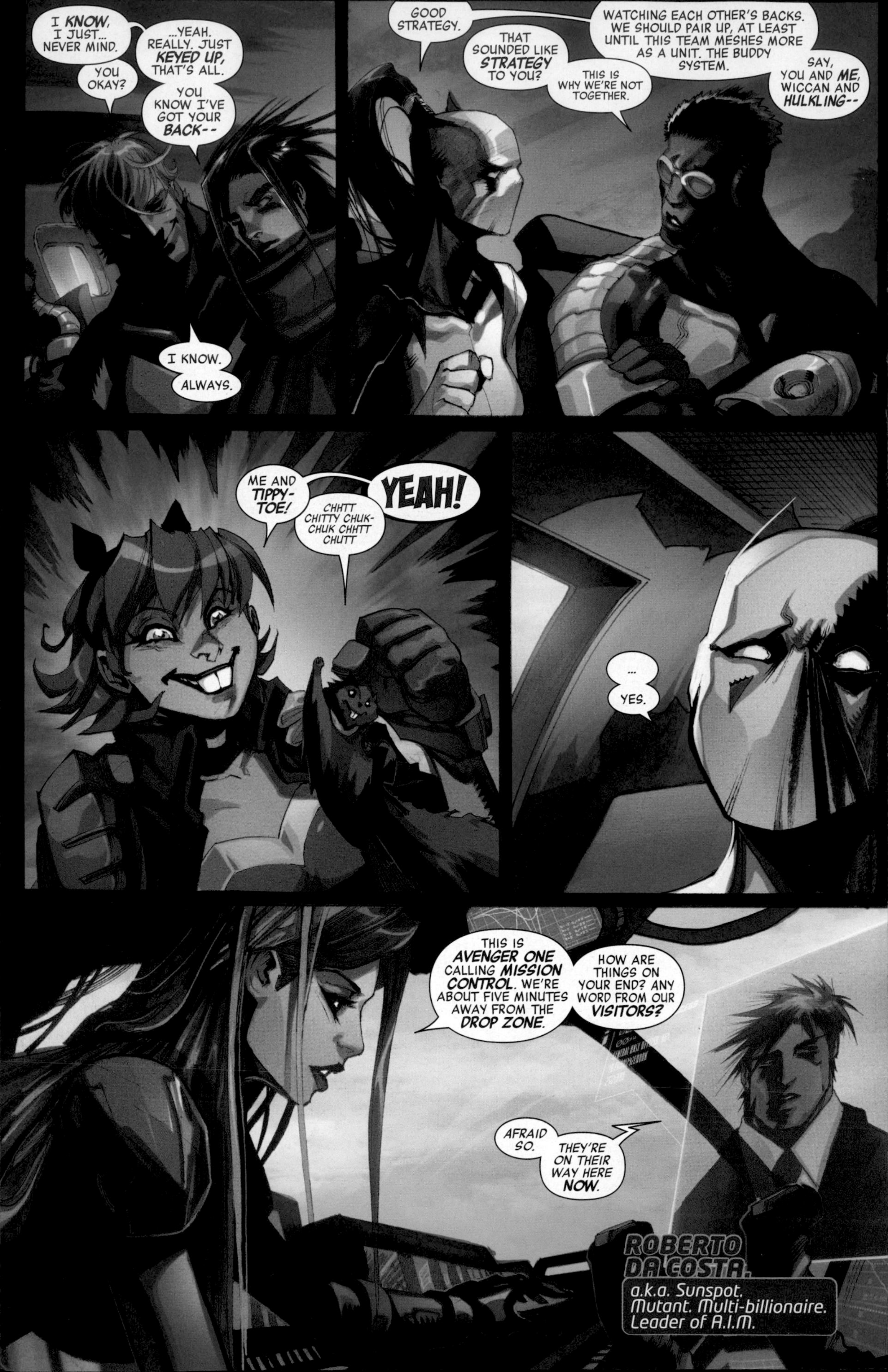
I KNOW, I JUST... NEVER MIND.
YOU OKAY?
...YEAH. REALLY. JUST KEYED UP, THAT'S ALL.
YOU KNOW I'VE GOT YOUR BACK--
I KNOW.
ALWAYS.
GOOD STRATEGY.
THAT SOUNDED LIKE STRATEGY TO YOU?
THIS IS WHY WE'RE NOT TOGETHER.
WATCHING EACH OTHER'S BACKS. WE SHOULD PAIR UP, AT LEAST UNTIL THIS TEAM MESHES MORE AS A UNIT. THE BUDDY SYSTEM.
SAY, YOU AND ME, WICCAN AND HULKLING--
ME AND TIPPY-TOE!
YEAH!
CHHTT CHITTY CHUK-CHUK CHHTT CHUTT
...
YES.
THIS IS AVENGER ONE CALLING MISSION CONTROL. WE'RE ABOUT FIVE MINUTES AWAY FROM THE DROP ZONE.
HOW ARE THINGS ON YOUR END? ANY WORD FROM OUR VISITORS?
AFRAID SO.
THEY'RE ON THEIR WAY HERE NOW.
ROBERTO DA COSTA.
a.k.a. Sunspot. Mutant. Multi-billionaire. Leader of A.I.M.

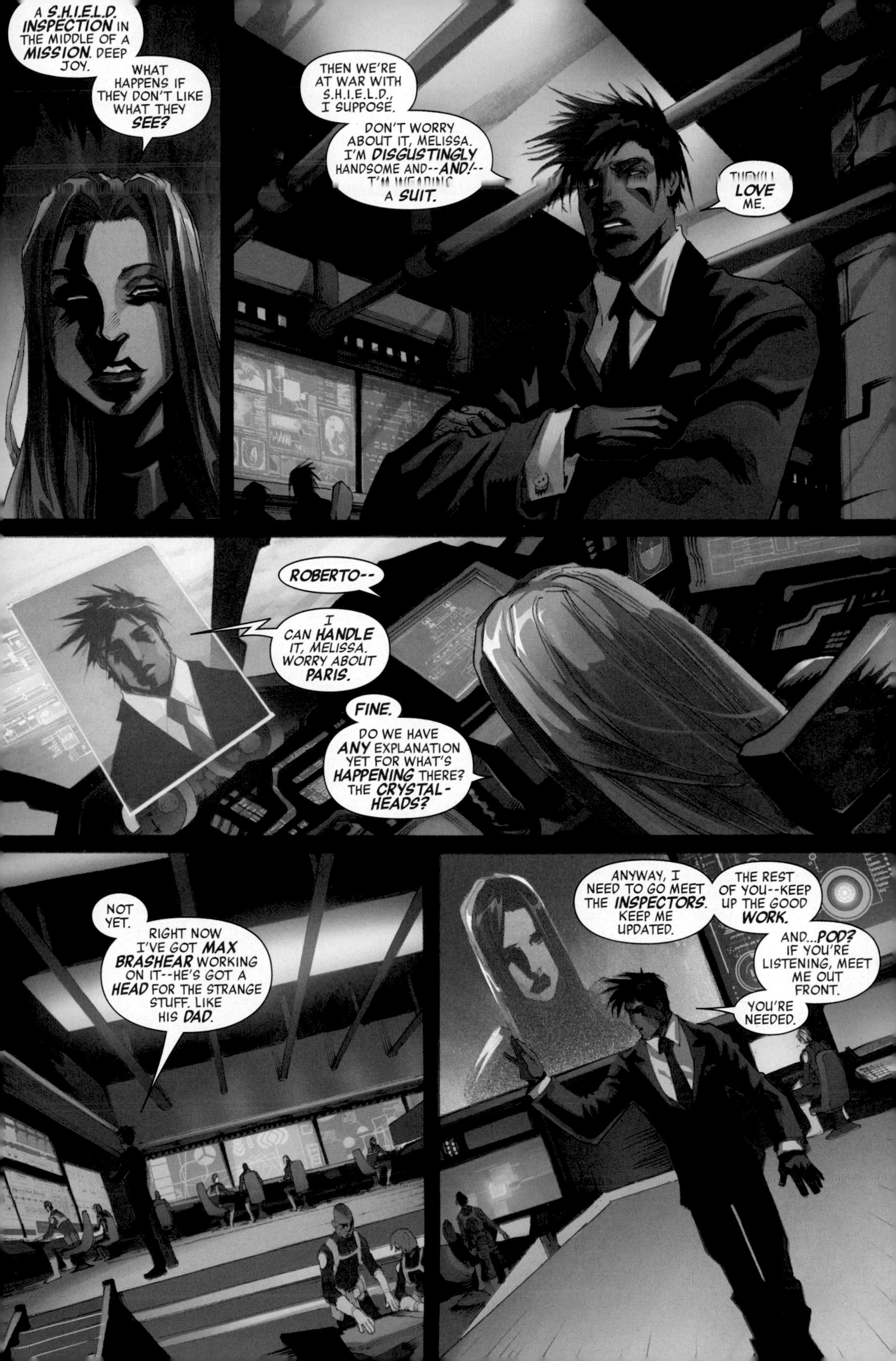
A S.H.I.E.L.D. INSPECTION IN THE MIDDLE OF A MISSION. DEEP JOY.
WHAT HAPPENS IF THEY DON'T LIKE WHAT THEY SEE?
THEN WE'RE AT WAR WITH S.H.I.E.L.D., I SUPPOSE.
DON'T WORRY ABOUT IT, MELISSA. I'M DISGUSTINGLY HANDSOME AND--AND!-- I'M WEARING A SUIT.
THEY'LL LOVE ME.
ROBERTO--
I CAN HANDLE IT, MELISSA. WORRY ABOUT PARIS.
FINE.
DO WE HAVE ANY EXPLANATION YET FOR WHAT'S HAPPENING THERE? THE CRYSTAL-HEADS?
NOT YET.
RIGHT NOW I'VE GOT MAX BRASHEAR WORKING ON IT--HE'S GOT A HEAD FOR THE STRANGE STUFF. LIKE HIS DAD.
ANYWAY, I NEED TO GO MEET THE INSPECTORS. KEEP ME UPDATED.
THE REST OF YOU--KEEP UP THE GOOD WORK.
AND...POD? IF YOU'RE LISTENING, MEET ME OUT FRONT.
YOU'RE NEEDED.

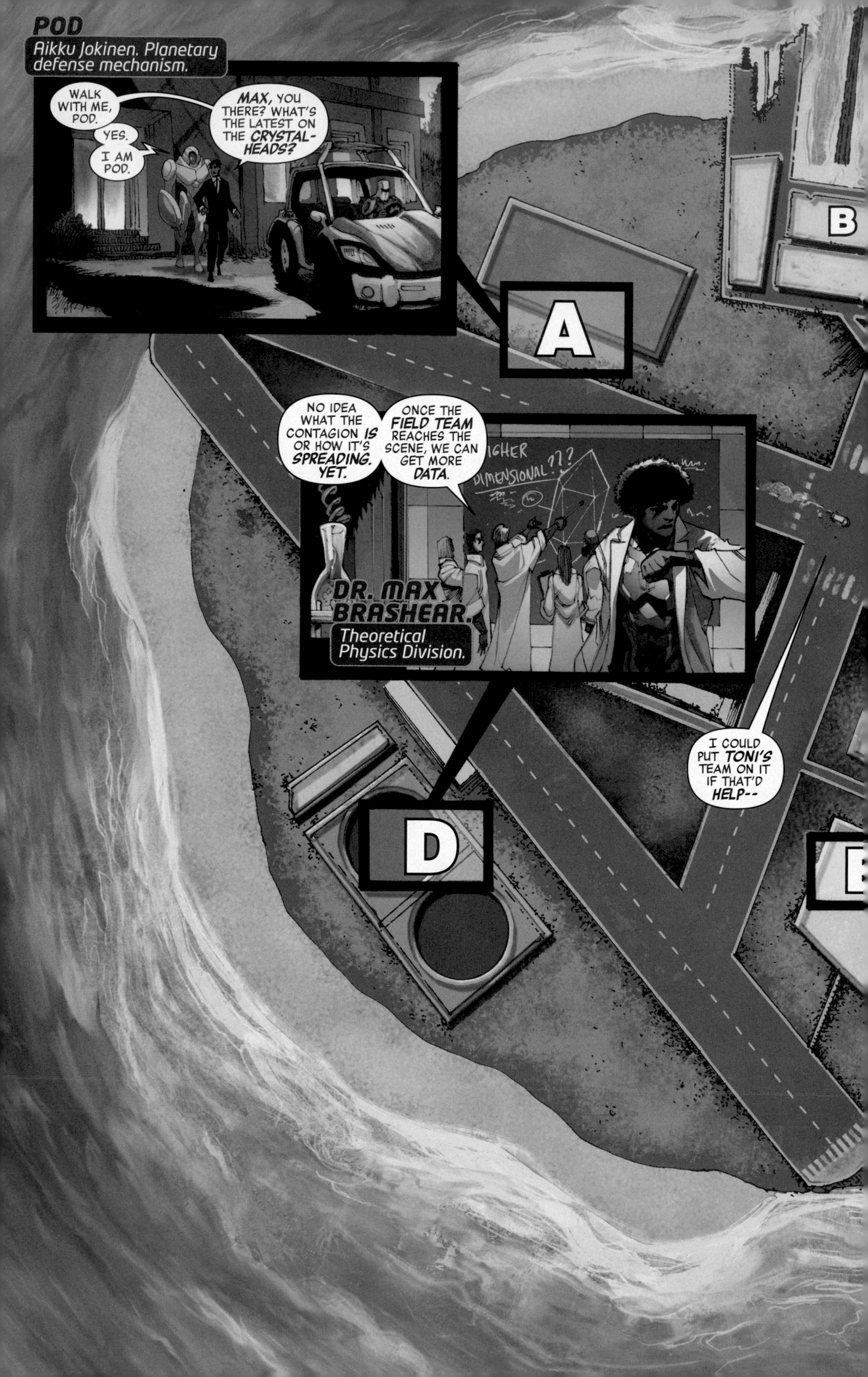
POD
Aikku Jokinen. Planetary defense mechanism.
WALK WITH ME, POD.
YES.
I AM POD.
MAX, YOU THERE? WHAT'S THE LATEST ON THE CRYSTAL-HEADS?
A
B
NO IDEA WHAT THE CONTAGION IS OR HOW IT'S SPREADING. YET.
ONCE THE FIELD TEAM REACHES THE SCENE, WE CAN GET MORE DATA.
HIGHER DIMENSIONAL???
DR. MAX BRASHEAR.
Theoretical Physics Division.
I COULD PUT TONI'S TEAM ON IT IF THAT'D HELP--
D
E

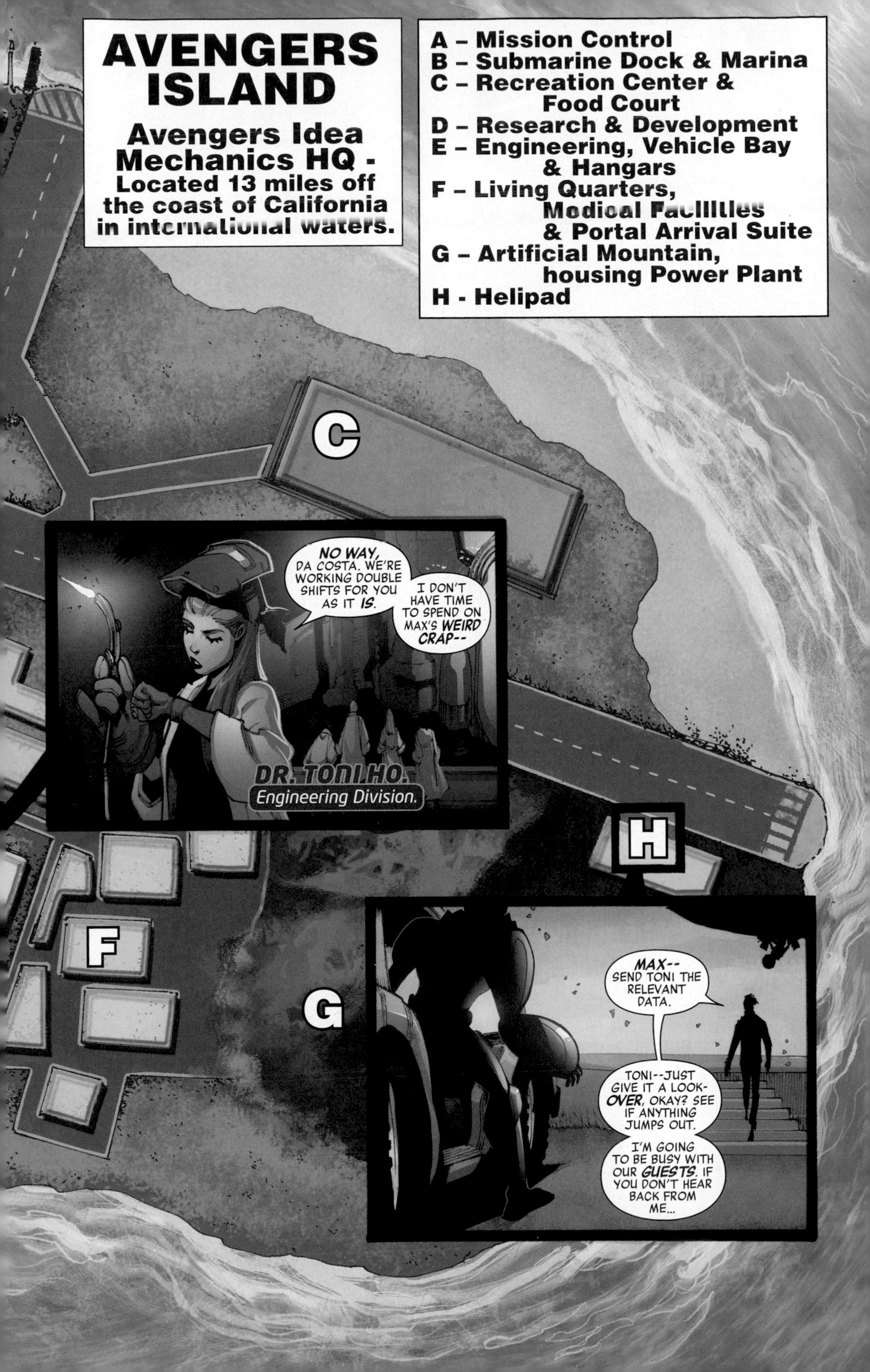

AVENGERS ISLAND
Avengers Idea Mechanics HQ - Located 13 miles off the coast of California in international waters.
A – Mission Control
B – Submarine Dock & Marina
C – Recreation Center & Food Court
D – Research & Development
E – Engineering, Vehicle Bay & Hangars
F – Living Quarters, Medical Facilities & Portal Arrival Suite
G – Artificial Mountain, housing Power Plant
H - Helipad
C
NO WAY, DA COSTA. WE'RE WORKING DOUBLE SHIFTS FOR YOU AS IT IS.
I DON'T HAVE TIME TO SPEND ON MAX'S WEIRD CRAP--
DR. TONI HO. Engineering Division.
H
F
G
MAX-- SEND TONI THE RELEVANT DATA.
TONI--JUST GIVE IT A LOOK-OVER, OKAY? SEE IF ANYTHING JUMPS OUT.
I'M GOING TO BE BUSY WITH OUR GUESTS. IF YOU DON'T HEAR BACK FROM ME...

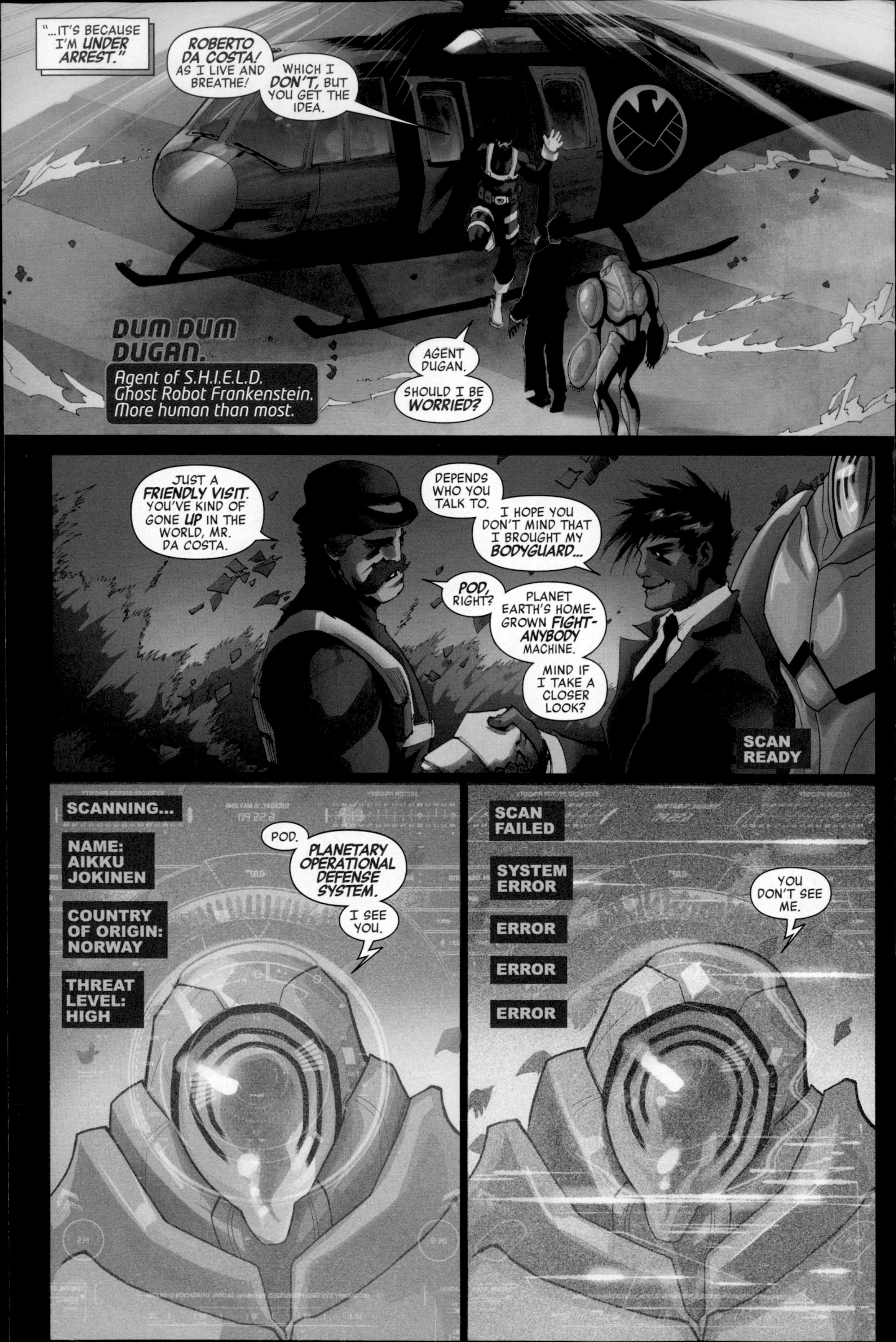

"...IT'S BECAUSE I'M UNDER ARREST."
ROBERTO DA COSTA! AS I LIVE AND BREATHE!
WHICH I DON'T, BUT YOU GET THE IDEA.
DUM DUM DUGAN.
Agent of S.H.I.E.L.D. Ghost Robot Frankenstein. More human than most.
AGENT DUGAN.
SHOULD I BE WORRIED?
JUST A FRIENDLY VISIT. YOU'VE KIND OF GONE UP IN THE WORLD, MR. DA COSTA.
DEPENDS WHO YOU TALK TO.
I HOPE YOU DON'T MIND THAT I BROUGHT MY BODYGUARD...
POD, RIGHT?
PLANET EARTH'S HOME-GROWN FIGHT-ANYBODY MACHINE.
MIND IF I TAKE A CLOSER LOOK?
SCAN READY
SCANNING...
NAME: AIKKU JOKINEN
COUNTRY OF ORIGIN: NORWAY
THREAT LEVEL: HIGH
POD.
PLANETARY OPERATIONAL DEFENSE SYSTEM.
I SEE YOU.
SCAN FAILED
SYSTEM ERROR
ERROR
ERROR
ERROR
YOU DON'T SEE ME.

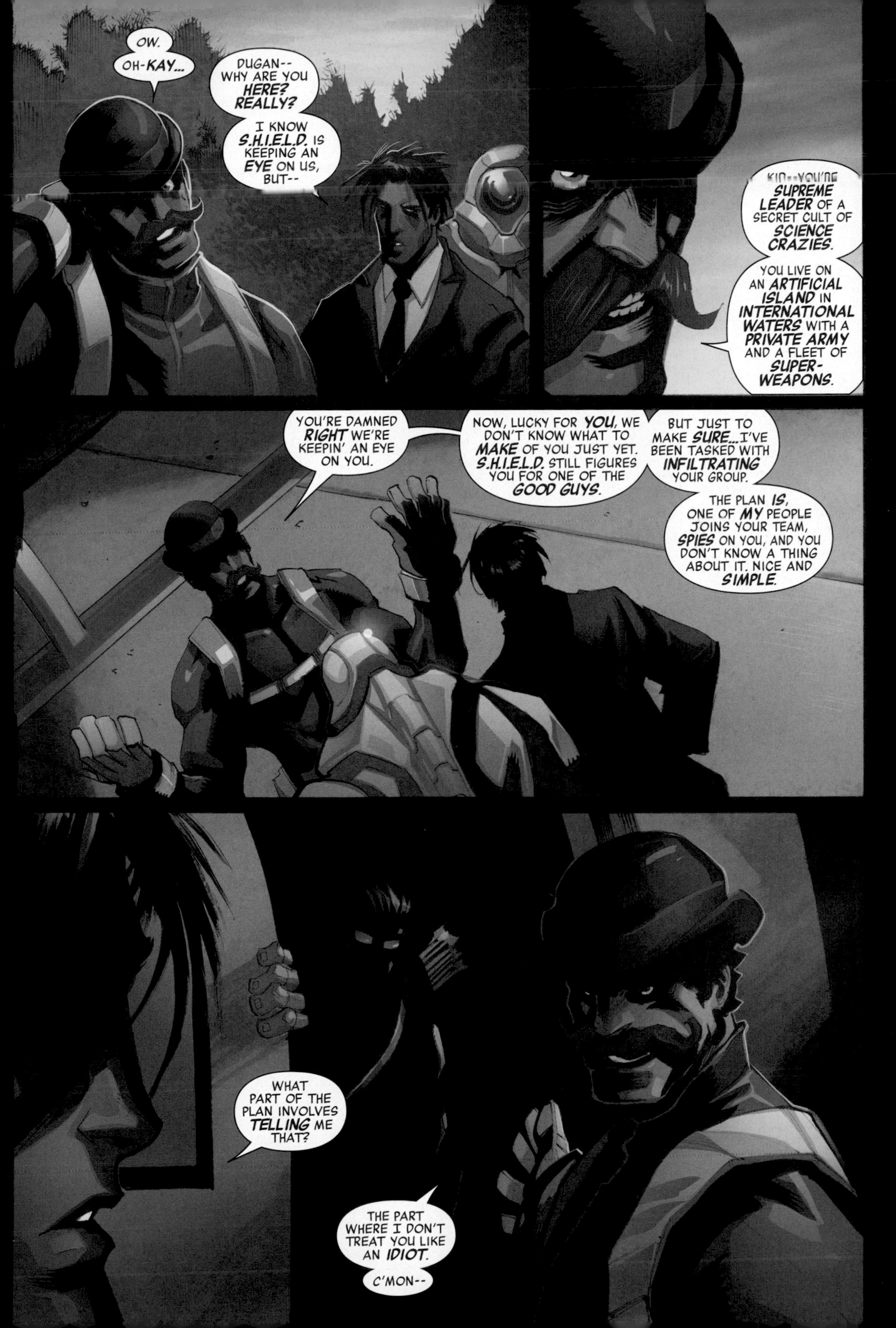
OW.
OH-KAY...
DUGAN-- WHY ARE YOU HERE? REALLY?
I KNOW S.H.I.E.L.D. IS KEEPING AN EYE ON US, BUT--
KID--YOU'RE SUPREME LEADER OF A SECRET CULT OF SCIENCE CRAZIES.
YOU LIVE ON AN ARTIFICIAL ISLAND IN INTERNATIONAL WATERS WITH A PRIVATE ARMY AND A FLEET OF SUPER-WEAPONS.
YOU'RE DAMNED RIGHT WE'RE KEEPIN' AN EYE ON YOU.
NOW, LUCKY FOR YOU, WE DON'T KNOW WHAT TO MAKE OF YOU JUST YET. S.H.I.E.L.D. STILL FIGURES YOU FOR ONE OF THE GOOD GUYS.
BUT JUST TO MAKE SURE...I'VE BEEN TASKED WITH INFILTRATING YOUR GROUP.
THE PLAN IS, ONE OF MY PEOPLE JOINS YOUR TEAM, SPIES ON YOU, AND YOU DON'T KNOW A THING ABOUT IT. NICE AND SIMPLE.
WHAT PART OF THE PLAN INVOLVES TELLING ME THAT?
THE PART WHERE I DON'T TREAT YOU LIKE AN IDIOT.
C'MON--

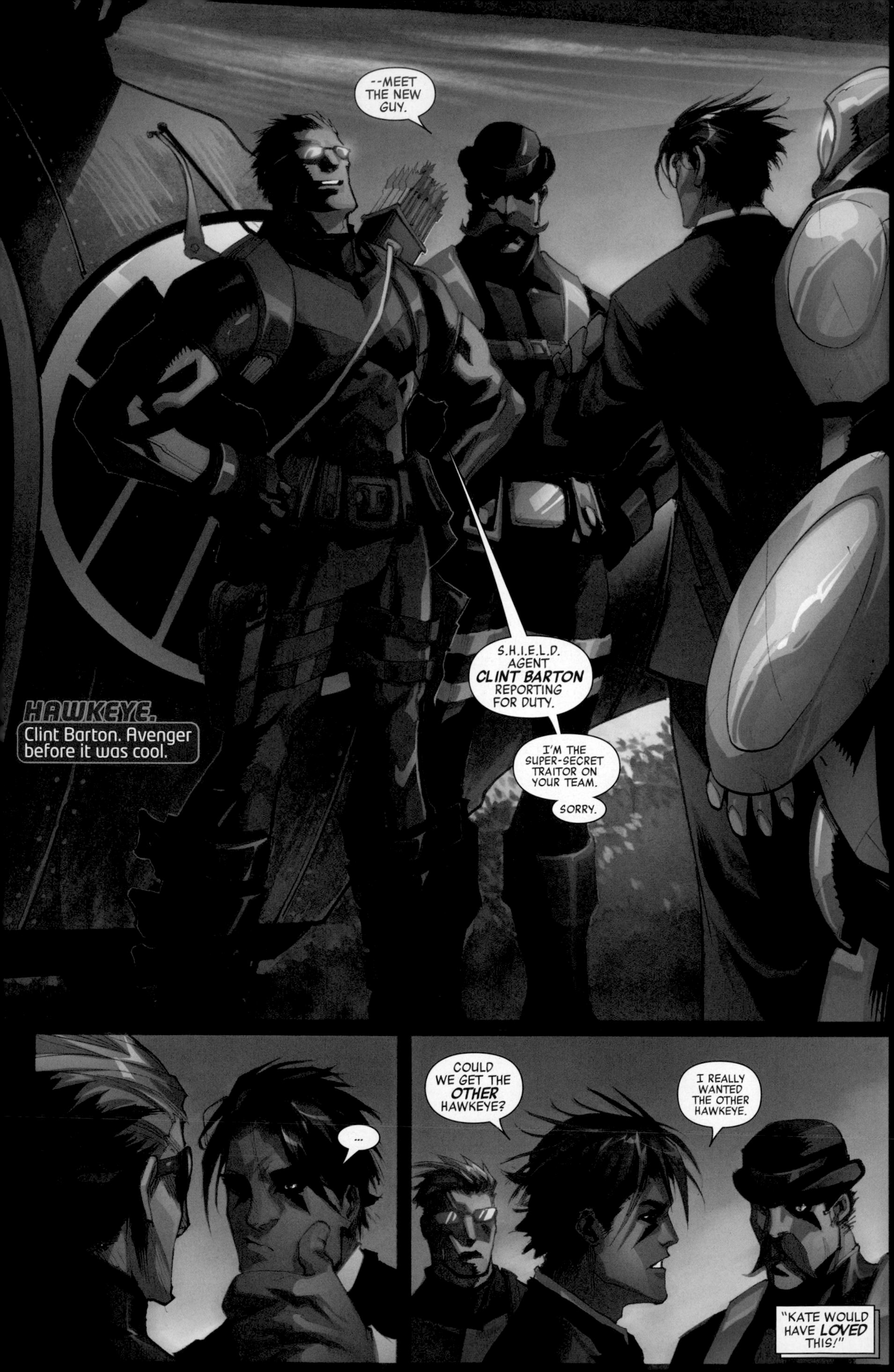
--MEET THE NEW GUY.
HAWKEYE.
Clint Barton. Avenger before it was cool.
S.H.I.E.L.D. AGENT CLINT BARTON REPORTING FOR DUTY.
I'M THE SUPER-SECRET TRAITOR ON YOUR TEAM.
SORRY.
...
COULD WE GET THE OTHER HAWKEYE?
I REALLY WANTED THE OTHER HAWKEYE.
"KATE WOULD HAVE LOVED THIS!"

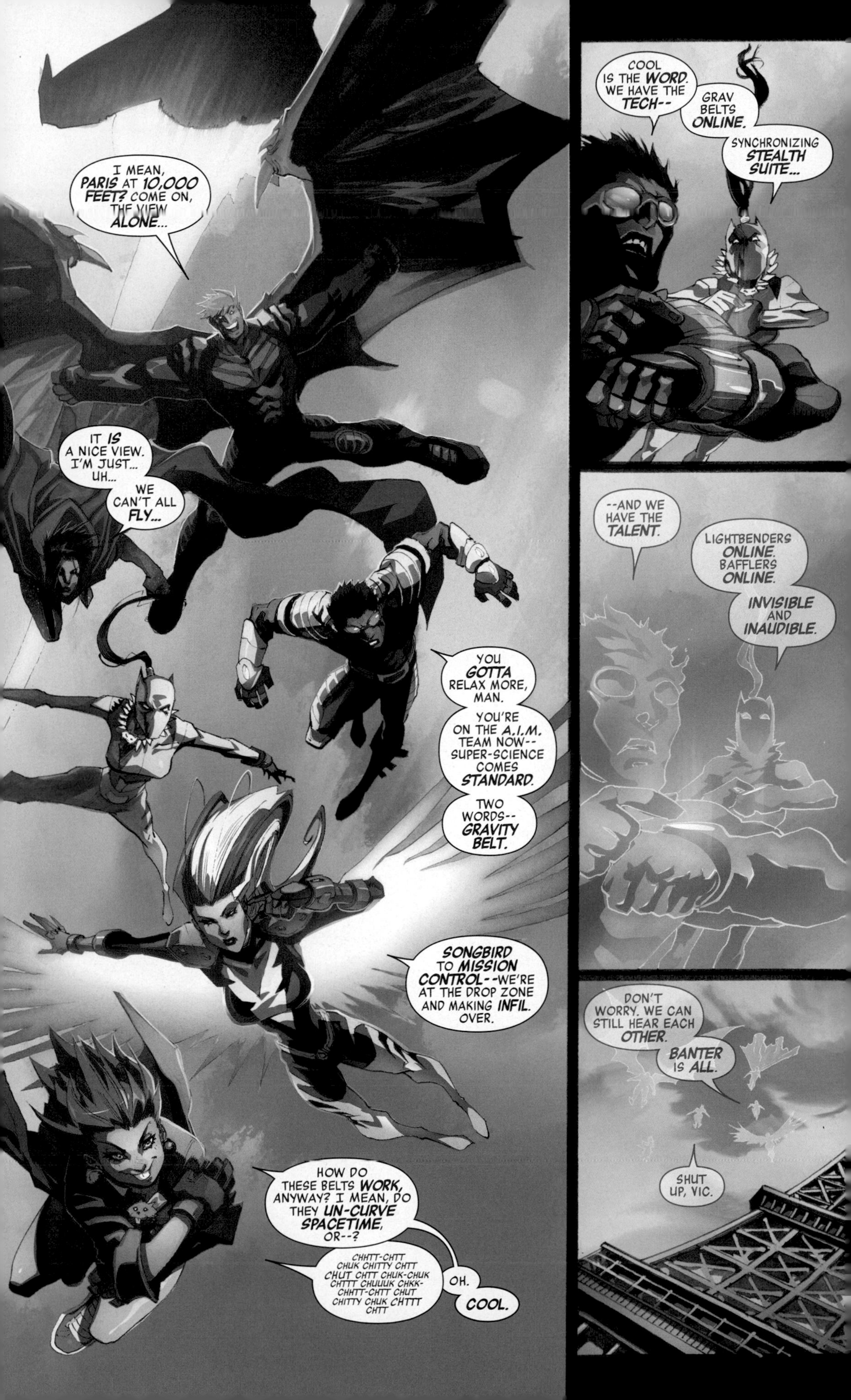
I MEAN, PARIS AT 10,000 FEET? COME ON, THE VIEW ALONE...
IT IS A NICE VIEW. I'M JUST... UH...
WE CAN'T ALL FLY...
YOU GOTTA RELAX MORE, MAN.
YOU'RE ON THE A.I.M. TEAM NOW-- SUPER-SCIENCE COMES STANDARD.
TWO WORDS-- GRAVITY BELT.
SONGBIRD TO MISSION CONTROL--WE'RE AT THE DROP ZONE AND MAKING INFIL. OVER.
HOW DO THESE BELTS WORK, ANYWAY? I MEAN, DO THEY UN-CURVE SPACETIME, OR--?
CHHTT-CHTT CHUK CHITTY CHTT CHUT CHTT CHUK-CHUK CHTTT CHUUUK CHKK-CHHTT-CHTT CHUT CHITTY CHUK CHTTT CHTT
OH.
COOL.
COOL IS THE WORD. WE HAVE THE TECH--
GRAV BELTS ONLINE.
SYNCHRONIZING STEALTH SUITE...
--AND WE HAVE THE TALENT.
LIGHTBENDERS ONLINE. BAFFLERS ONLINE.
INVISIBLE AND INAUDIBLE.
DON'T WORRY. WE CAN STILL HEAR EACH OTHER.
BANTER IS ALL.
SHUT UP, VIC.

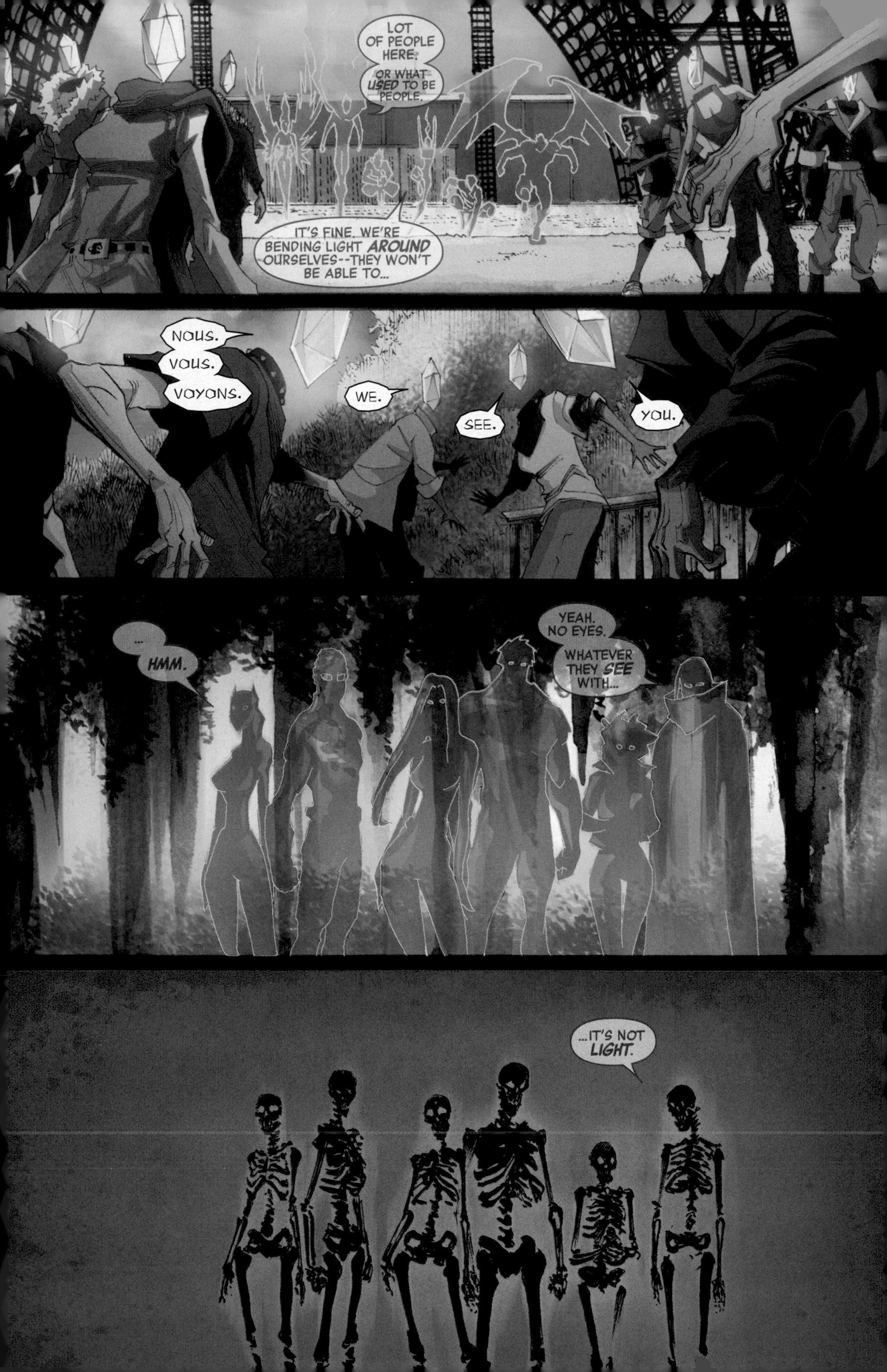
LOT OF PEOPLE HERE.
OR WHAT USED TO BE PEOPLE.
IT'S FINE. WE'RE BENDING LIGHT AROUND OURSELVES--THEY WON'T BE ABLE TO...
NOUS.
VOUS.
VOYONS.
WE.
SEE.
YOU.
... HMM.
YEAH. NO EYES.
WHATEVER THEY SEE WITH...
...IT'S NOT LIGHT.

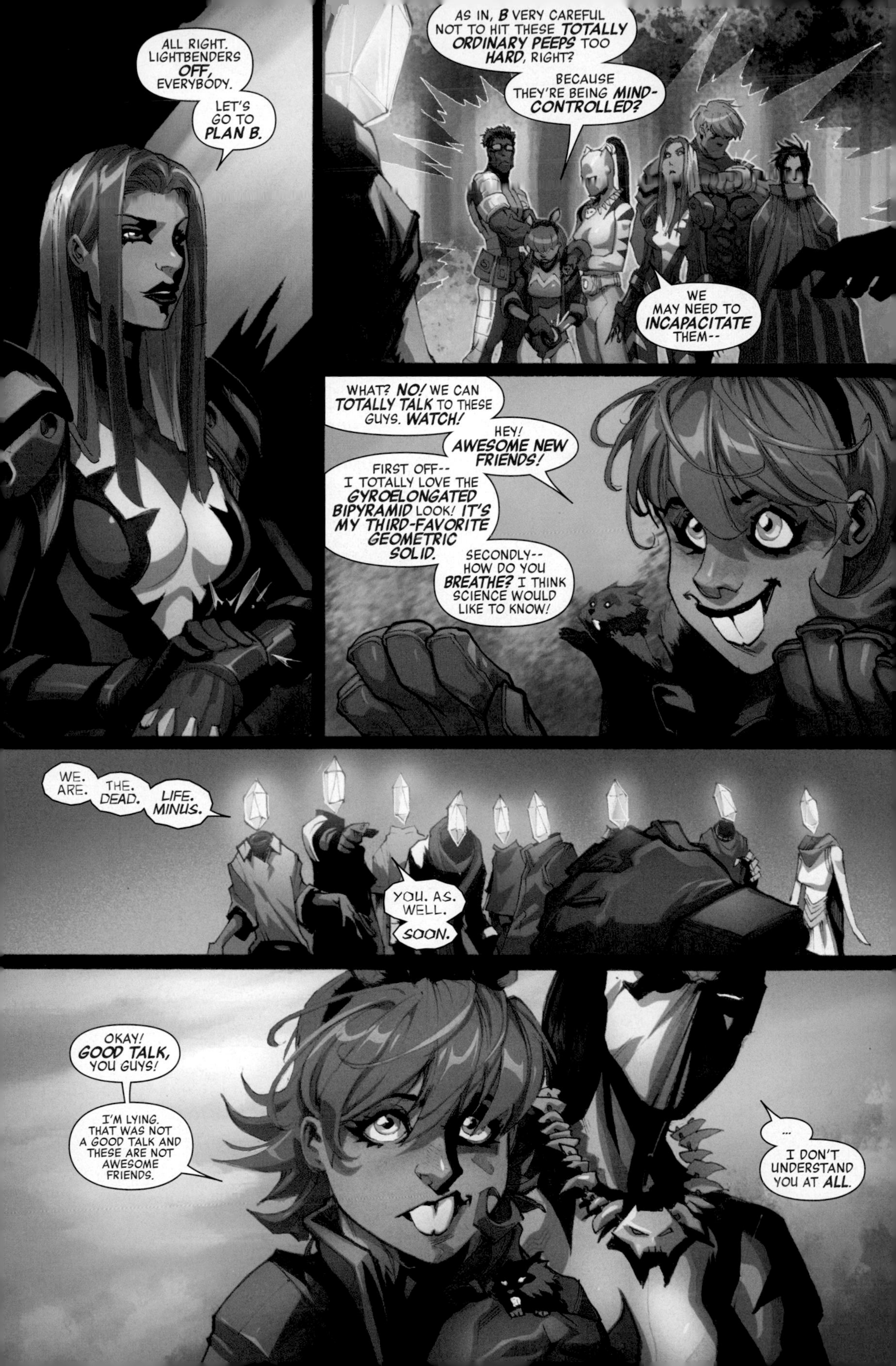
ALL RIGHT. LIGHTBENDERS OFF, EVERYBODY.
LET'S GO TO PLAN B.
AS IN, B VERY CAREFUL NOT TO HIT THESE TOTALLY ORDINARY PEEPS TOO HARD, RIGHT?
BECAUSE THEY'RE BEING MIND-CONTROLLED?
WE MAY NEED TO INCAPACITATE THEM--
WHAT? NO! WE CAN TOTALLY TALK TO THESE GUYS. WATCH!
HEY! AWESOME NEW FRIENDS!
FIRST OFF-- I TOTALLY LOVE THE GYROELONGATED BIPYRAMID LOOK! IT'S MY THIRD-FAVORITE GEOMETRIC SOLID.
SECONDLY-- HOW DO YOU BREATHE? I THINK SCIENCE WOULD LIKE TO KNOW!
WE. ARE.
THE. DEAD.
LIFE. MINUS.
YOU. AS. WELL.
SOON.
OKAY! GOOD TALK, YOU GUYS!
I'M LYING. THAT WAS NOT A GOOD TALK AND THESE ARE NOT AWESOME FRIENDS.
...
I DON'T UNDERSTAND YOU AT ALL.

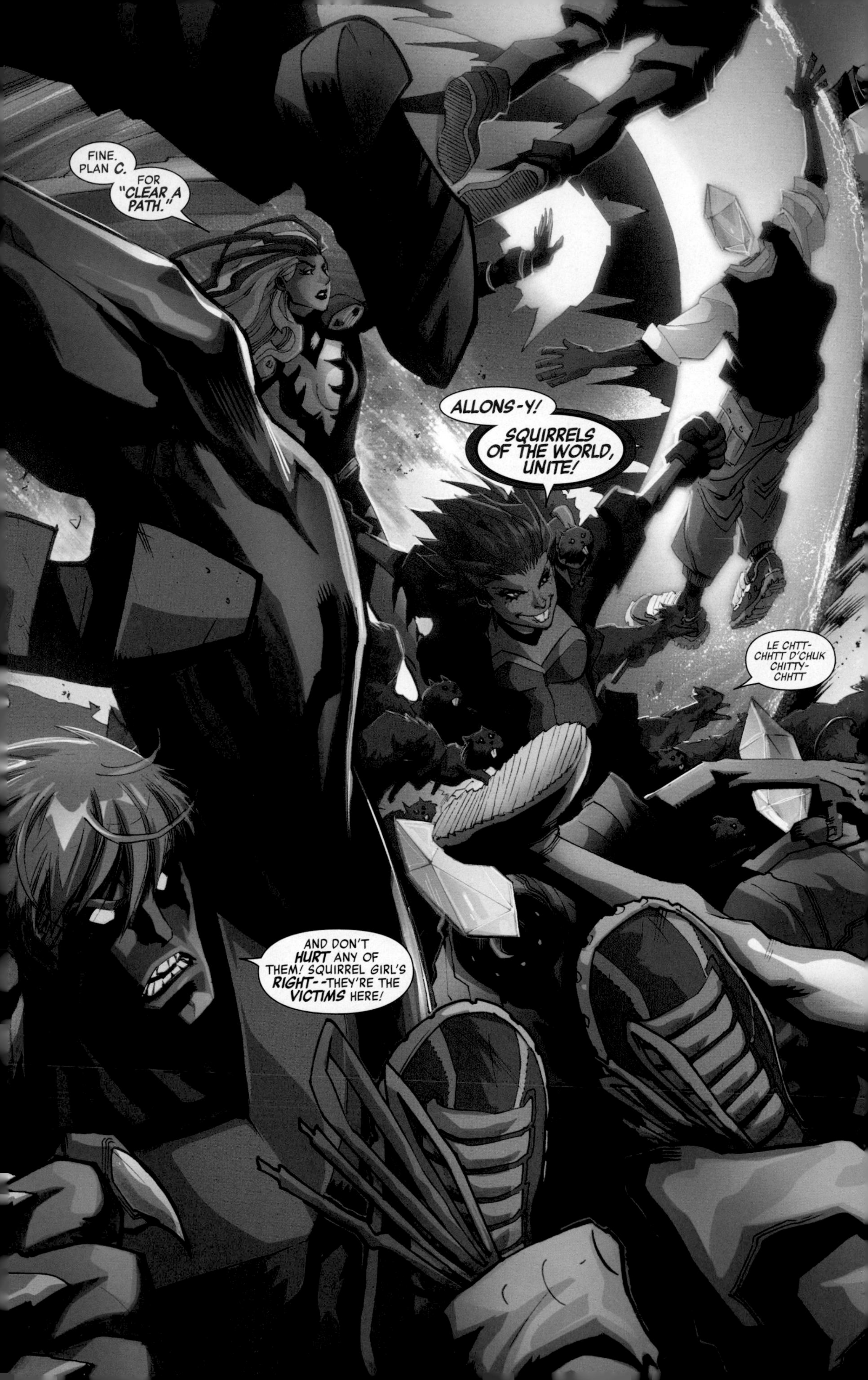
FINE. PLAN C. FOR "CLEAR A PATH."
ALLONS-Y! SQUIRRELS OF THE WORLD, UNITE!
LE CHTT-CHHTT D'CHUK CHITTY-CHHTT
AND DON'T HURT ANY OF THEM! SQUIRREL GIRL'S RIGHT--THEY'RE THE VICTIMS HERE!

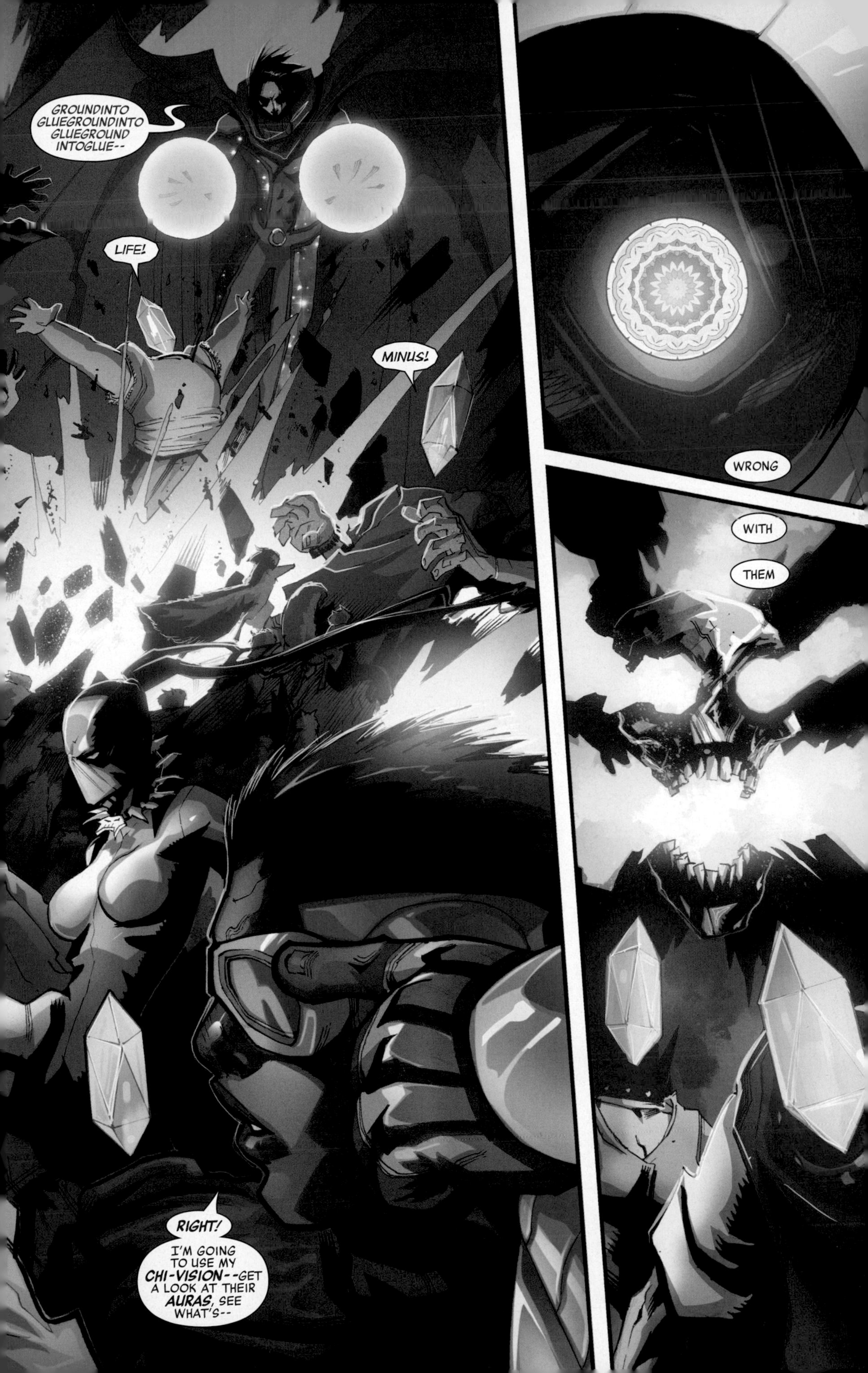
GROUNDINTO GLUEGROUNDINTO GLUEGROUND INTOGLUE--
LIFE!
MINUS!
RIGHT!
I'M GOING TO USE MY CHI-VISION--GET A LOOK AT THEIR AURAS, SEE WHAT'S--
WRONG
WITH
THEM

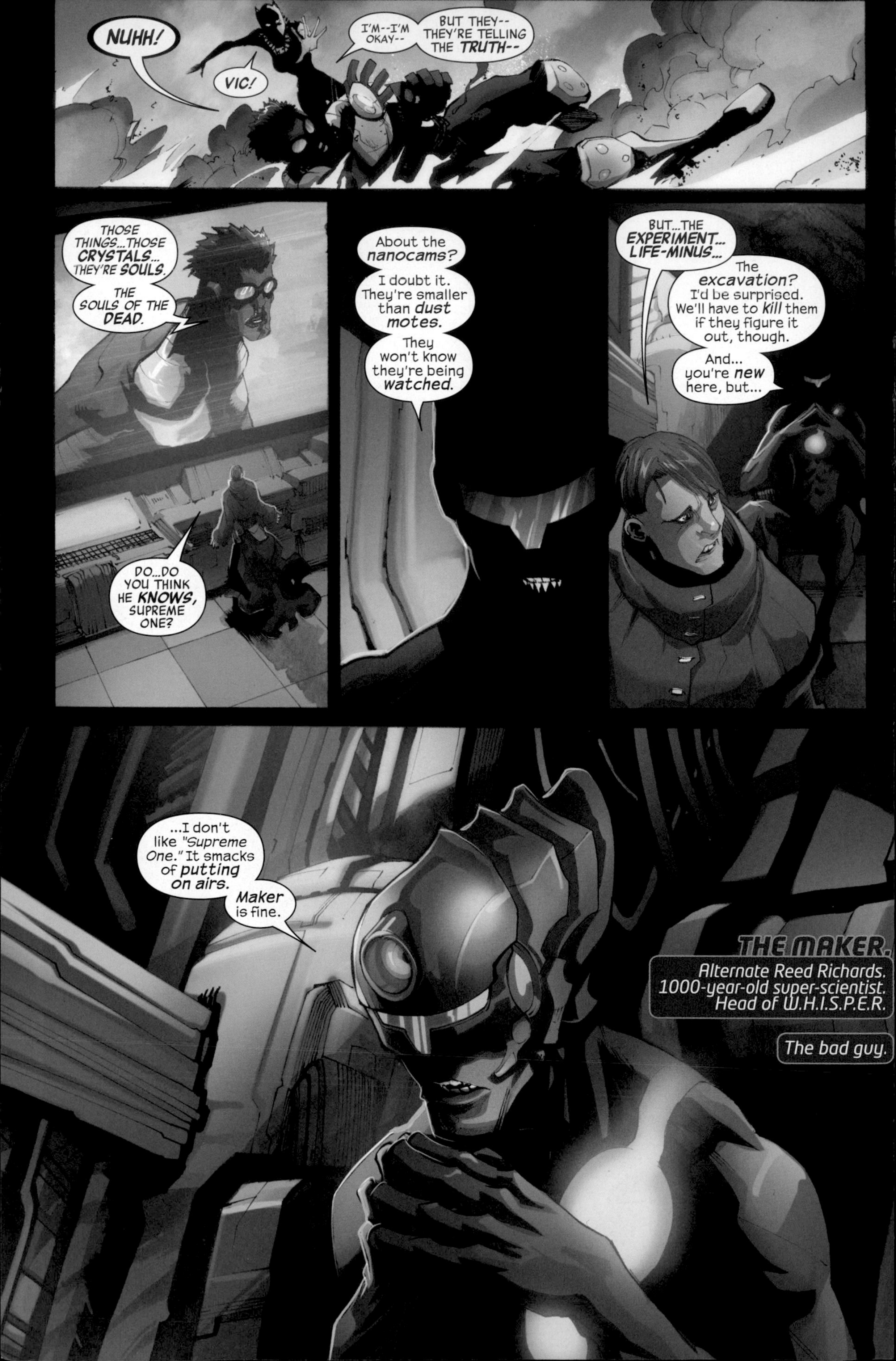
NUHH!
VIC!
I'M--I'M OKAY--
BUT THEY-- THEY'RE TELLING THE TRUTH--
THOSE THINGS...THOSE CRYSTALS... THEY'RE SOULS.
THE SOULS OF THE DEAD.
DO...DO YOU THINK HE KNOWS, SUPREME ONE?
About the nanocams?
I doubt it. They're smaller than dust motes.
They won't know they're being watched.
BUT...THE EXPERIMENT... LIFE-MINUS...
The excavation? I'd be surprised. We'll have to kill them if they figure it out, though.
And... you're new here, but...
...I don't like "Supreme One." It smacks of putting on airs.
Maker is fine.
THE MAKER.
Alternate Reed Richards. 1000-year-old super-scientist. Head of W.H.I.S.P.E.R.
The bad guy.

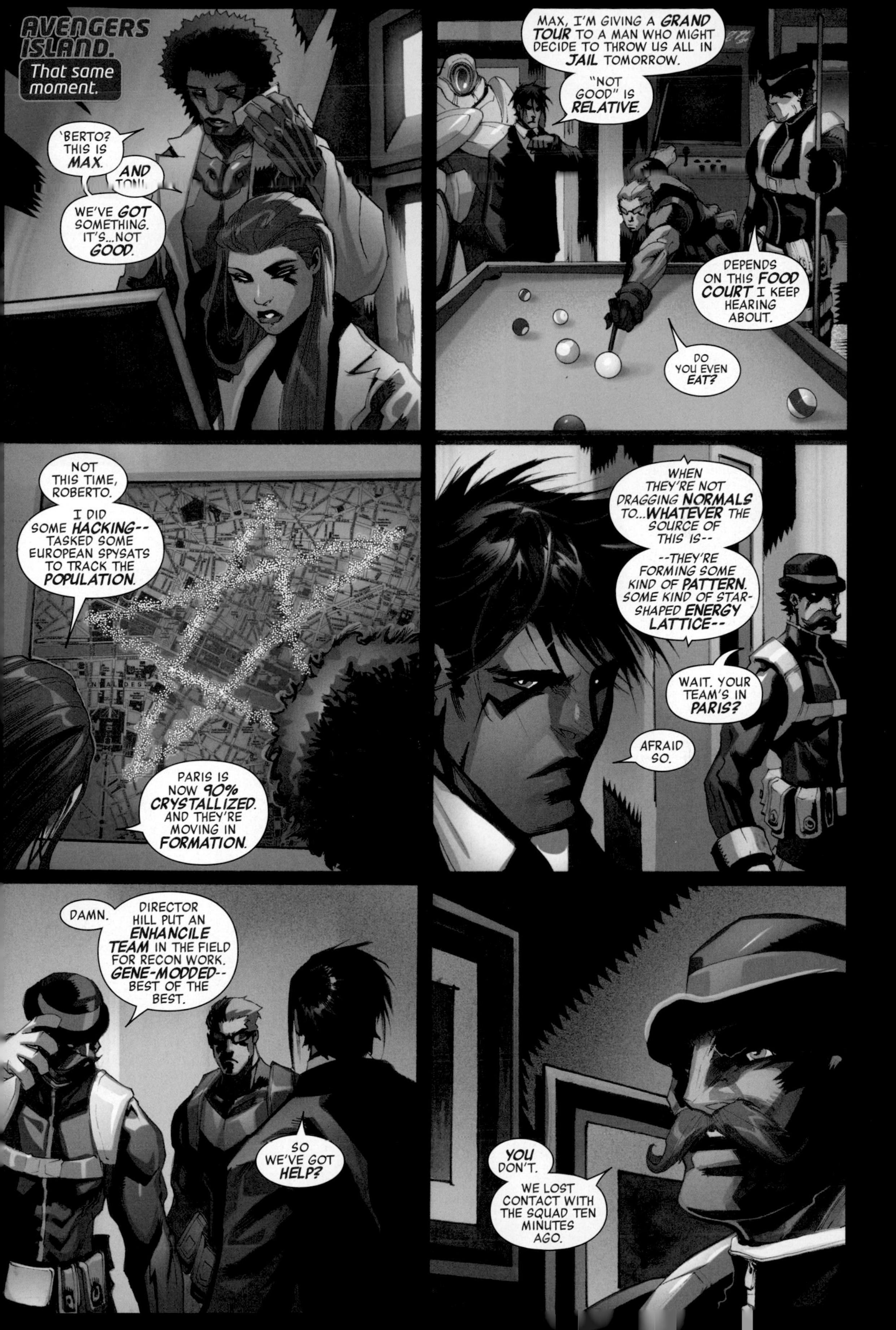
AVENGERS ISLAND.
That same moment.
'BERTO? THIS IS MAX.
AND TONI.
WE'VE GOT SOMETHING. IT'S...NOT GOOD.
MAX, I'M GIVING A GRAND TOUR TO A MAN WHO MIGHT DECIDE TO THROW US ALL IN JAIL TOMORROW.
"NOT GOOD" IS RELATIVE.
DEPENDS ON THIS FOOD COURT I KEEP HEARING ABOUT.
DO YOU EVEN EAT?
NOT THIS TIME, ROBERTO.
I DID SOME HACKING--TASKED SOME EUROPEAN SPYSATS TO TRACK THE POPULATION.
PARIS IS NOW 90% CRYSTALLIZED. AND THEY'RE MOVING IN FORMATION.
WHEN THEY'RE NOT DRAGGING NORMALS TO...WHATEVER THE SOURCE OF THIS IS--
--THEY'RE FORMING SOME KIND OF PATTERN. SOME KIND OF STAR-SHAPED ENERGY LATTICE--
WAIT. YOUR TEAM'S IN PARIS?
AFRAID SO.
DAMN.
DIRECTOR HILL PUT AN ENHANCILE TEAM IN THE FIELD FOR RECON WORK. GENE-MODDED--BEST OF THE BEST.
SO WE'VE GOT HELP?
YOU DON'T.
WE LOST CONTACT WITH THE SQUAD TEN MINUTES AGO.

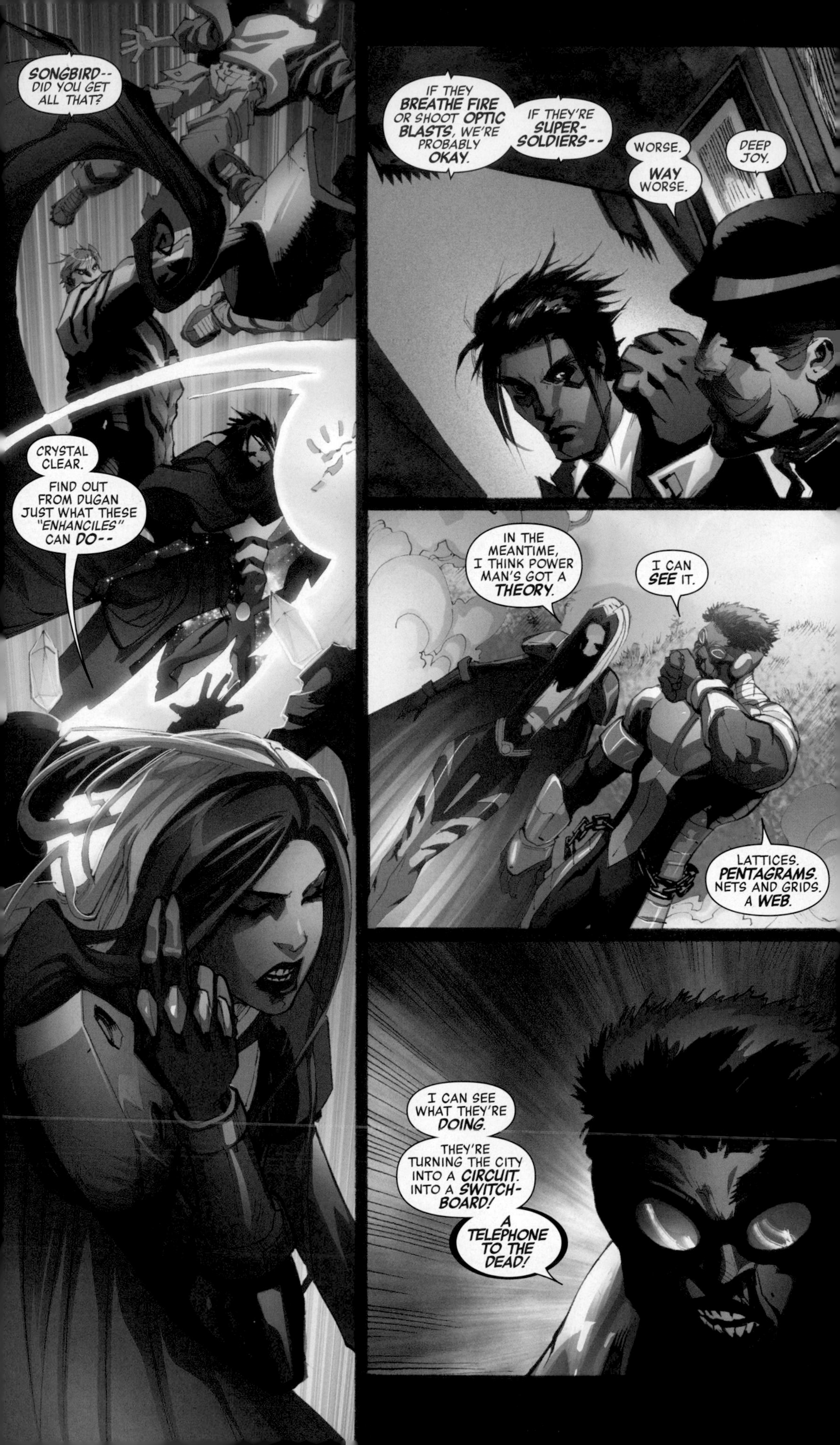
SONGBIRD-- DID YOU GET ALL THAT?
CRYSTAL CLEAR.
FIND OUT FROM DUGAN JUST WHAT THESE "ENHANCILES" CAN DO--
IF THEY BREATHE FIRE OR SHOOT OPTIC BLASTS, WE'RE PROBABLY OKAY.
IF THEY'RE SUPER-SOLDIERS--
WORSE.
WAY WORSE.
DEEP JOY.
IN THE MEANTIME, I THINK POWER MAN'S GOT A THEORY.
I CAN SEE IT.
LATTICES. PENTAGRAMS. NETS AND GRIDS. A WEB.
I CAN SEE WHAT THEY'RE DOING.
THEY'RE TURNING THE CITY INTO A CIRCUIT. INTO A SWITCH-BOARD!
A TELEPHONE TO THE DEAD!

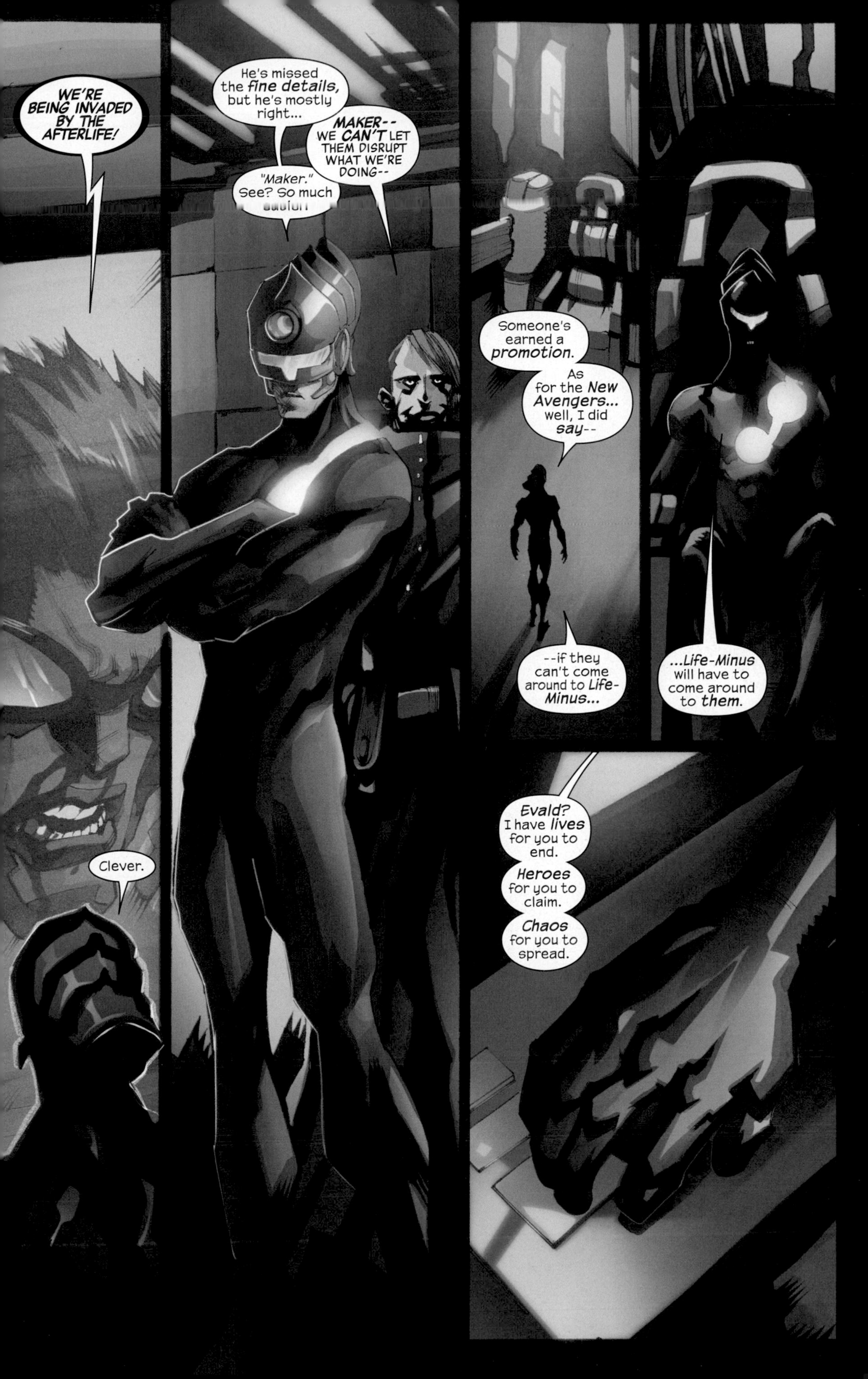
WE'RE BEING INVADED BY THE AFTERLIFE!
He's missed the fine details, but he's mostly right...
"Maker." See? So much
MAKER-- WE CAN'T LET THEM DISRUPT WHAT WE'RE DOING--
Clever.
Someone's earned a promotion.
As for the New Avengers... well, I did say--
--if they can't come around to Life-Minus...
...Life-Minus will have to come around to them.
Evald? I have lives for you to end.
Heroes for you to claim.
Chaos for you to spread.

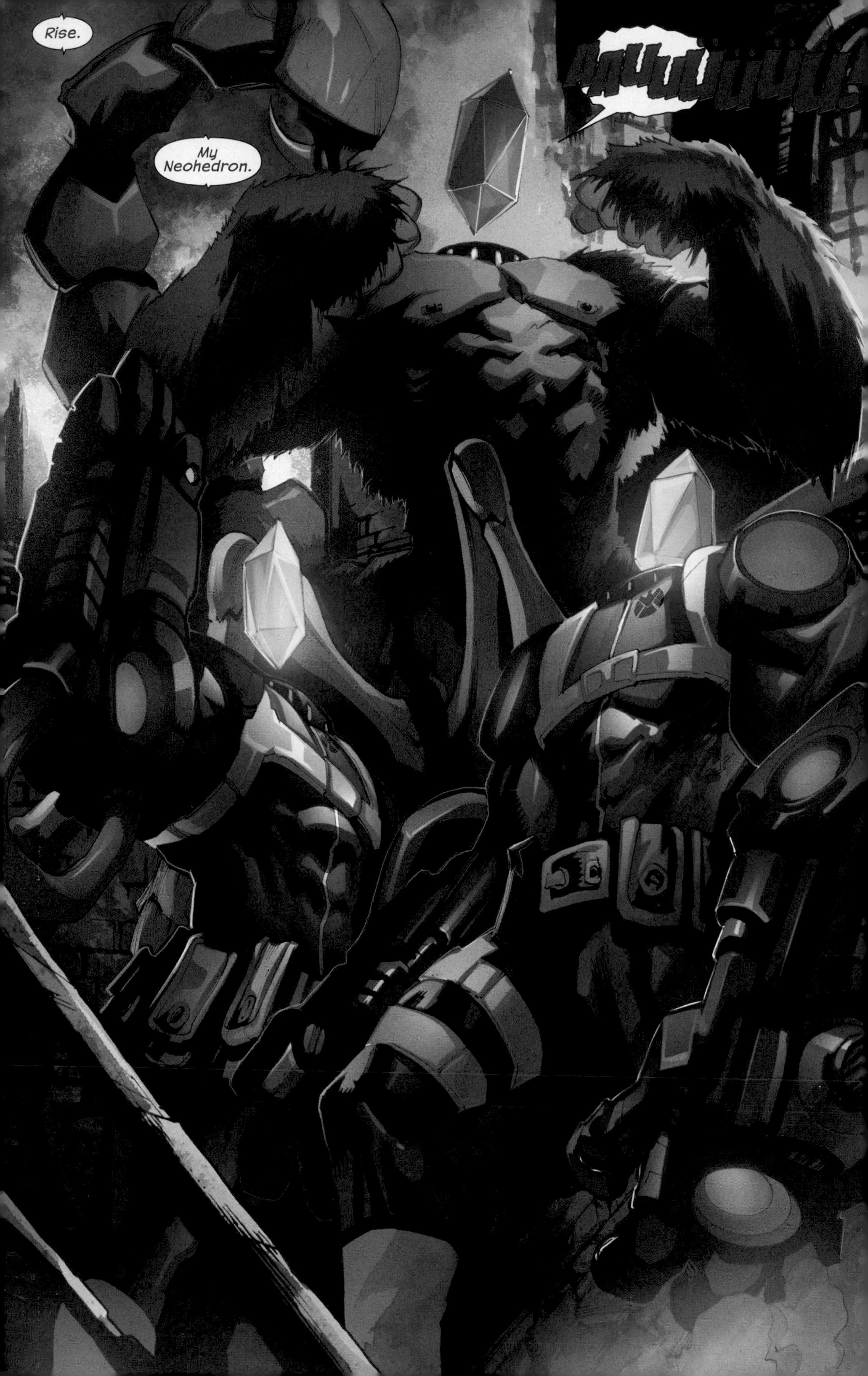
Rise.
My Neohedron.

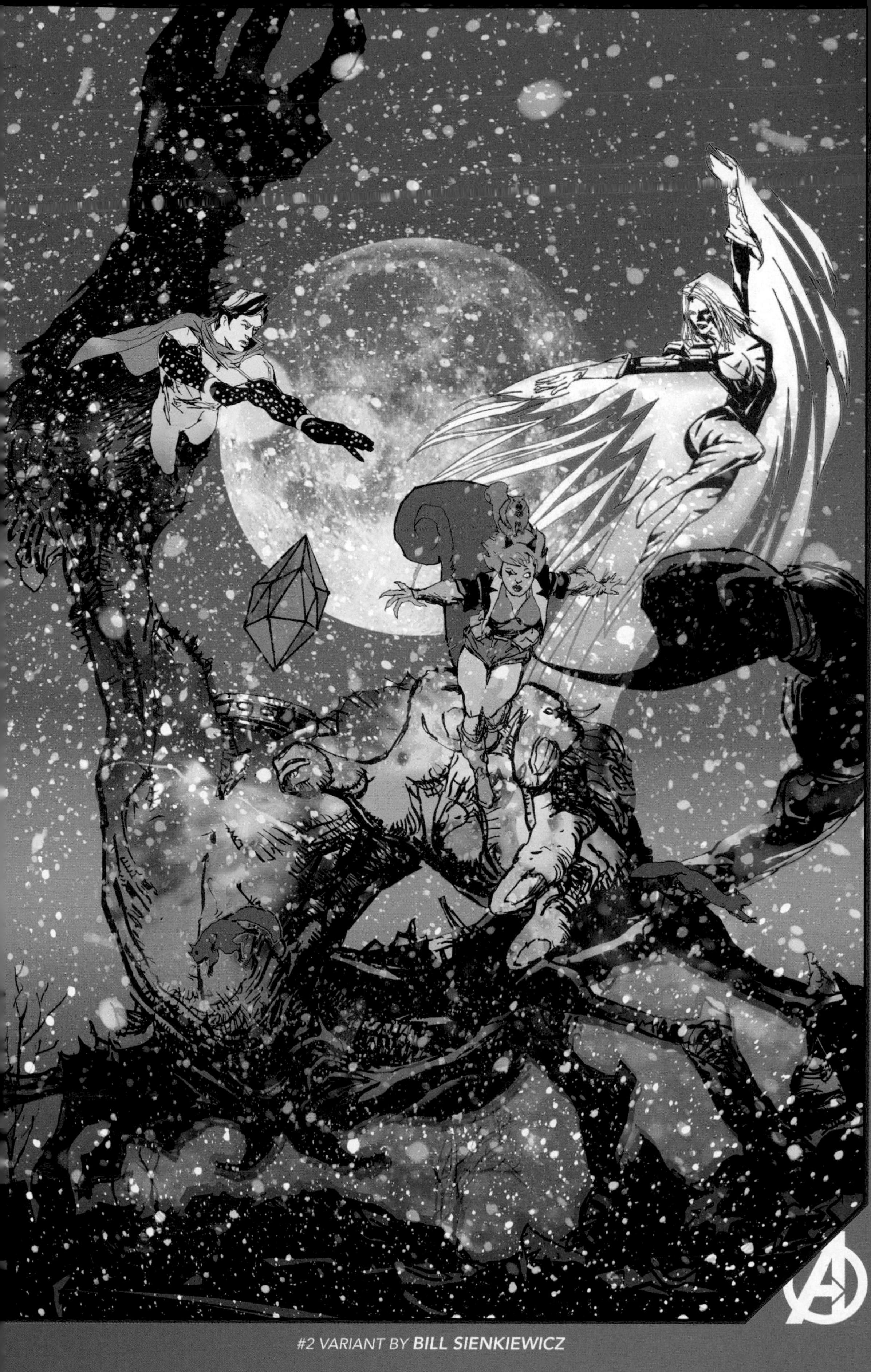

#2 VARIANT BY **BILL SIENKIEWICZ**

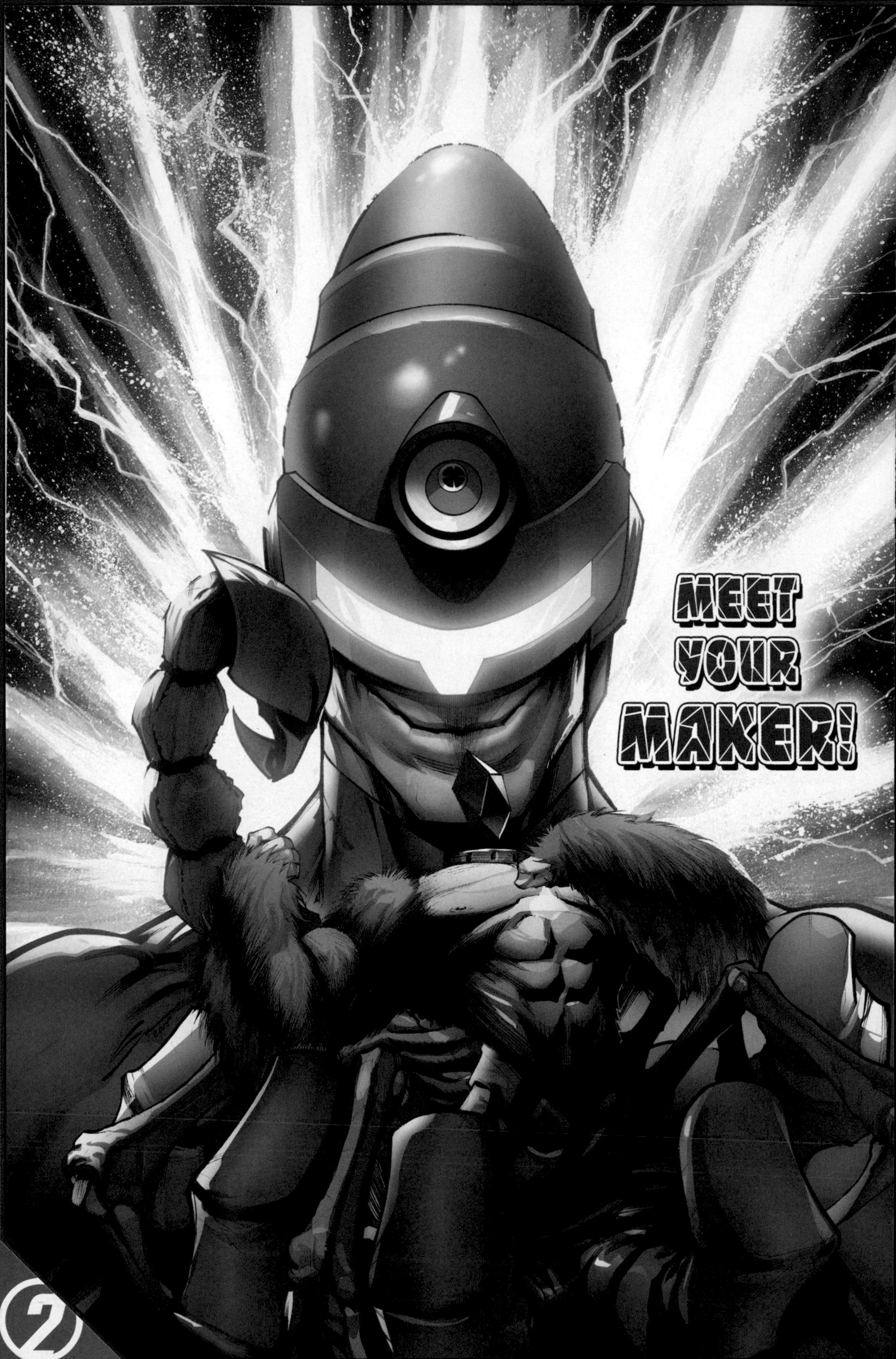
MEET YOUR MAKER!
2

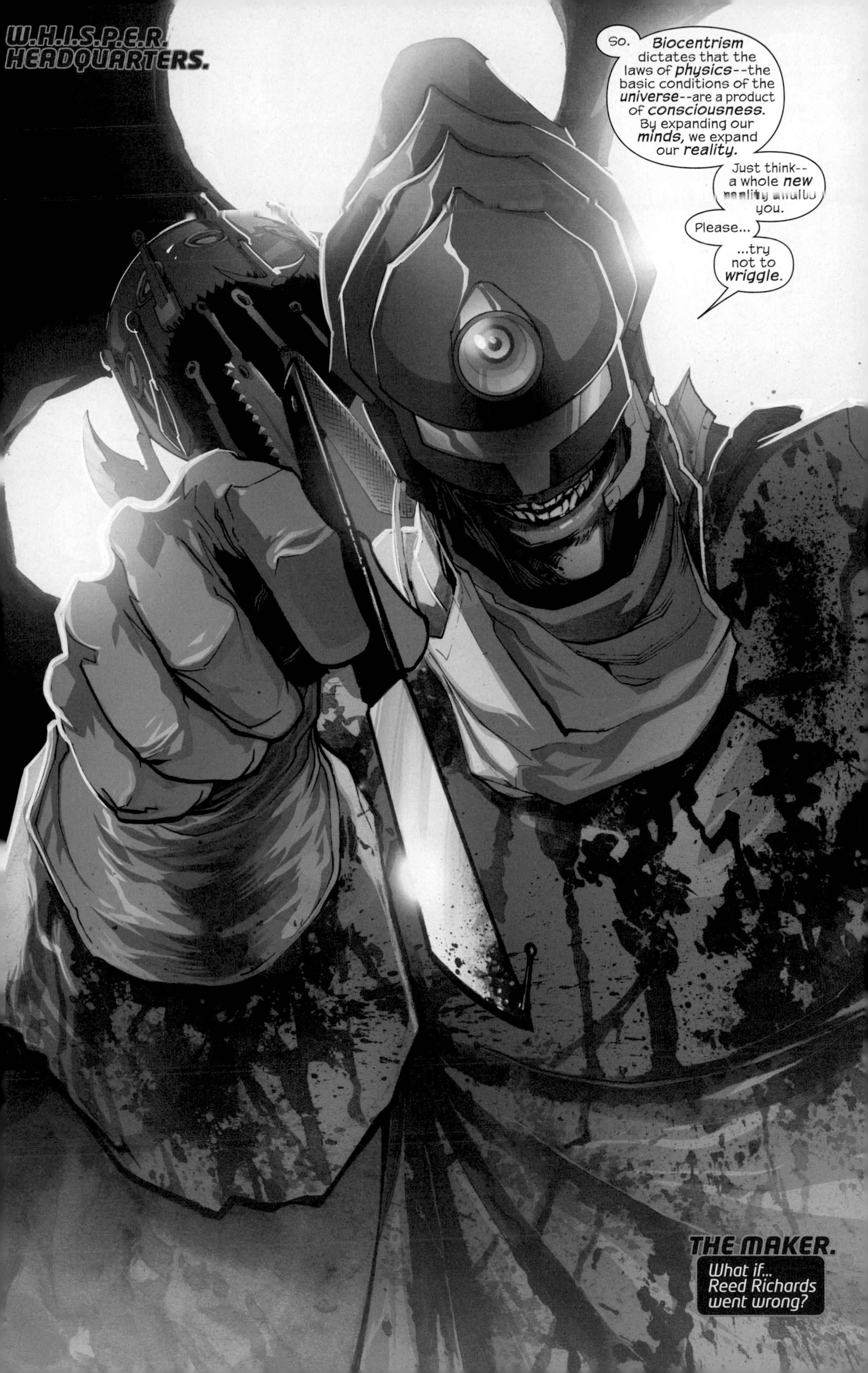
W.H.I.S.P.E.R. HEADQUARTERS.
So. Biocentrism dictates that the laws of physics--the basic conditions of the universe--are a product of consciousness. By expanding our minds, we expand our reality.
Just think--a whole new you.
Please...
...try not to wriggle.
THE MAKER.
What if... Reed Richards went wrong?

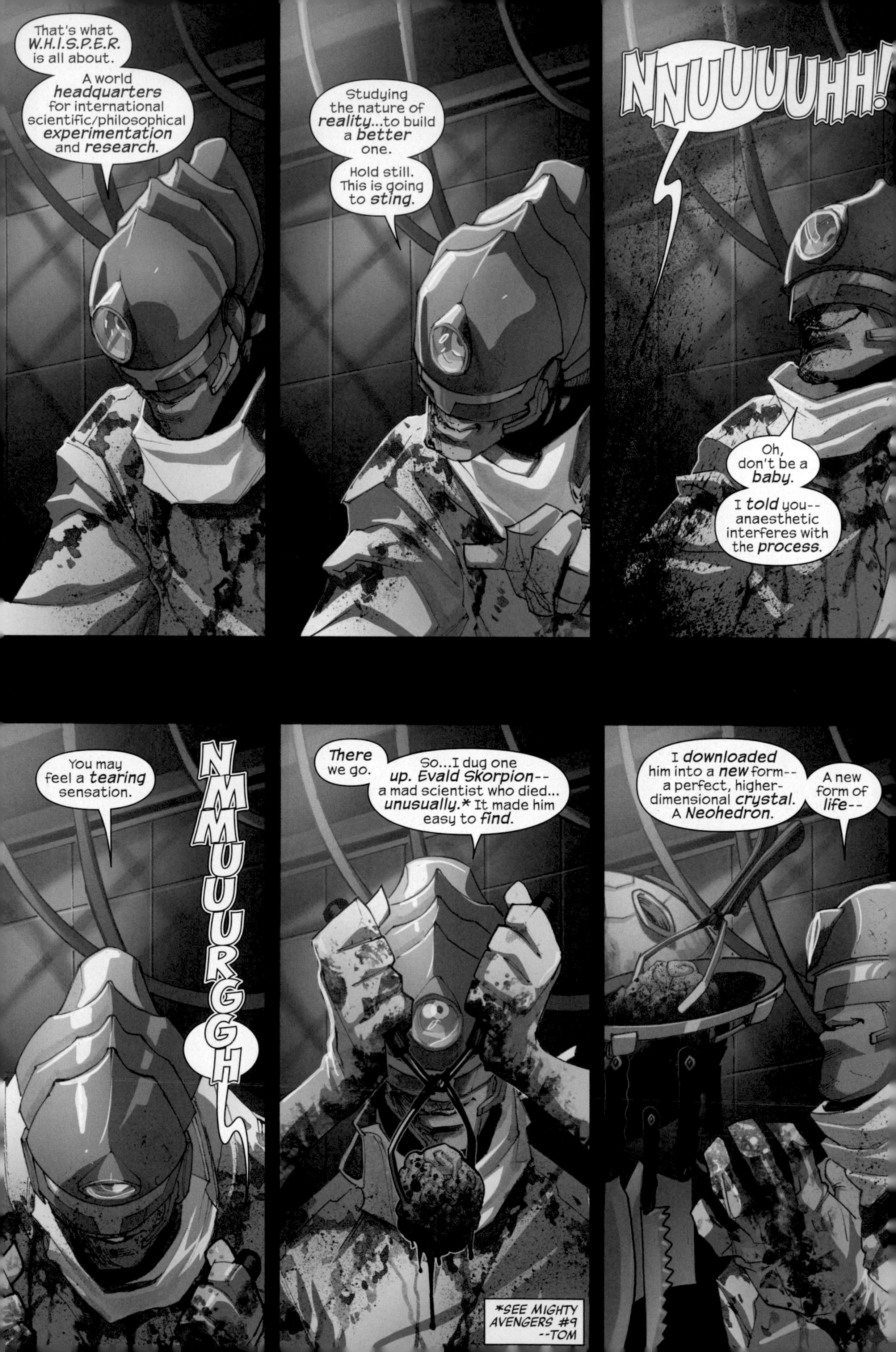
That's what W.H.I.S.P.E.R. is all about.
A world headquarters for international scientific/philosophical experimentation and research.
Studying the nature of reality...to build a better one.
Hold still. This is going to sting.
NNUUUUUHH!
Oh, don't be a baby.
I told you--anaesthetic interferes with the process.
You may feel a tearing sensation.
NMMUUURGGH
There we go.
So...I dug one up. Evald Skorpion--a mad scientist who died... unusually.* It made him easy to find.
*SEE MIGHTY AVENGERS #9 --TOM
I downloaded him into a new form--a perfect, higher-dimensional crystal. A Neohedron.
A new form of life--

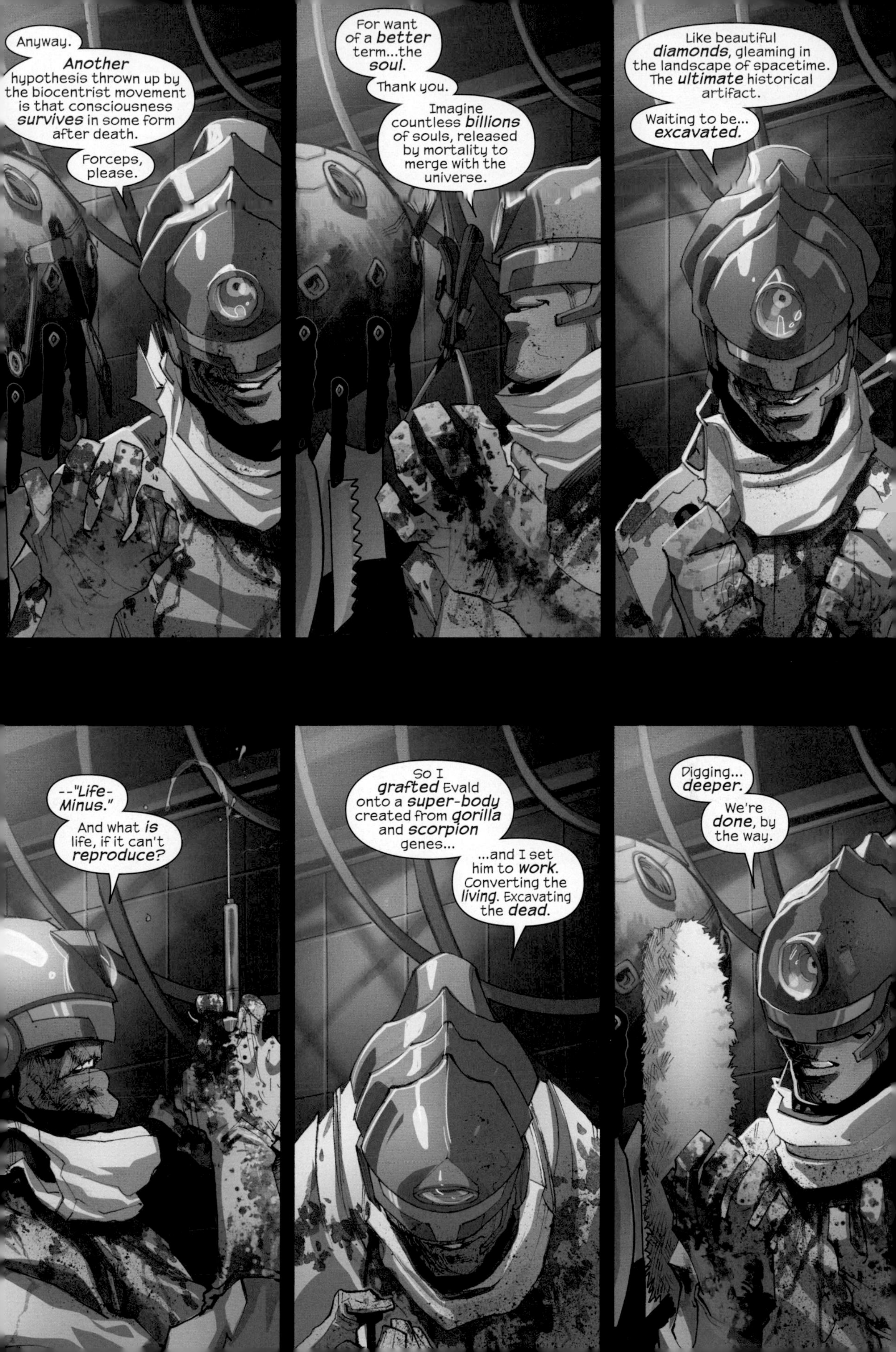
Anyway.
Another hypothesis thrown up by the biocentrist movement is that consciousness survives in some form after death.
Forceps, please.
For want of a better term...the soul.
Thank you.
Imagine countless billions of souls, released by mortality to merge with the universe.
Like beautiful diamonds, gleaming in the landscape of spacetime. The ultimate historical artifact.
Waiting to be... excavated.
--"Life-Minus."
And what is life, if it can't reproduce?
So I grafted Evald onto a super-body created from gorilla and scorpion genes...
...and I set him to work. Converting the living. Excavating the dead.
Digging... deeper.
We're done, by the way.

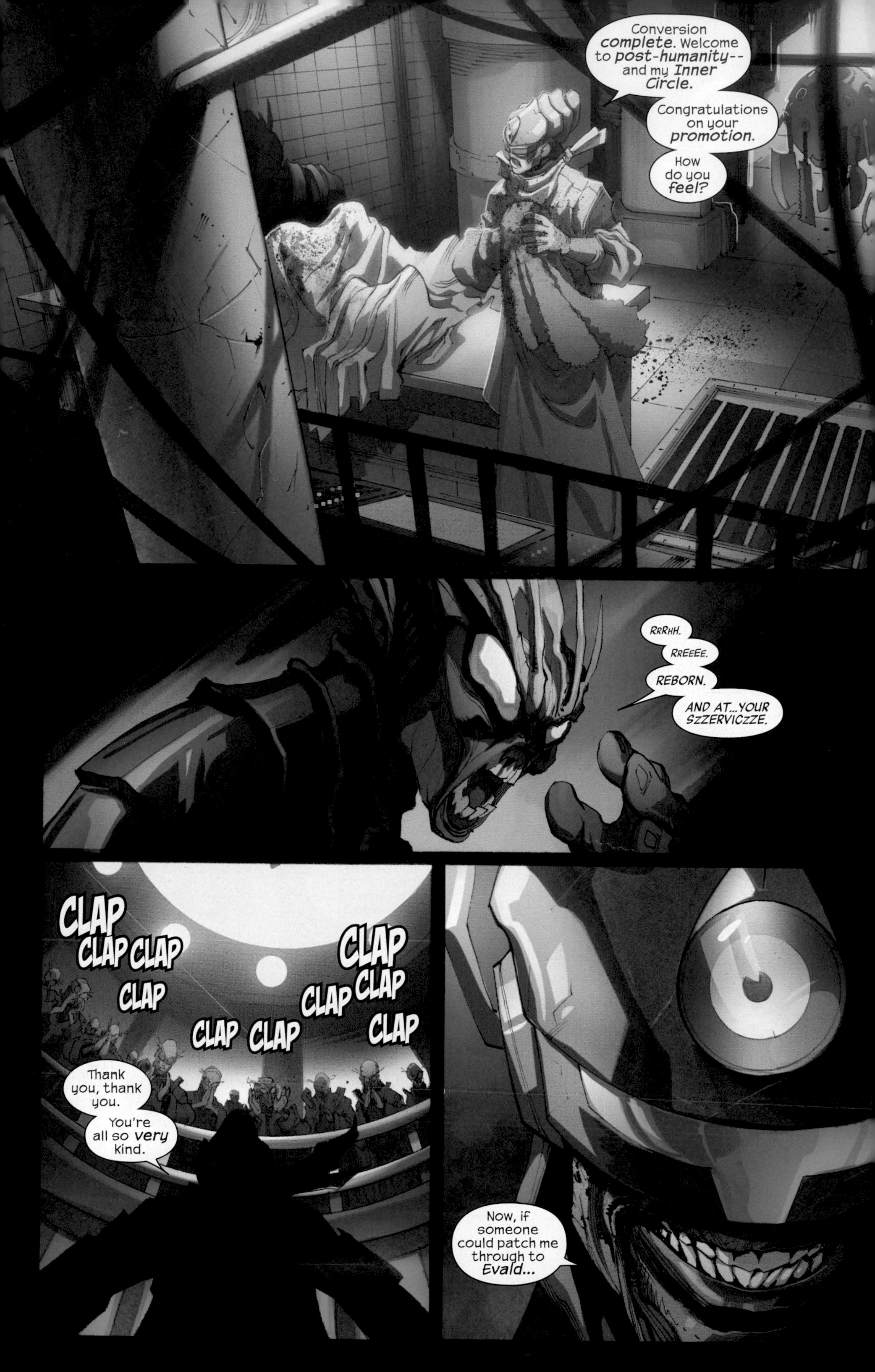
Conversion complete. Welcome to post-humanity--and my Inner Circle.
Congratulations on your promotion.
How do you feel?
RRRHH.
RREEEE.
REBORN.
AND AT...YOUR SZZERVICZZE.
CLAP CLAP CLAP CLAP CLAP CLAP CLAP CLAP CLAP CLAP
Thank you, thank you.
You're all so very kind.
Now, if someone could patch me through to Evald...

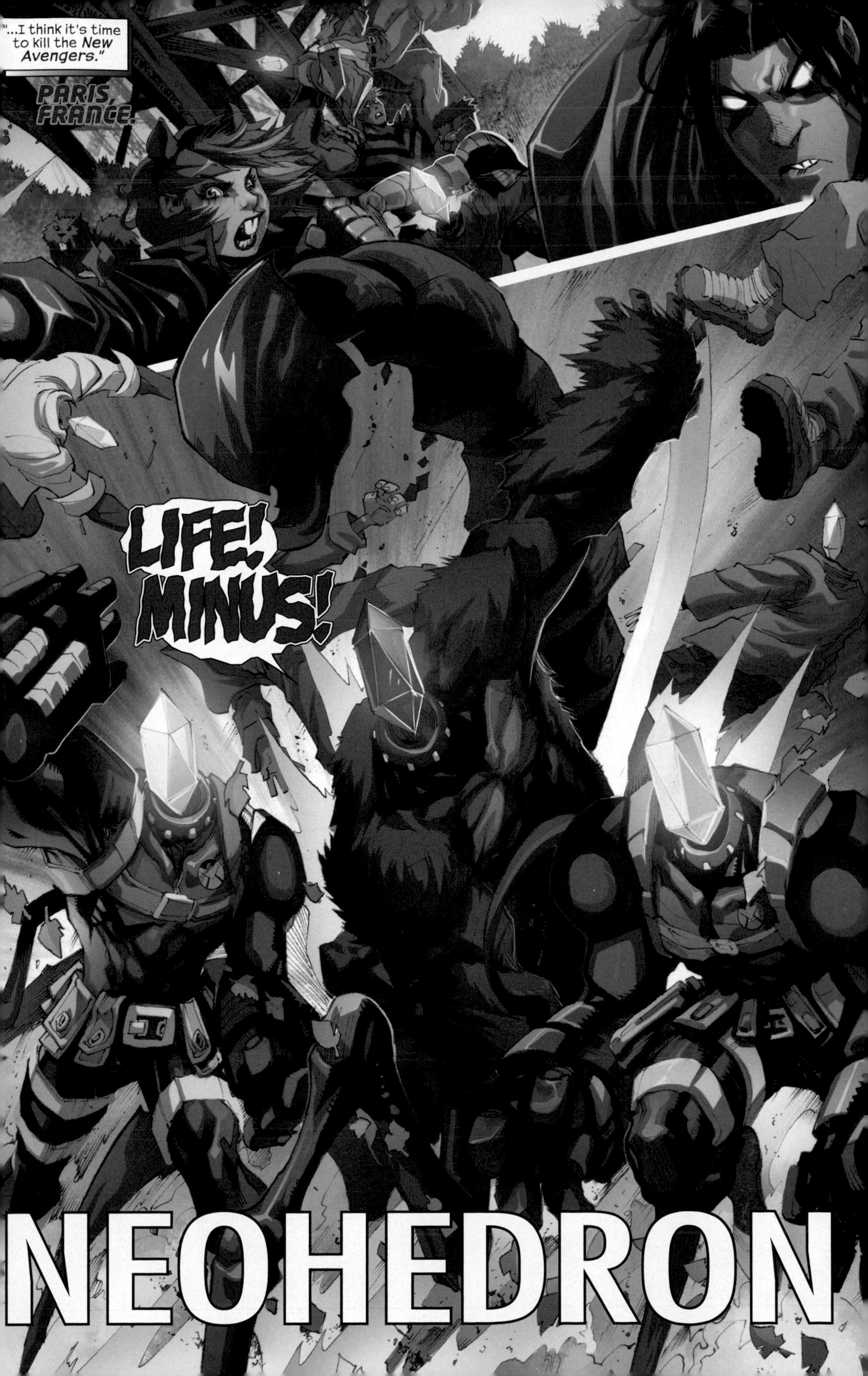
"...I think it's time to kill the *New Avengers*."
PARIS, FRANCE.
LIFE! MINUS!
NEOHEDRON

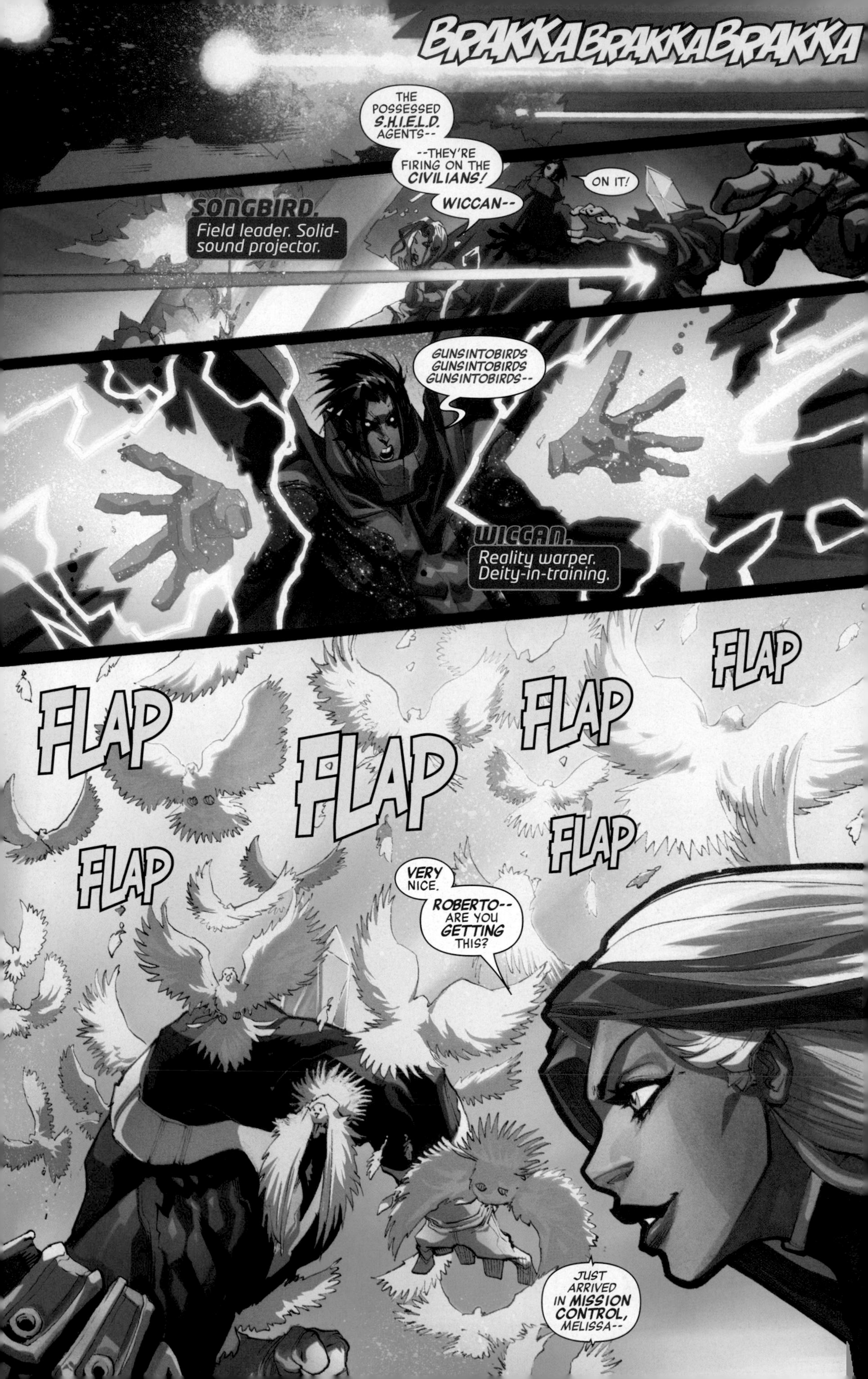
BRAKKA BRAKKA BRAKKA
THE POSSESSED S.H.I.E.L.D. AGENTS--
--THEY'RE FIRING ON THE CIVILIANS!
WICCAN--
ON IT!
SONGBIRD.
Field leader. Solid-sound projector.
GUNSINTOBIRDS GUNSINTOBIRDS GUNSINTOBIRDS--
WICCAN.
Reality warper. Deity-in-training.
FLAP
FLAP
FLAP
FLAP
FLAP
FLAP
VERY NICE.
ROBERTO-- ARE YOU GETTING THIS?
JUST ARRIVED IN MISSION CONTROL, MELISSA--

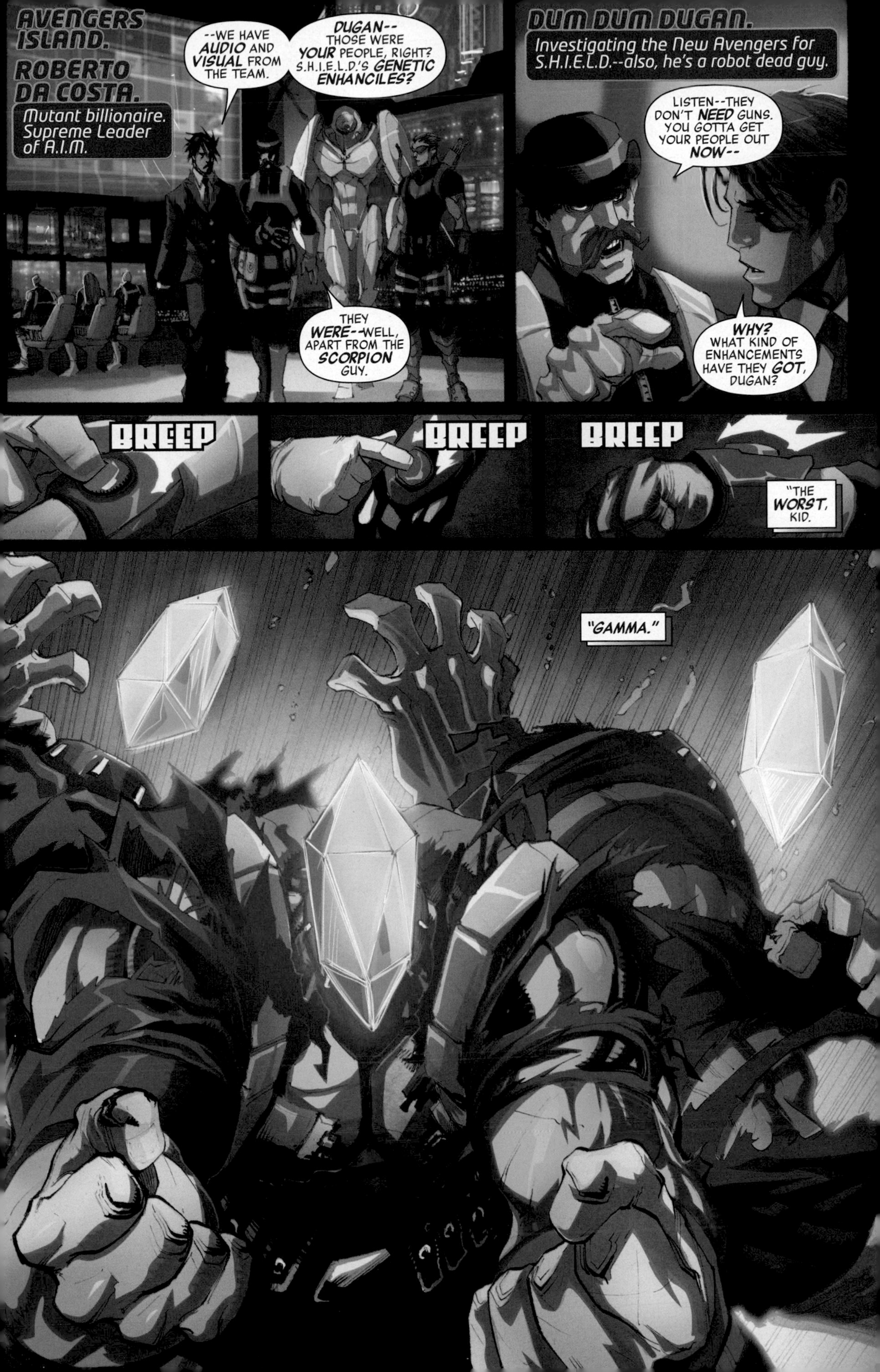
AVENGERS ISLAND.
ROBERTO DA COSTA.
Mutant billionaire. Supreme Leader of A.I.M.
--WE HAVE AUDIO AND VISUAL FROM THE TEAM.
DUGAN-- THOSE WERE YOUR PEOPLE, RIGHT? S.H.I.E.L.D.'S GENETIC ENHANCILES?
THEY WERE--WELL, APART FROM THE SCORPION GUY.
DUM DUM DUGAN.
Investigating the New Avengers for S.H.I.E.L.D.--also, he's a robot dead guy.
LISTEN--THEY DON'T NEED GUNS. YOU GOTTA GET YOUR PEOPLE OUT NOW--
WHY? WHAT KIND OF ENHANCEMENTS HAVE THEY GOT, DUGAN?
BREEP
BREEP
BREEP
"THE WORST, KID.
"GAMMA."

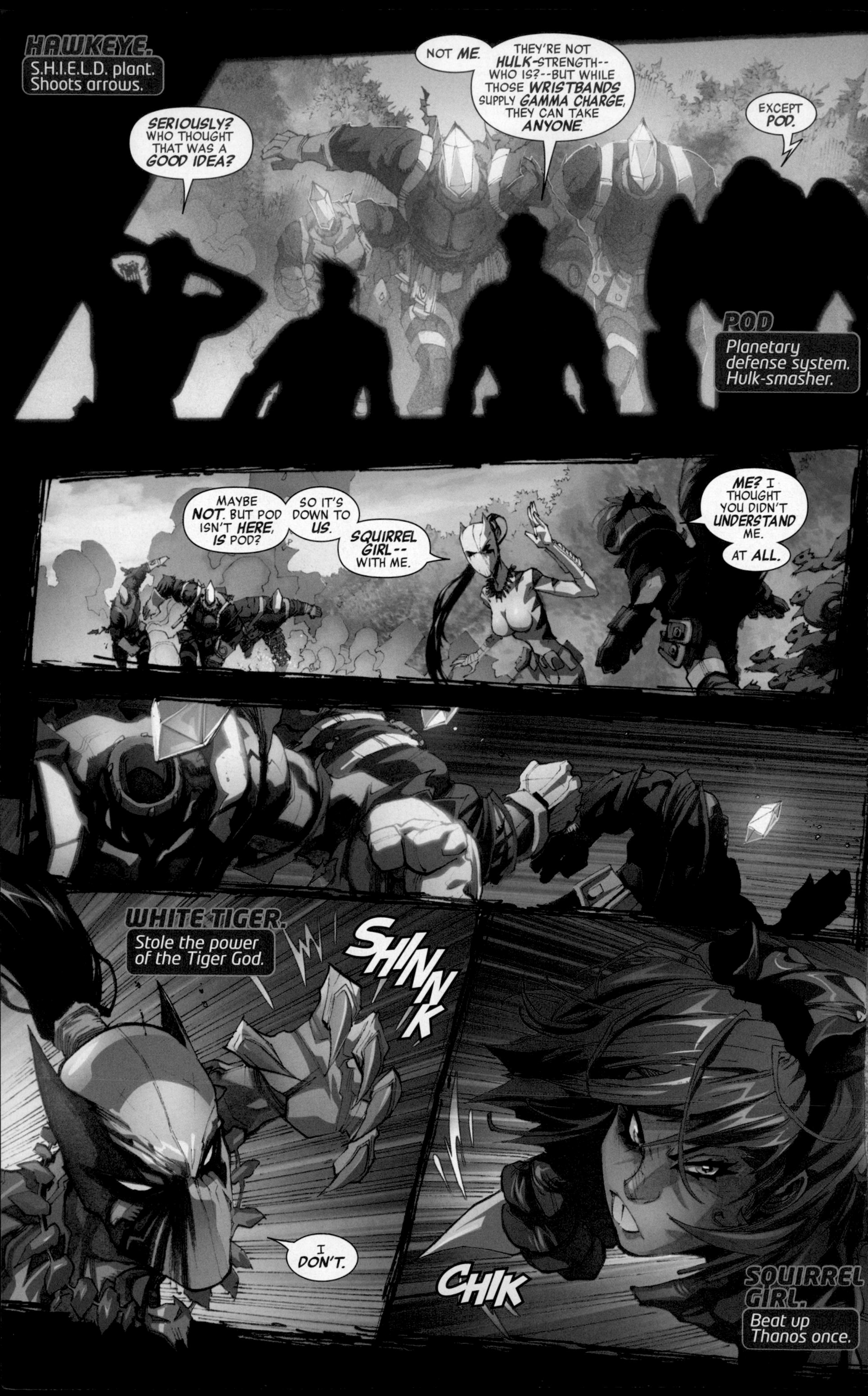
HAWKEYE.
S.H.I.E.L.D. plant. Shoots arrows.
SERIOUSLY? WHO THOUGHT THAT WAS A GOOD IDEA?
NOT ME.
THEY'RE NOT HULK-STRENGTH-- WHO IS?--BUT WHILE THOSE WRISTBANDS SUPPLY GAMMA CHARGE, THEY CAN TAKE ANYONE.
EXCEPT POD.
POD
Planetary defense system. Hulk-smasher.
MAYBE NOT. BUT POD ISN'T HERE, IS POD?
SO IT'S DOWN TO US.
SQUIRREL GIRL-- WITH ME.
ME? I THOUGHT YOU DIDN'T UNDERSTAND ME.
AT ALL.
WHITE TIGER.
Stole the power of the Tiger God.
SHINNK
I DON'T.
CHIK
SQUIRREL GIRL.
Beat up Thanos once.

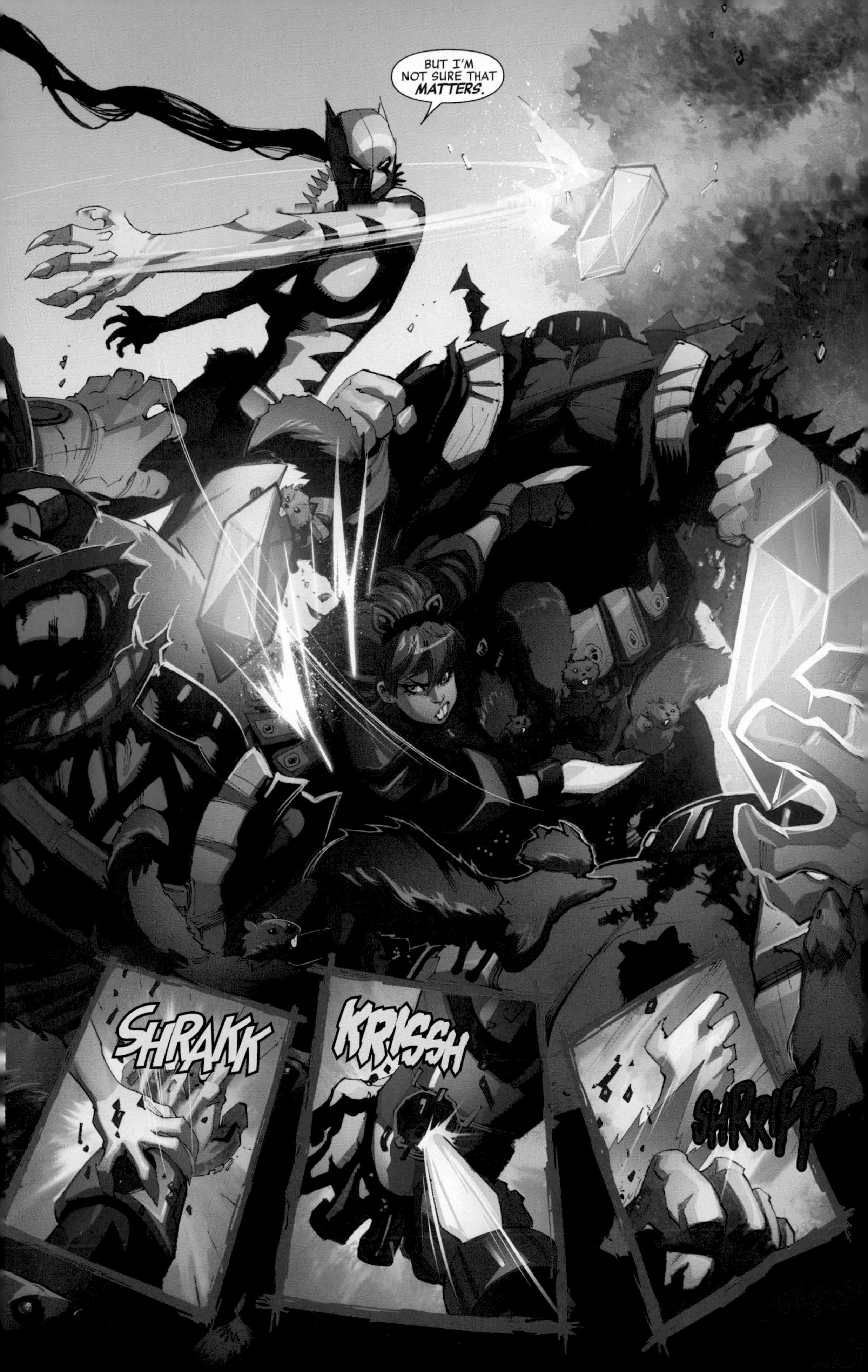
BUT I'M NOT SURE THAT MATTERS.
SHRAKK
KRISSH
SHRIPP

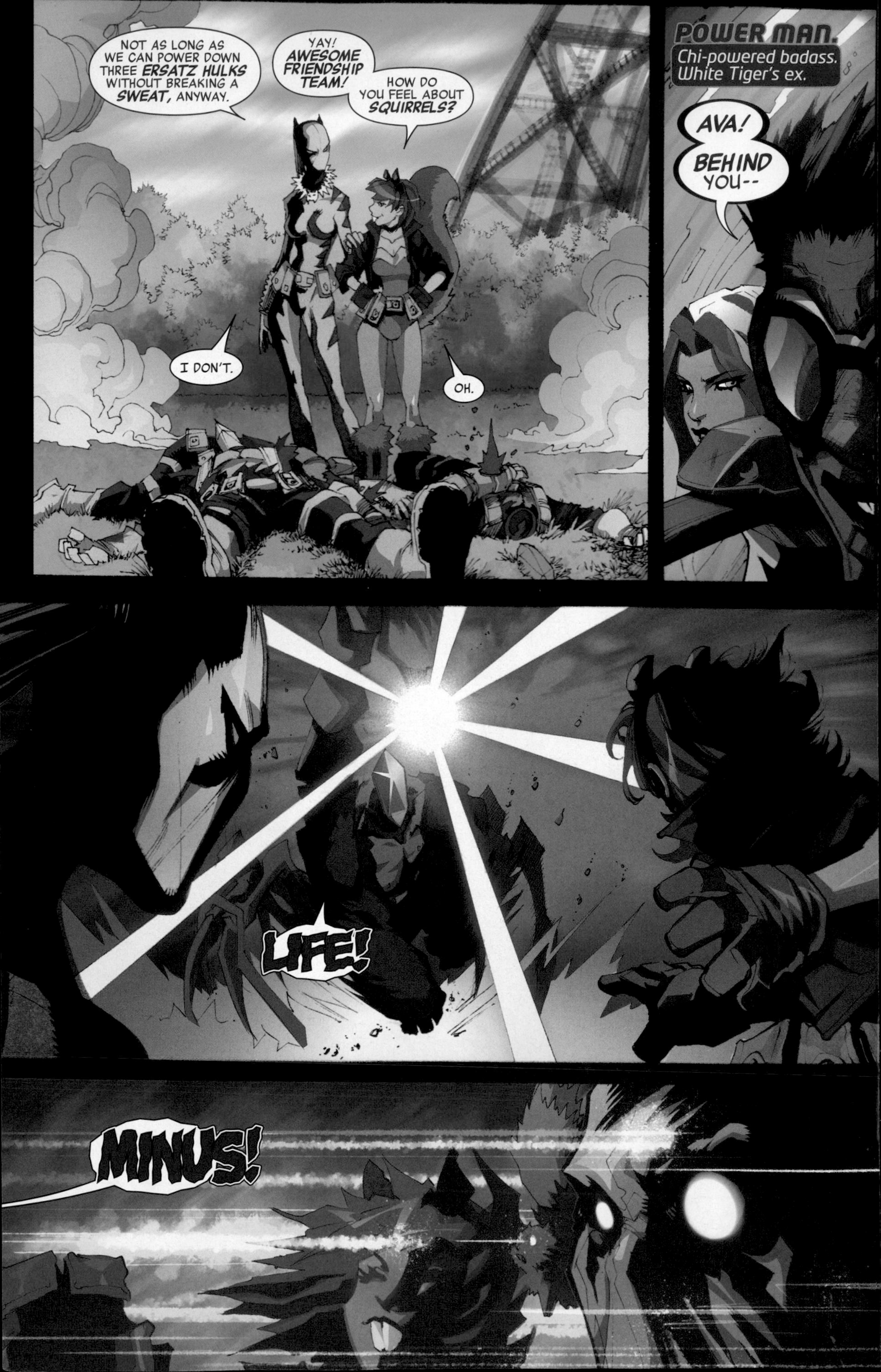
NOT AS LONG AS WE CAN POWER DOWN THREE ERSATZ HULKS WITHOUT BREAKING A SWEAT, ANYWAY.
YAY! AWESOME FRIENDSHIP TEAM!
HOW DO YOU FEEL ABOUT SQUIRRELS?
I DON'T.
OH.
POWER MAN.
Chi-powered badass. White Tiger's ex.
AVA! BEHIND YOU--
LIFE!
MINUS!

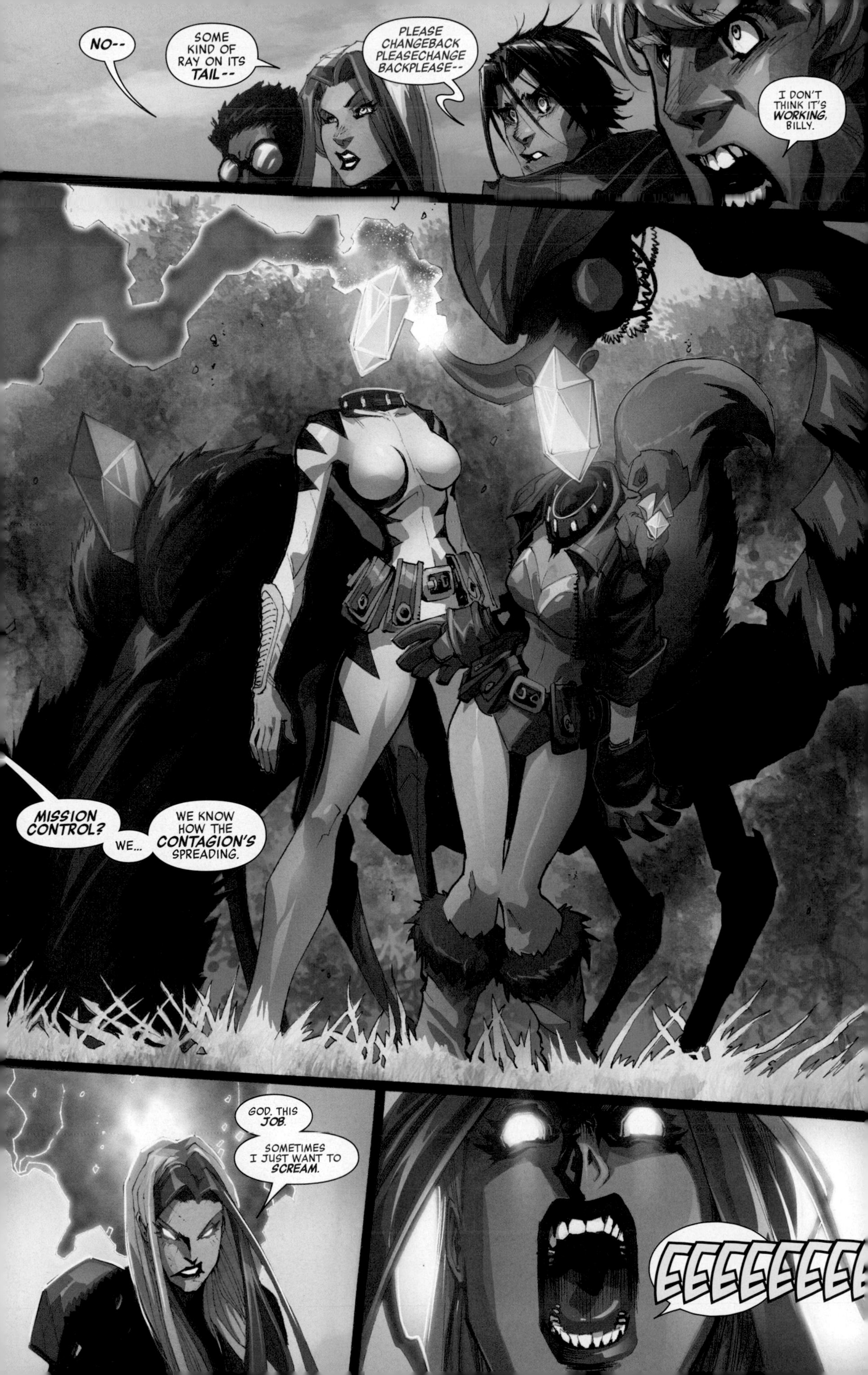
NO--
SOME KIND OF RAY ON ITS TAIL--
PLEASE CHANGEBACK PLEASECHANGE BACKPLEASE--
I DON'T THINK IT'S WORKING, BILLY.
MISSION CONTROL?
WE...
WE KNOW HOW THE CONTAGION'S SPREADING.
GOD. THIS JOB.
SOMETIMES I JUST WANT TO SCREAM.
EEEEEEEE

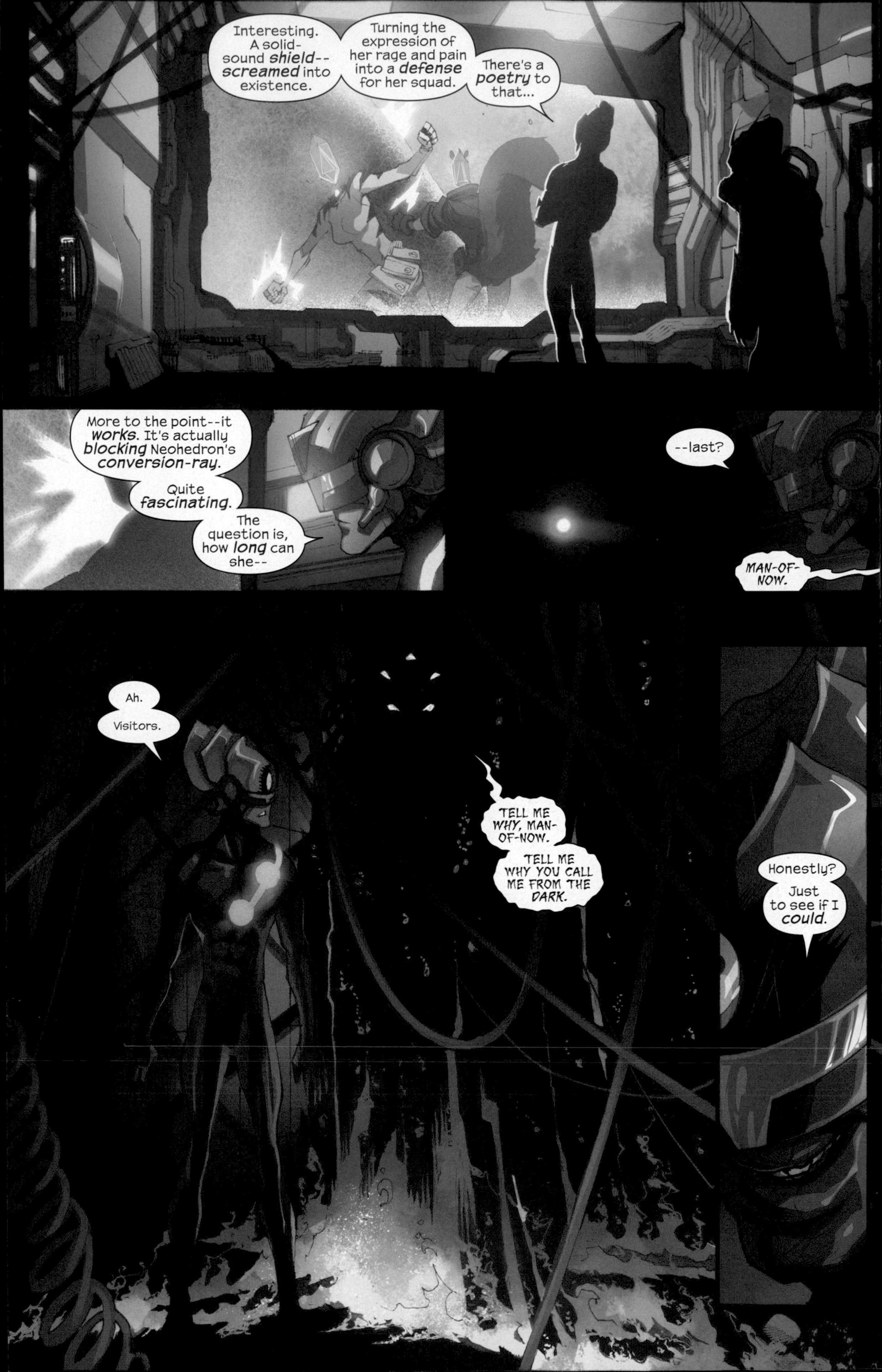
Interesting. A solid-sound shield--screamed into existence.
Turning the expression of her rage and pain into a defense for her squad.
There's a poetry to that...
More to the point--it works. It's actually blocking Neohedron's conversion-ray.
Quite fascinating.
The question is, how long can she--
--last?
MAN-OF-NOW.
Ah.
Visitors.
TELL ME WHY, MAN-OF-NOW.
TELL ME WHY YOU CALL ME FROM THE DARK.
Honestly?
Just to see if I could.

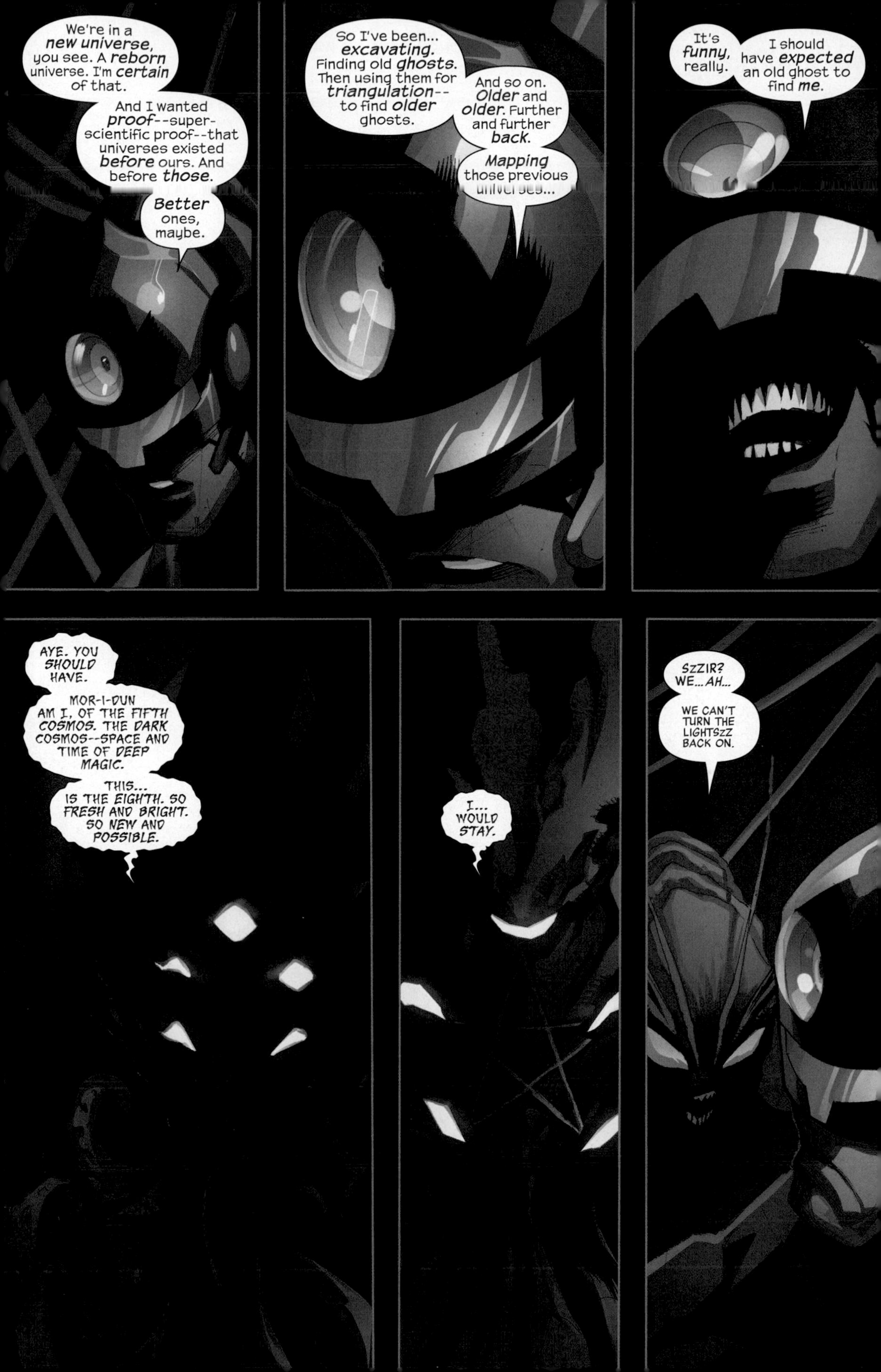
We're in a new universe, you see. A reborn universe. I'm certain of that.
And I wanted proof--super-scientific proof--that universes existed before ours. And before those.
Better ones, maybe.
So I've been... excavating. Finding old ghosts. Then using them for triangulation-- to find older ghosts.
And so on. Older and older. Further and further back.
Mapping those previous universes...
It's funny, really.
I should have expected an old ghost to find me.
AYE. YOU SHOULD HAVE.
MOR-I-DUN AM I, OF THE FIFTH COSMOS. THE DARK COSMOS--SPACE AND TIME OF DEEP MAGIC.
THIS... IS THE EIGHTH. SO FRESH AND BRIGHT. SO NEW AND POSSIBLE.
I... WOULD STAY.
SzZIR? WE... AH...
WE CAN'T TURN THE LIGHTSzZ BACK ON.

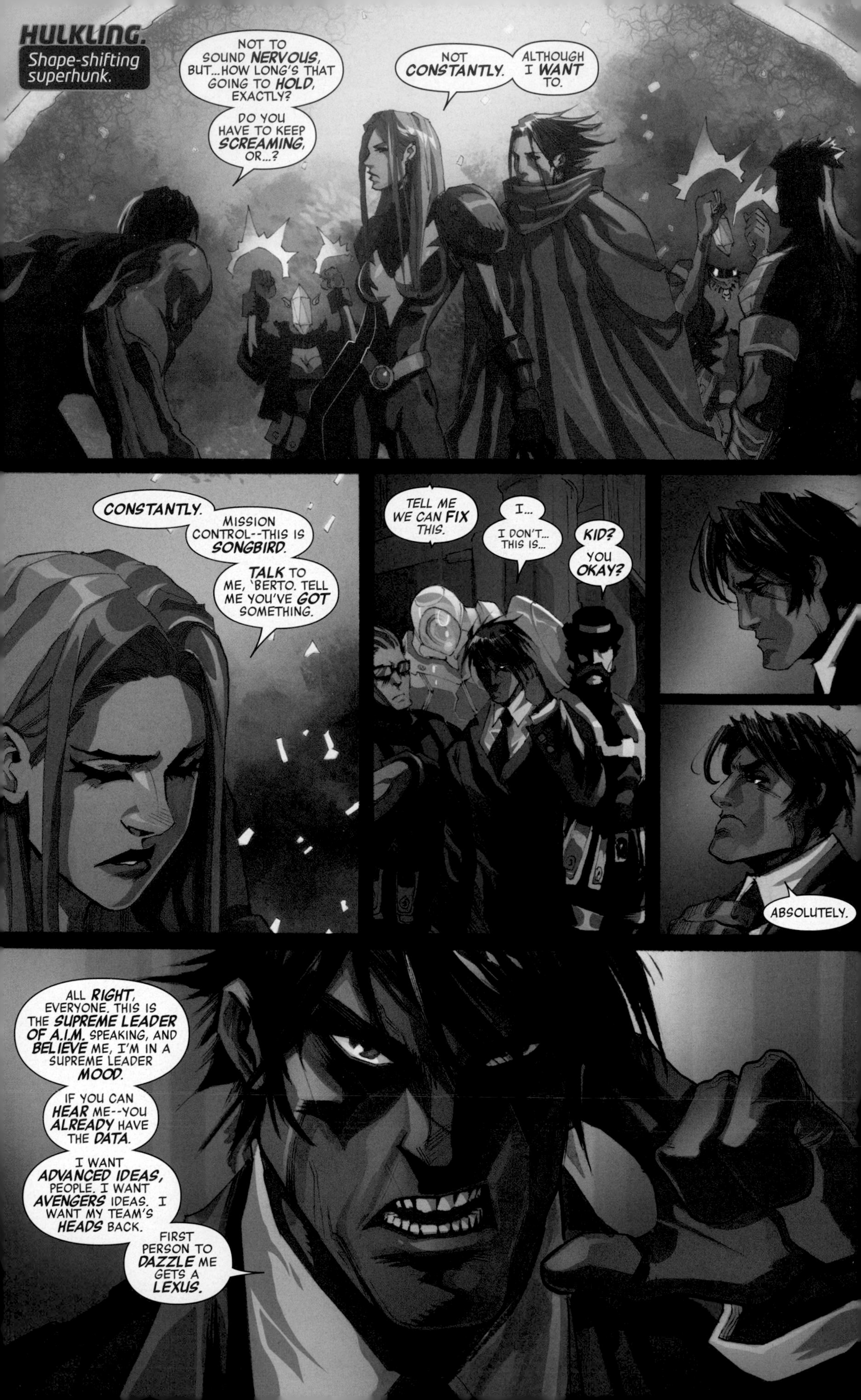
HULKLING. Shape-shifting superhunk.
NOT TO SOUND NERVOUS, BUT...HOW LONG'S THAT GOING TO HOLD, EXACTLY?
DO YOU HAVE TO KEEP SCREAMING, OR...?
NOT CONSTANTLY.
ALTHOUGH I WANT TO.
CONSTANTLY.
MISSION CONTROL--THIS IS SONGBIRD.
TALK TO ME, 'BERTO. TELL ME YOU'VE GOT SOMETHING.
TELL ME WE CAN FIX THIS.
I...
I DON'T... THIS IS...
KID?
YOU OKAY?
ABSOLUTELY.
ALL RIGHT, EVERYONE. THIS IS THE SUPREME LEADER OF A.I.M. SPEAKING, AND BELIEVE ME, I'M IN A SUPREME LEADER MOOD.
IF YOU CAN HEAR ME--YOU ALREADY HAVE THE DATA.
I WANT ADVANCED IDEAS, PEOPLE. I WANT AVENGERS IDEAS. I WANT MY TEAM'S HEADS BACK.
FIRST PERSON TO DAZZLE ME GETS A LEXUS.

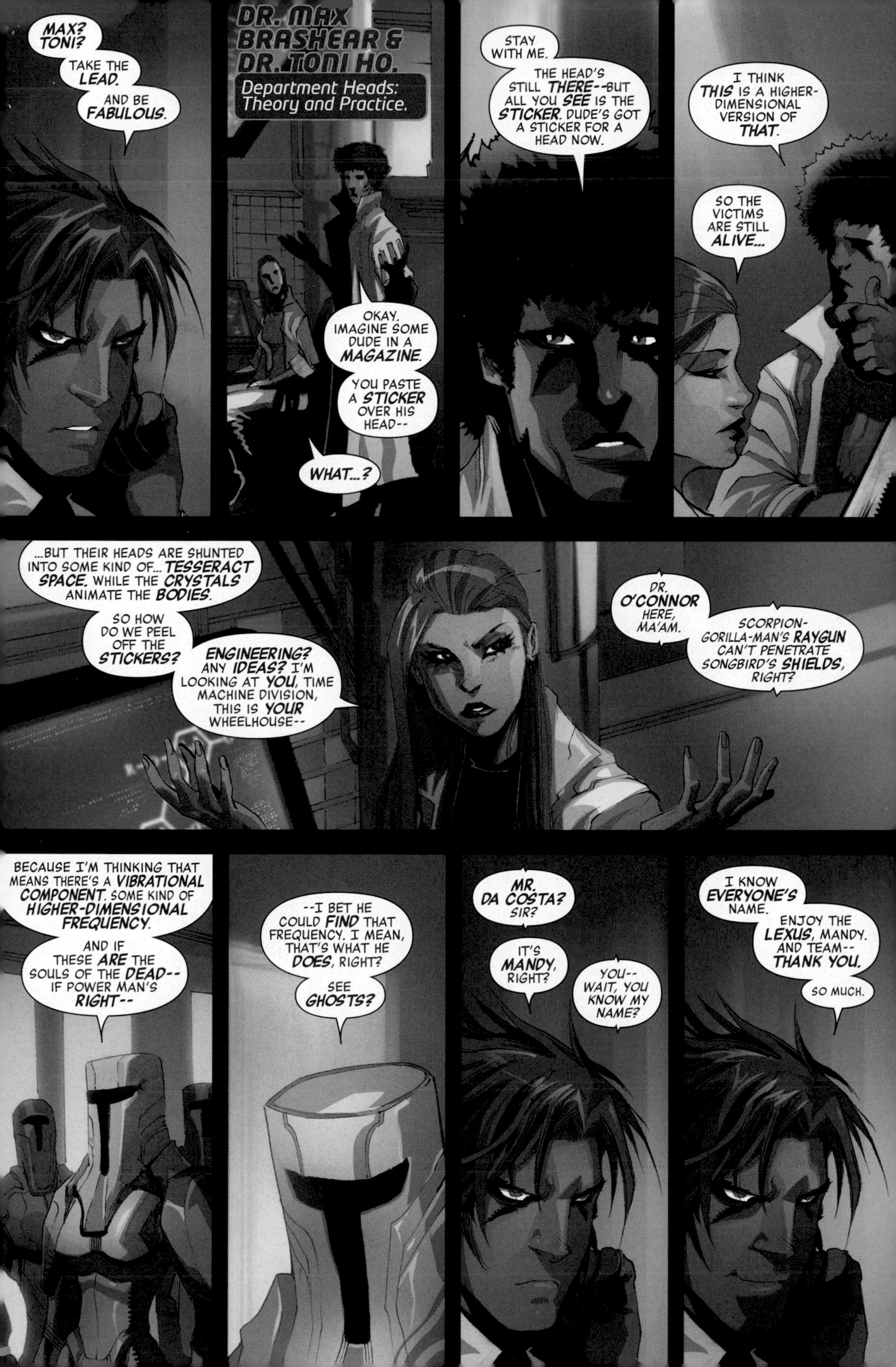
MAX? TONI?
TAKE THE LEAD.
AND BE FABULOUS.
DR. MAX BRASHEAR & DR. TONI HO.
Department Heads: Theory and Practice.
OKAY. IMAGINE SOME DUDE IN A MAGAZINE.
YOU PASTE A STICKER OVER HIS HEAD--
WHAT...?
STAY WITH ME.
THE HEAD'S STILL THERE--BUT ALL YOU SEE IS THE STICKER. DUDE'S GOT A STICKER FOR A HEAD NOW.
I THINK THIS IS A HIGHER-DIMENSIONAL VERSION OF THAT.
SO THE VICTIMS ARE STILL ALIVE...
...BUT THEIR HEADS ARE SHUNTED INTO SOME KIND OF... TESSERACT SPACE. WHILE THE CRYSTALS ANIMATE THE BODIES.
SO HOW DO WE PEEL OFF THE STICKERS?
ENGINEERING? ANY IDEAS? I'M LOOKING AT YOU, TIME MACHINE DIVISION, THIS IS YOUR WHEELHOUSE--
DR. O'CONNOR HERE, MA'AM.
SCORPION-GORILLA-MAN'S RAYGUN CAN'T PENETRATE SONGBIRD'S SHIELDS, RIGHT?
BECAUSE I'M THINKING THAT MEANS THERE'S A VIBRATIONAL COMPONENT. SOME KIND OF HIGHER-DIMENSIONAL FREQUENCY.
AND IF THESE ARE THE SOULS OF THE DEAD--IF POWER MAN'S RIGHT--
--I BET HE COULD FIND THAT FREQUENCY. I MEAN, THAT'S WHAT HE DOES, RIGHT?
SEE GHOSTS?
MR. DA COSTA? SIR?
IT'S MANDY, RIGHT?
YOU--WAIT, YOU KNOW MY NAME?
I KNOW EVERYONE'S NAME.
ENJOY THE LEXUS, MANDY. AND TEAM--THANK YOU.
SO MUCH.

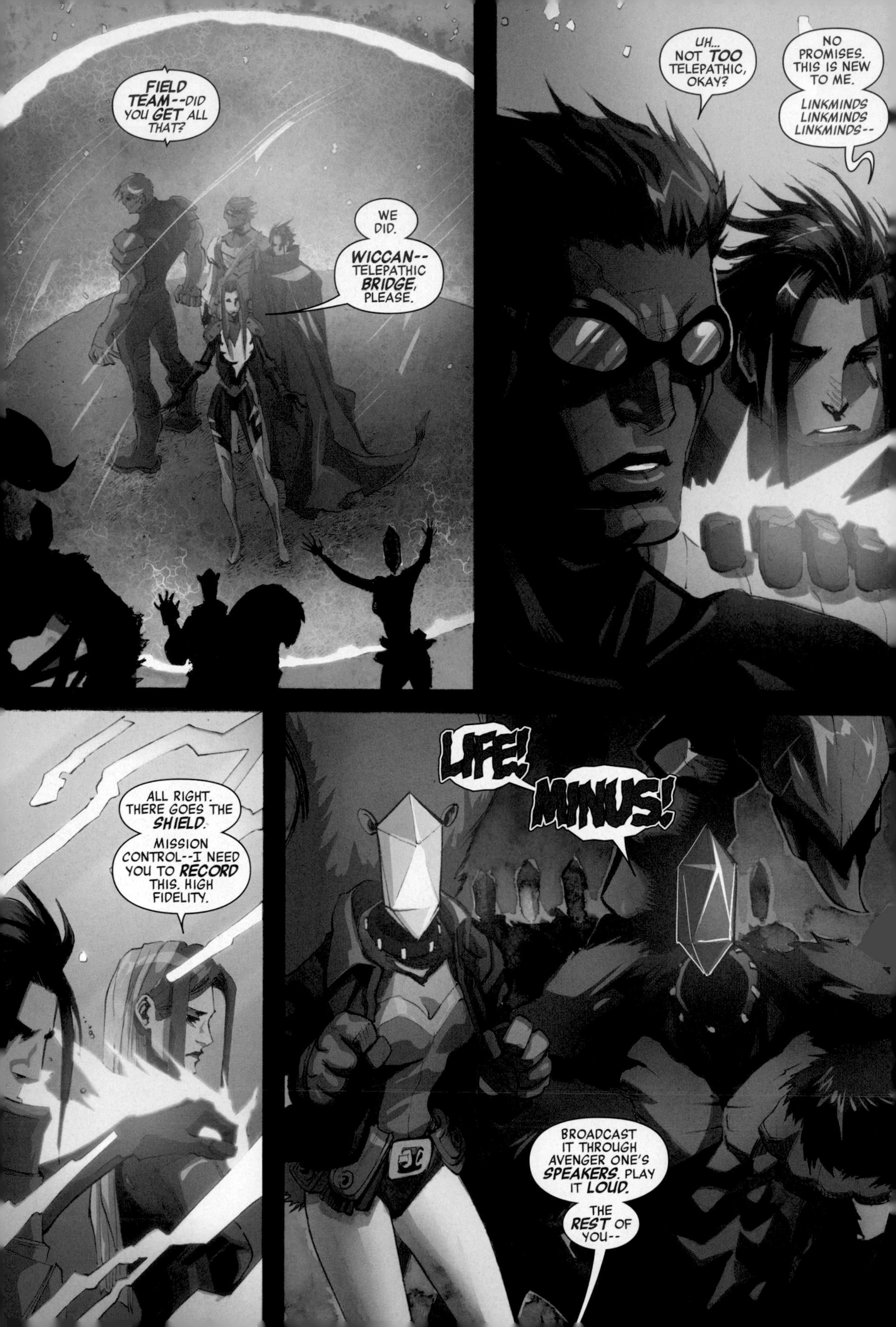
FIELD TEAM--DID YOU GET ALL THAT?
WE DID.
WICCAN--TELEPATHIC BRIDGE, PLEASE.
UH... NOT TOO TELEPATHIC, OKAY?
NO PROMISES. THIS IS NEW TO ME.
LINKMINDS LINKMINDS LINKMINDS--
ALL RIGHT. THERE GOES THE SHIELD.
MISSION CONTROL--I NEED YOU TO RECORD THIS. HIGH FIDELITY.
LIFE! MINUS!
BROADCAST IT THROUGH AVENGER ONE'S SPEAKERS. PLAY IT LOUD.
THE REST OF YOU--

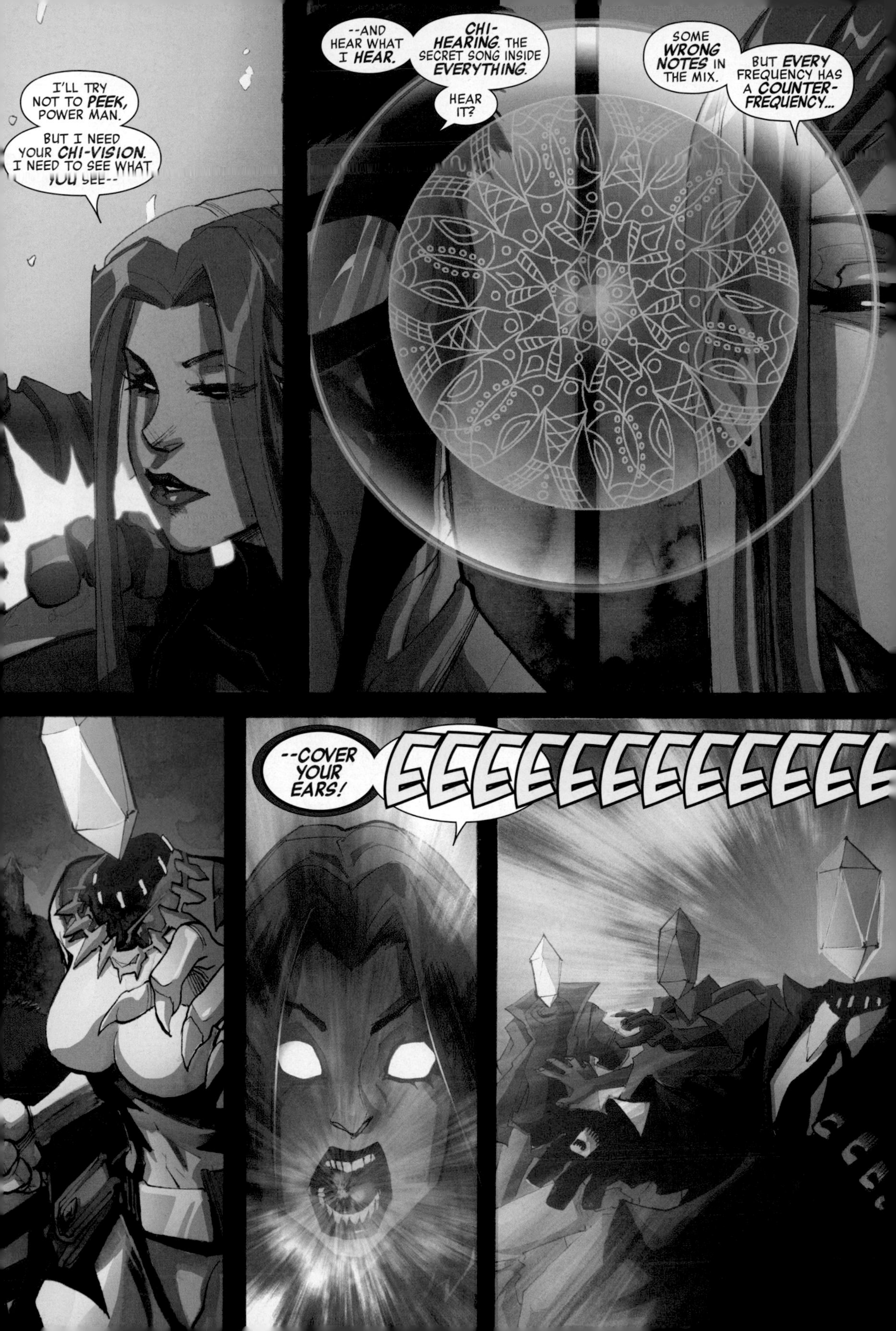
I'LL TRY NOT TO PEEK, POWER MAN.
BUT I NEED YOUR CHI-VISION. I NEED TO SEE WHAT YOU SEE--
--AND HEAR WHAT I HEAR.
CHI-HEARING. THE SECRET SONG INSIDE EVERYTHING.
HEAR IT?
SOME WRONG NOTES IN THE MIX.
BUT EVERY FREQUENCY HAS A COUNTER-FREQUENCY...
--COVER YOUR EARS!
EEEEEEEEEEEEEE

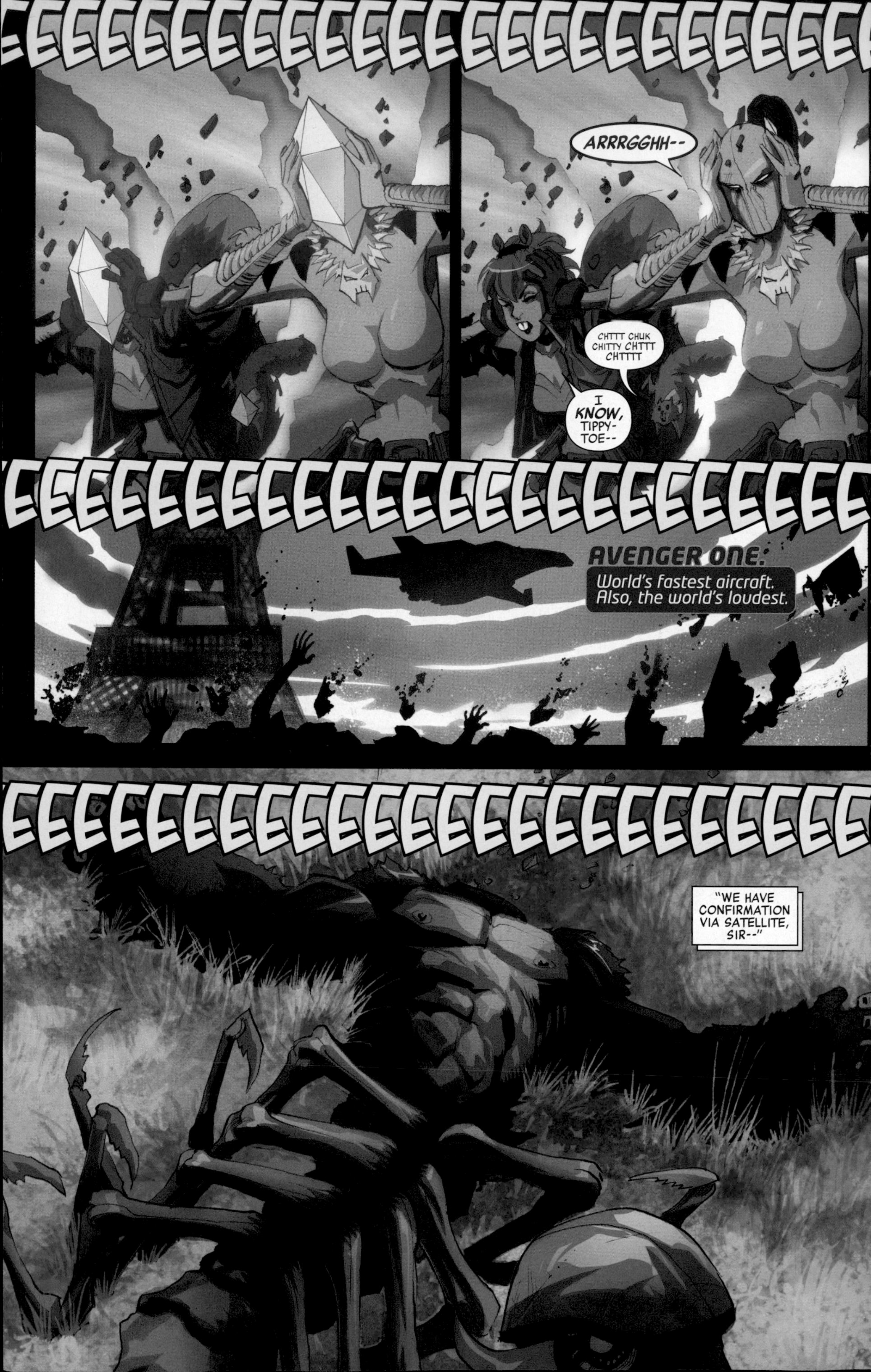
EEEEEEEEEEEEEEEEEEEEEEEEEEEEEEEE
ARRRGGHH--
CHTTT CHUK CHITTY CHTTT CHTTTT
I KNOW, TIPPY-TOE--
EEEEEEEEEEEEEEEEEEEEEEEEEEEEEEE
AVENGER ONE.
World's fastest aircraft. Also, the world's loudest.
EEEEEEEEEEEEEEEEEEEEEEEEEEEEEEE
"WE HAVE CONFIRMATION VIA SATELLITE, SIR--"

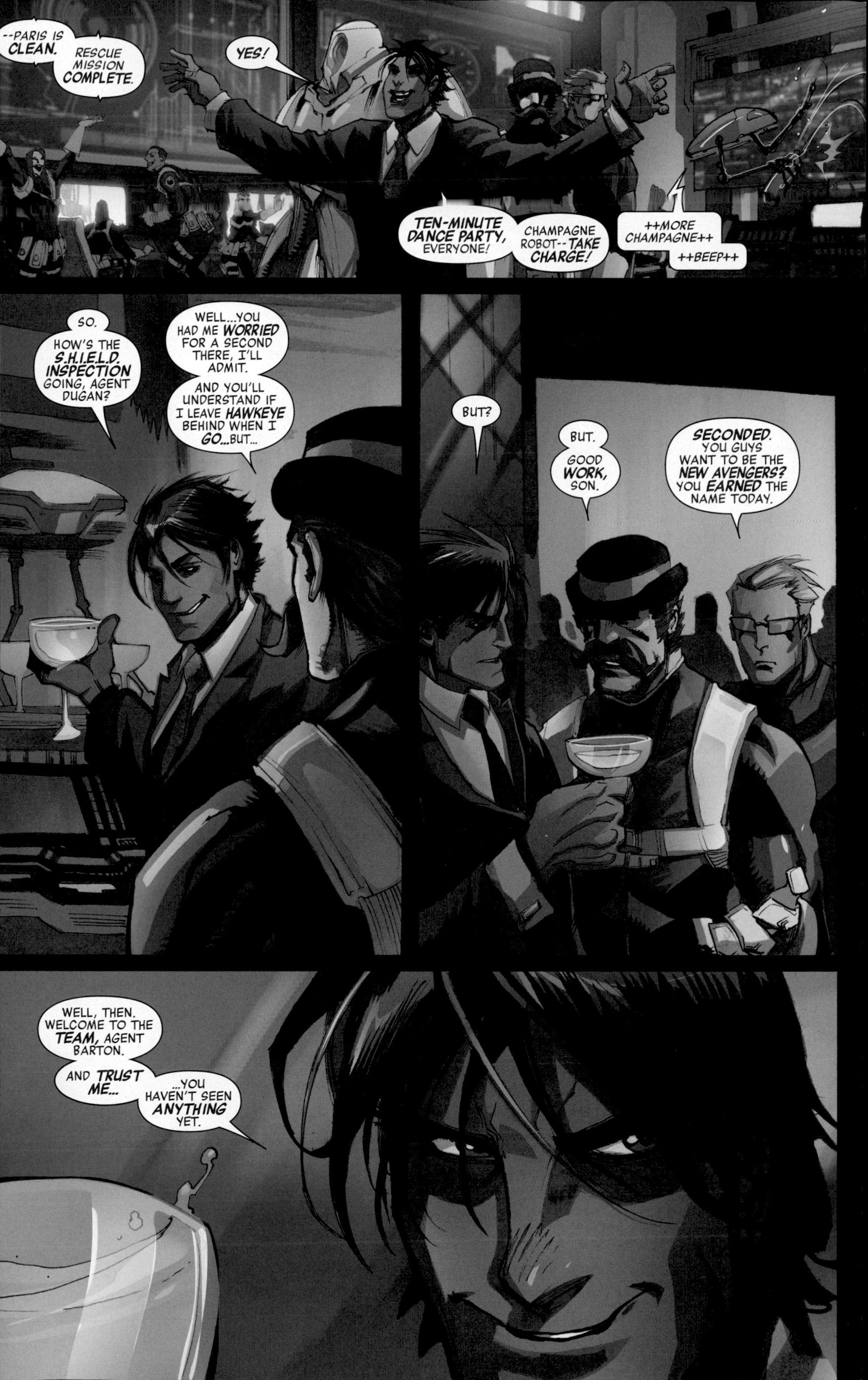
--PARIS IS CLEAN. RESCUE MISSION COMPLETE.
YES!
TEN-MINUTE DANCE PARTY, EVERYONE!
CHAMPAGNE ROBOT--TAKE CHARGE!
++MORE CHAMPAGNE++
++BEEP++
SO.
HOW'S THE S.H.I.E.L.D. INSPECTION GOING, AGENT DUGAN?
WELL...YOU HAD ME WORRIED FOR A SECOND THERE, I'LL ADMIT.
AND YOU'LL UNDERSTAND IF I LEAVE HAWKEYE BEHIND WHEN I GO...BUT...
BUT?
BUT.
GOOD WORK, SON.
SECONDED. YOU GUYS WANT TO BE THE NEW AVENGERS? YOU EARNED THE NAME TODAY.
WELL, THEN. WELCOME TO THE TEAM, AGENT BARTON.
AND TRUST ME...
...YOU HAVEN'T SEEN ANYTHING YET.

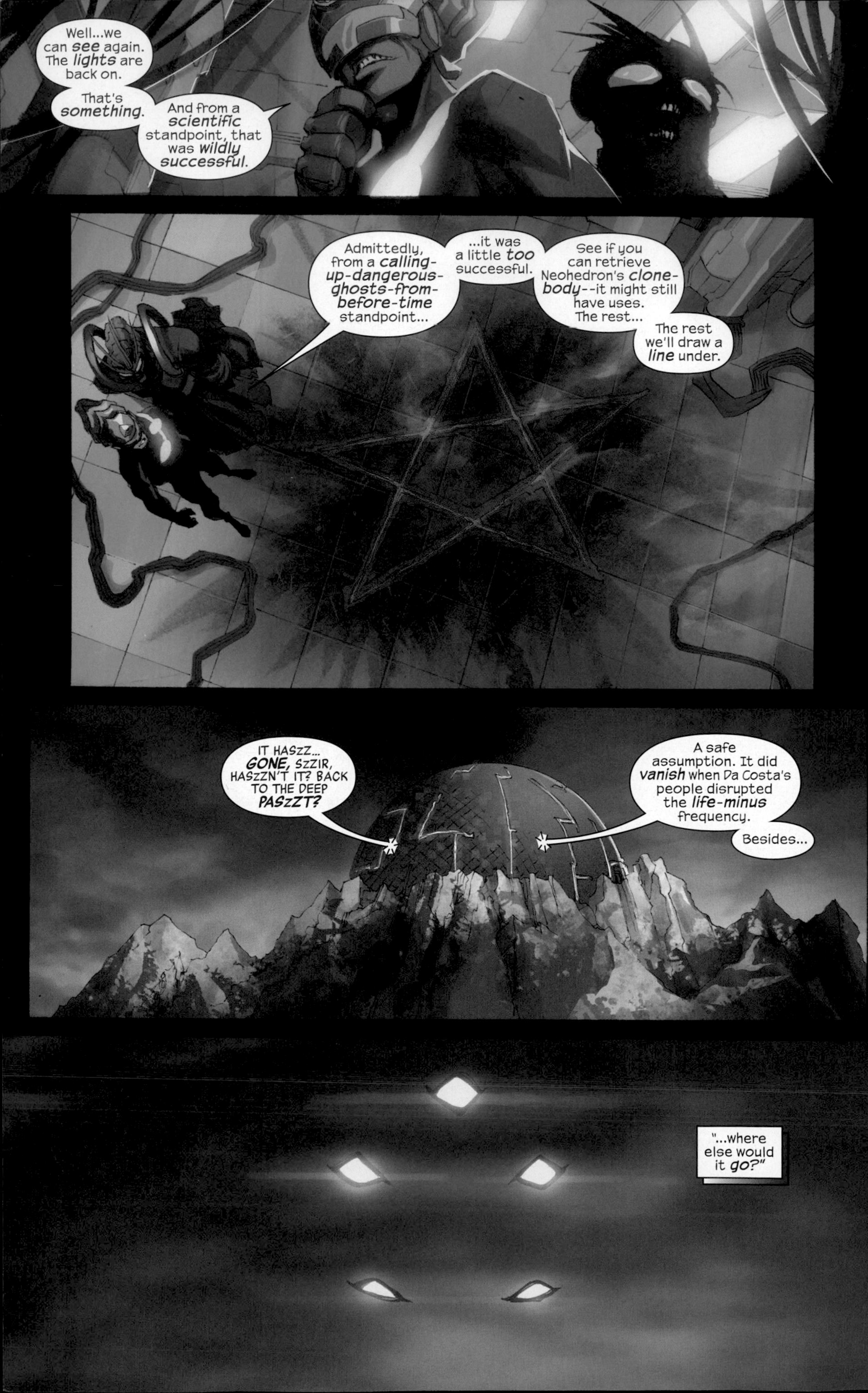
Well...we can see again. The lights are back on.
That's something.
And from a scientific standpoint, that was wildly successful.
Admittedly, from a calling-up-dangerous-ghosts-from-before-time standpoint...
...it was a little too successful.
See if you can retrieve Neohedron's clone-body--it might still have uses. The rest...
The rest we'll draw a line under.
IT HASzZ... GONE, SzZIR, HASzZN'T IT? BACK TO THE DEEP PASzZT?
A safe assumption. It did vanish when Da Costa's people disrupted the life-minus frequency.
Besides...
"...where else would it go?"

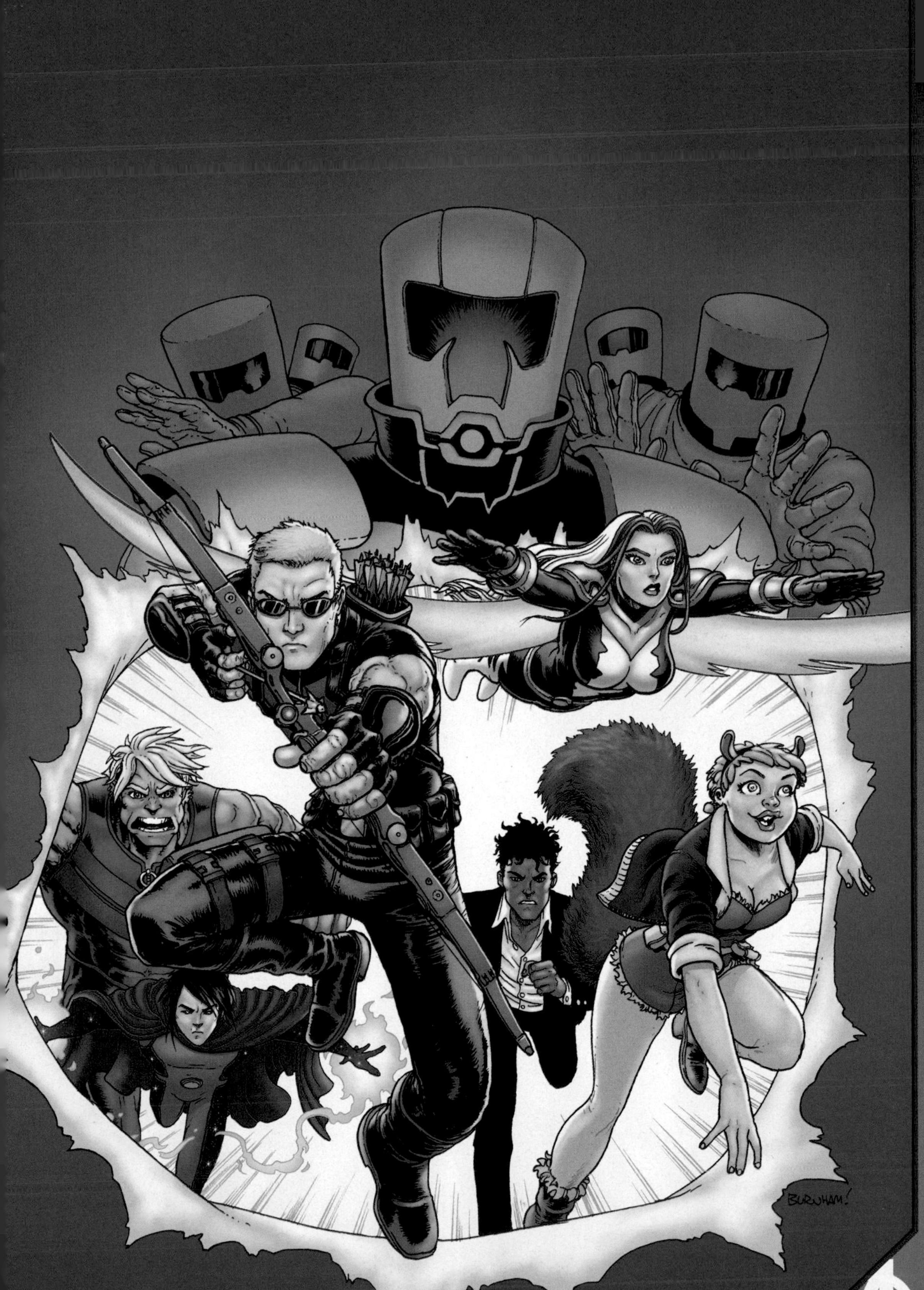
BURNHAM!

#3 VARIANT BY **CHRIS BURNHAM** & **NATHAN FAIRBAIRN**

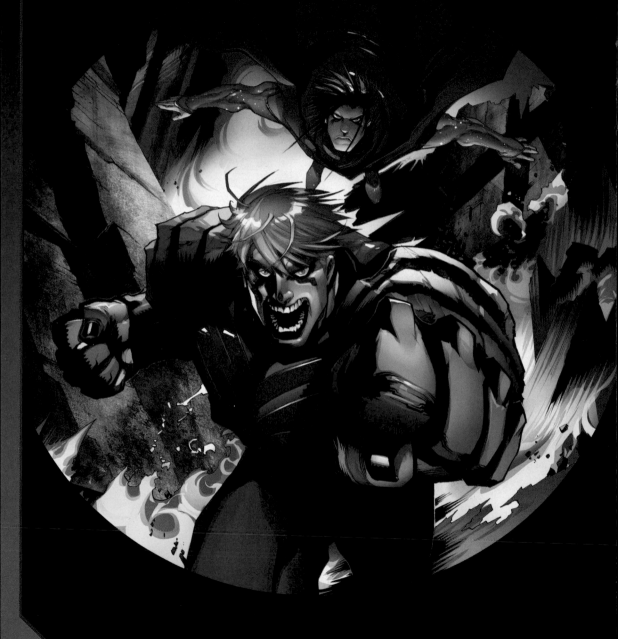

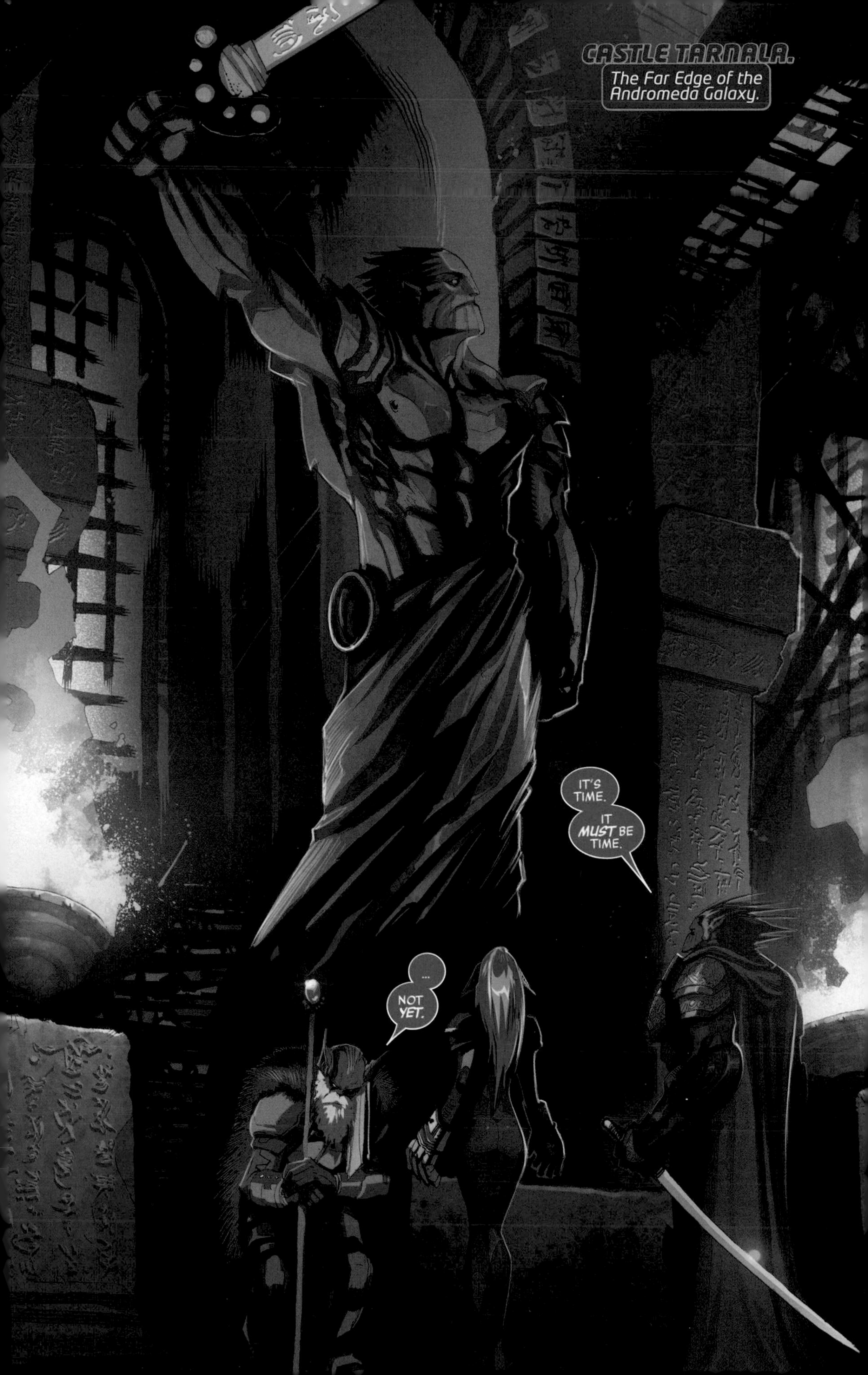
CASTLE TARNALA.
The Far Edge of the Andromeda Galaxy.
IT'S TIME.
IT MUST BE TIME.
... NOT YET.

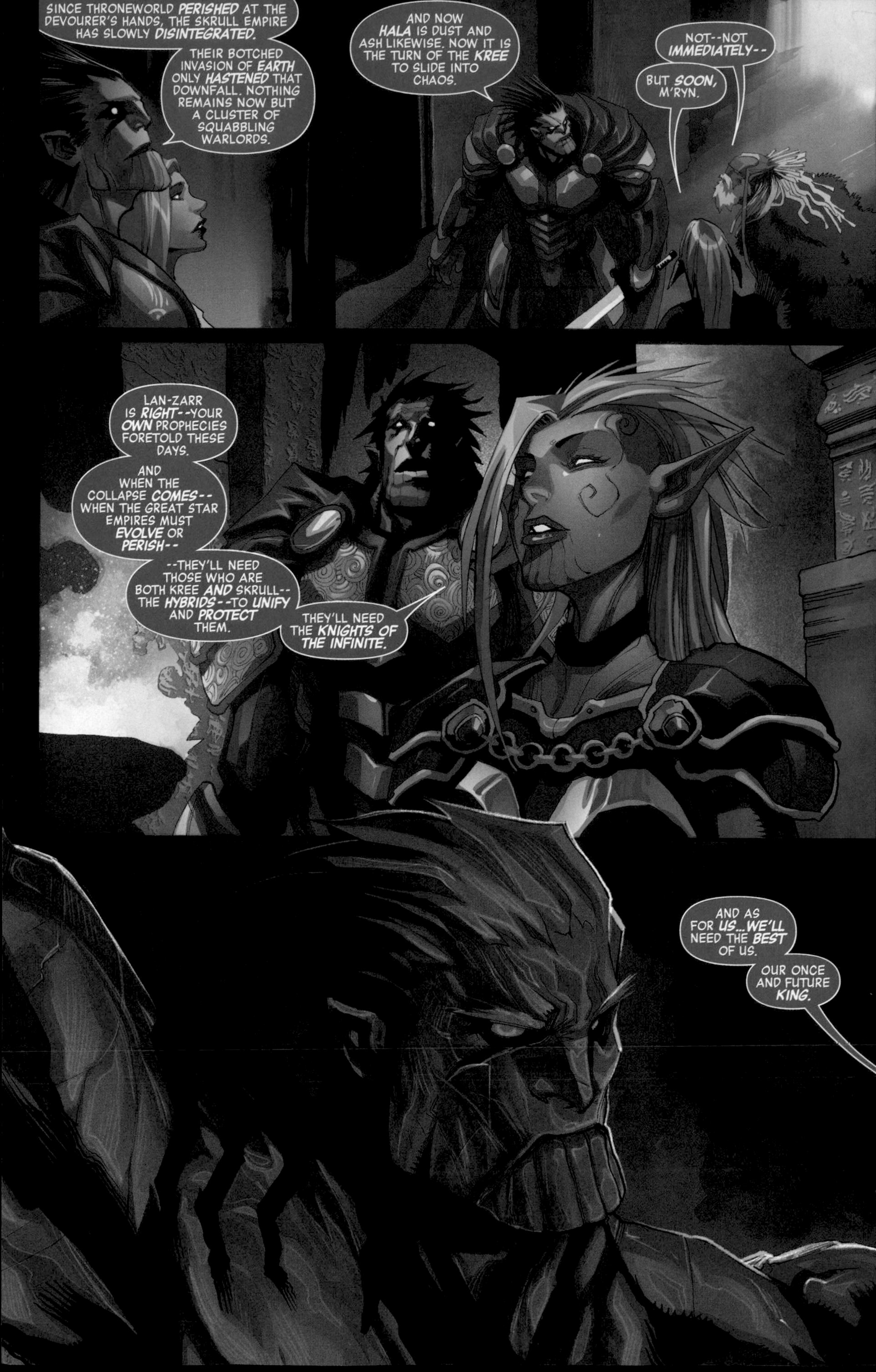
SINCE THRONEWORLD PERISHED AT THE DEVOURER'S HANDS, THE SKRULL EMPIRE HAS SLOWLY DISINTEGRATED.
THEIR BOTCHED INVASION OF EARTH ONLY HASTENED THAT DOWNFALL. NOTHING REMAINS NOW BUT A CLUSTER OF SQUABBLING WARLORDS.
AND NOW HALA IS DUST AND ASH LIKEWISE. NOW IT IS THE TURN OF THE KREE TO SLIDE INTO CHAOS.
NOT--NOT IMMEDIATELY--
BUT SOON, M'RYN.
LAN-ZARR IS RIGHT--YOUR OWN PROPHECIES FORETOLD THESE DAYS.
AND WHEN THE COLLAPSE COMES-- WHEN THE GREAT STAR EMPIRES MUST EVOLVE OR PERISH--
--THEY'LL NEED THOSE WHO ARE BOTH KREE AND SKRULL-- THE HYBRIDS--TO UNIFY AND PROTECT THEM.
THEY'LL NEED THE KNIGHTS OF THE INFINITE.
AND AS FOR US...WE'LL NEED THE BEST OF US.
OUR ONCE AND FUTURE KING.

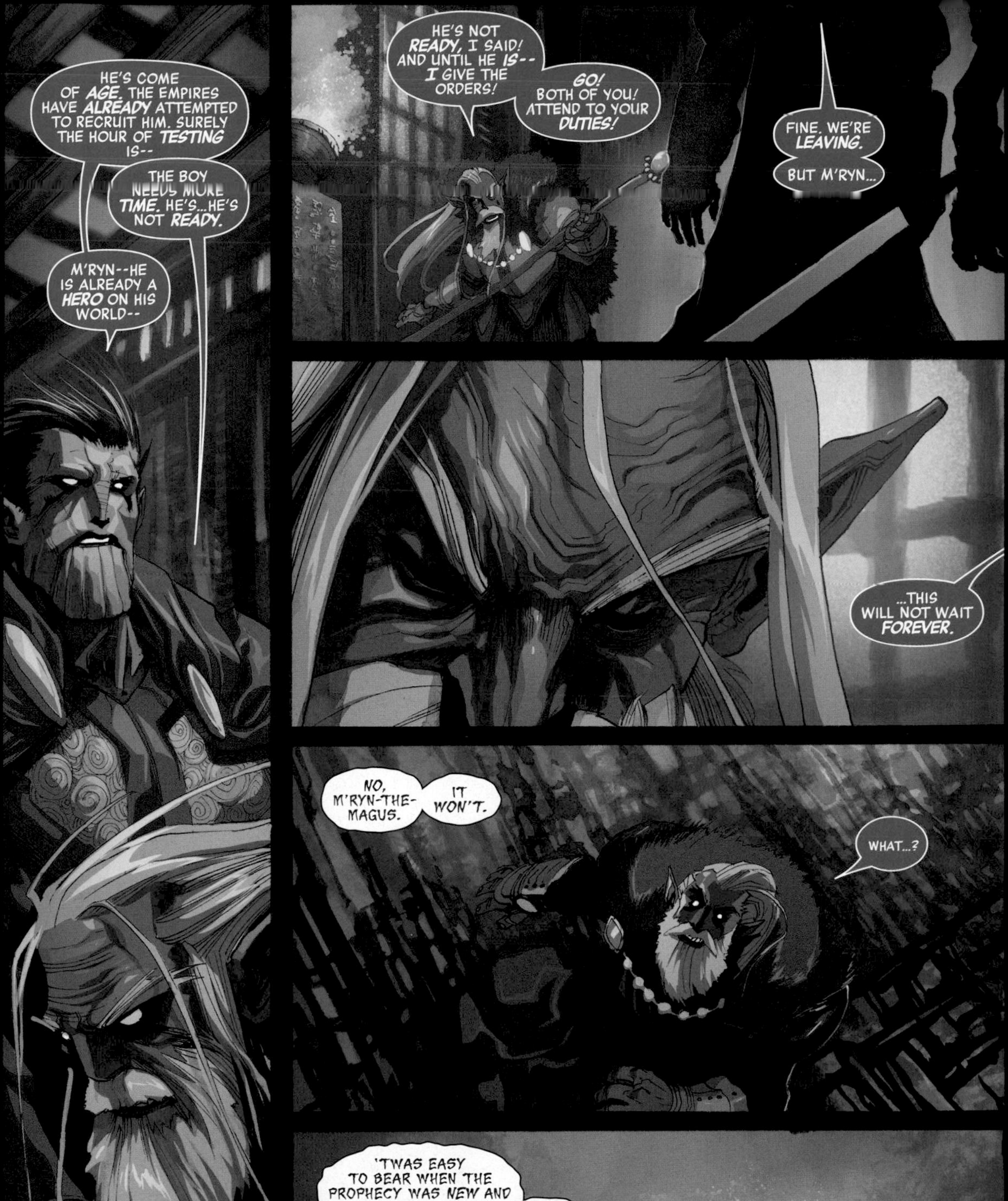
HE'S COME OF AGE. THE EMPIRES HAVE ALREADY ATTEMPTED TO RECRUIT HIM. SURELY THE HOUR OF TESTING IS--
THE BOY NEEDS MORE TIME. HE'S...HE'S NOT READY.
M'RYN--HE IS ALREADY A HERO ON HIS WORLD--
HE'S NOT READY, I SAID! AND UNTIL HE IS-- I GIVE THE ORDERS!
GO! BOTH OF YOU! ATTEND TO YOUR DUTIES!
FINE. WE'RE LEAVING.
BUT M'RYN...
...THIS WILL NOT WAIT FOREVER.
NO, M'RYN-THE-MAGUS.
IT WON'T.
WHAT...?
'TWAS EASY TO BEAR WHEN THE PROPHECY WAS NEW AND LONG-AHEAD. FAR IN YOUR FUTURE.
EASY TO BEAR THE TRUTH.
WHO--WHO SPEAKS?
I WARN YOU--I AM NO HARMLESS ELDER! I KEEP THE SECRET FIRE OF MAGIC!
I HAVE POWERS BEYOND POWERS--

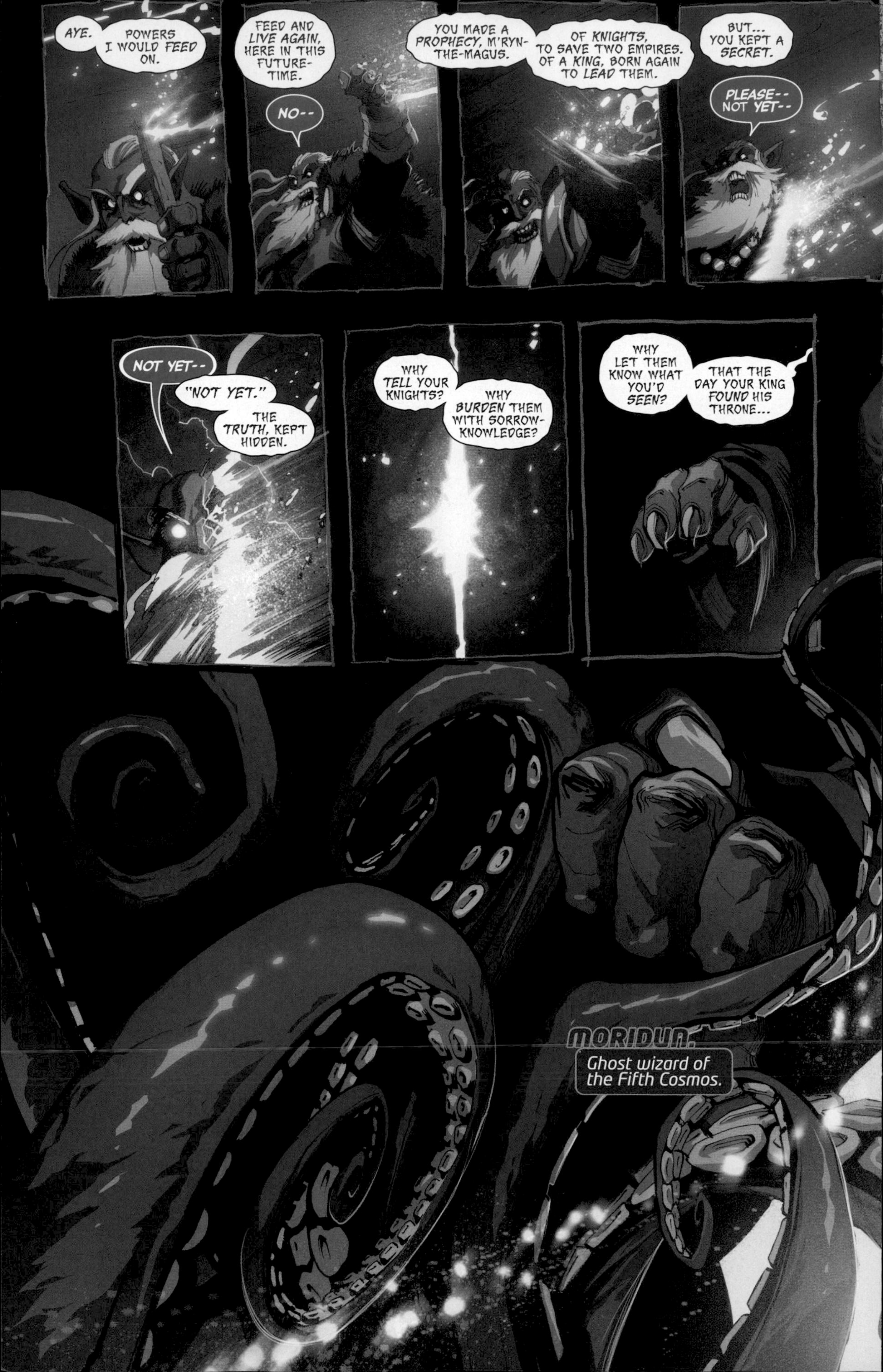

AYE.
POWERS I WOULD FEED ON.
FEED AND LIVE AGAIN, HERE IN THIS FUTURE-TIME.
NO--
YOU MADE A PROPHECY, M'RYN-THE-MAGUS.
OF KNIGHTS, TO SAVE TWO EMPIRES. OF A KING, BORN AGAIN TO LEAD THEM.
BUT... YOU KEPT A SECRET.
PLEASE-- NOT YET--
NOT YET--
"NOT YET."
THE TRUTH, KEPT HIDDEN.
WHY TELL YOUR KNIGHTS?
WHY BURDEN THEM WITH SORROW-KNOWLEDGE?
WHY LET THEM KNOW WHAT YOU'D SEEN?
THAT THE DAY YOUR KING FOUND HIS THRONE...
MORIDUN.
Ghost wizard of the Fifth Cosmos.

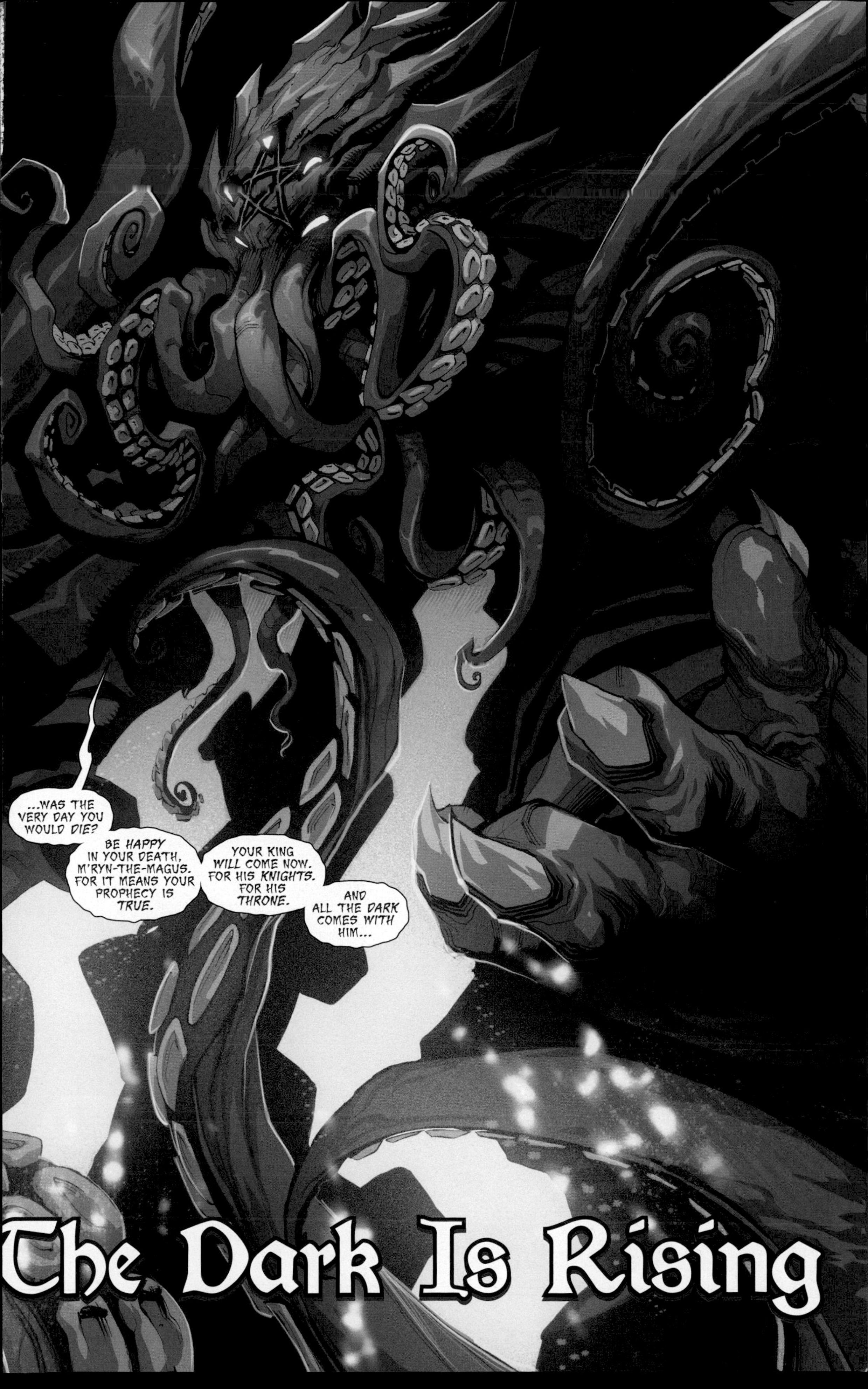
...WAS THE VERY DAY YOU WOULD DIE?
BE HAPPY IN YOUR DEATH, M'RYN-THE-MAGUS. FOR IT MEANS YOUR PROPHECY IS TRUE.
YOUR KING WILL COME NOW. FOR HIS KNIGHTS. FOR HIS THRONE.
AND ALL THE DARK COMES WITH HIM...
The Dark Is Rising

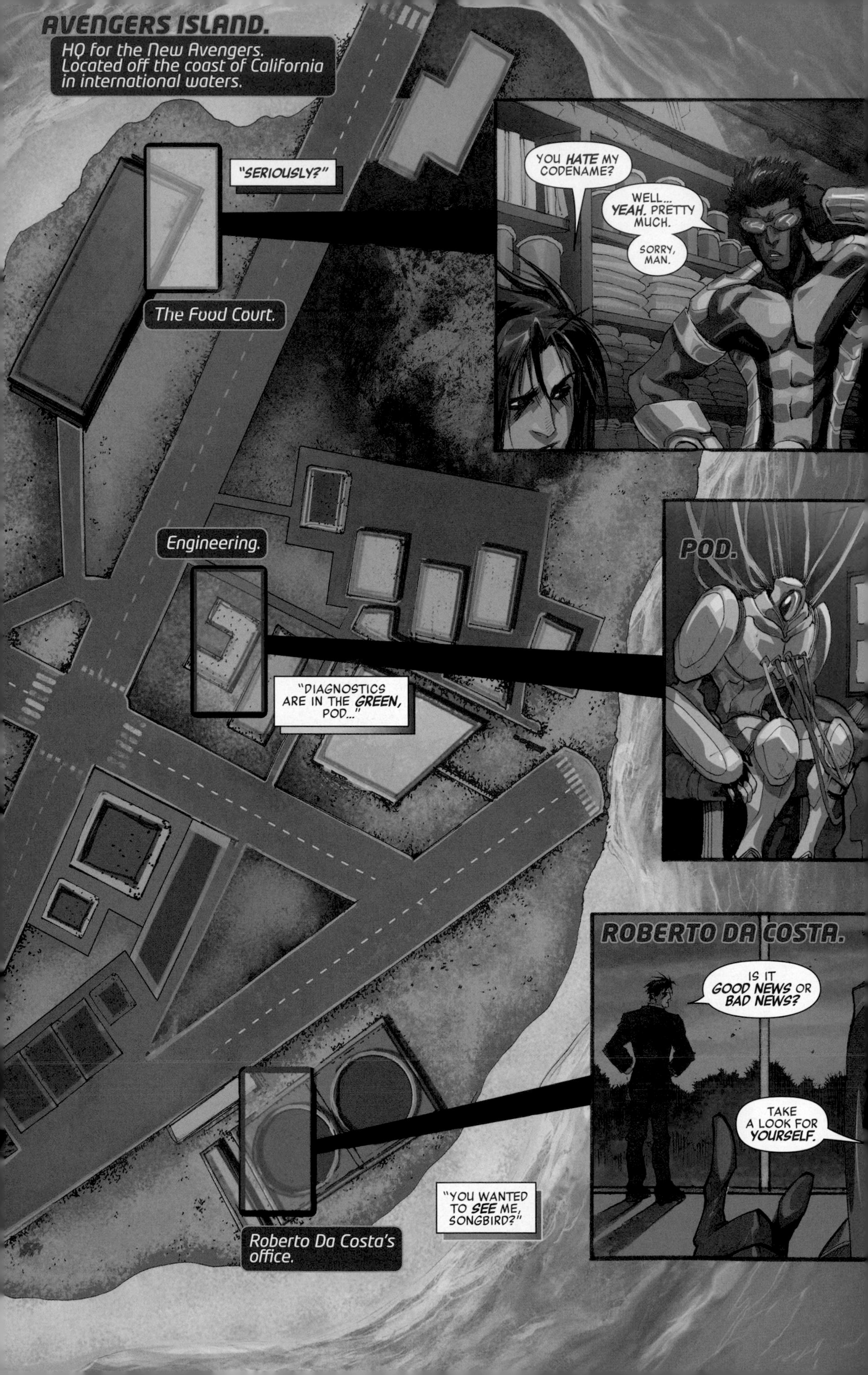
AVENGERS ISLAND.
HQ for the New Avengers. Located off the coast of California in international waters.
"SERIOUSLY?"
The Food Court.
YOU HATE MY CODENAME?
WELL... YEAH. PRETTY MUCH.
SORRY, MAN.
Engineering.
"DIAGNOSTICS ARE IN THE GREEN, POD..."
POD.
ROBERTO DA COSTA.
IS IT GOOD NEWS OR BAD NEWS?
TAKE A LOOK FOR YOURSELF.
"YOU WANTED TO SEE ME, SONGBIRD?"
Roberto Da Costa's office.

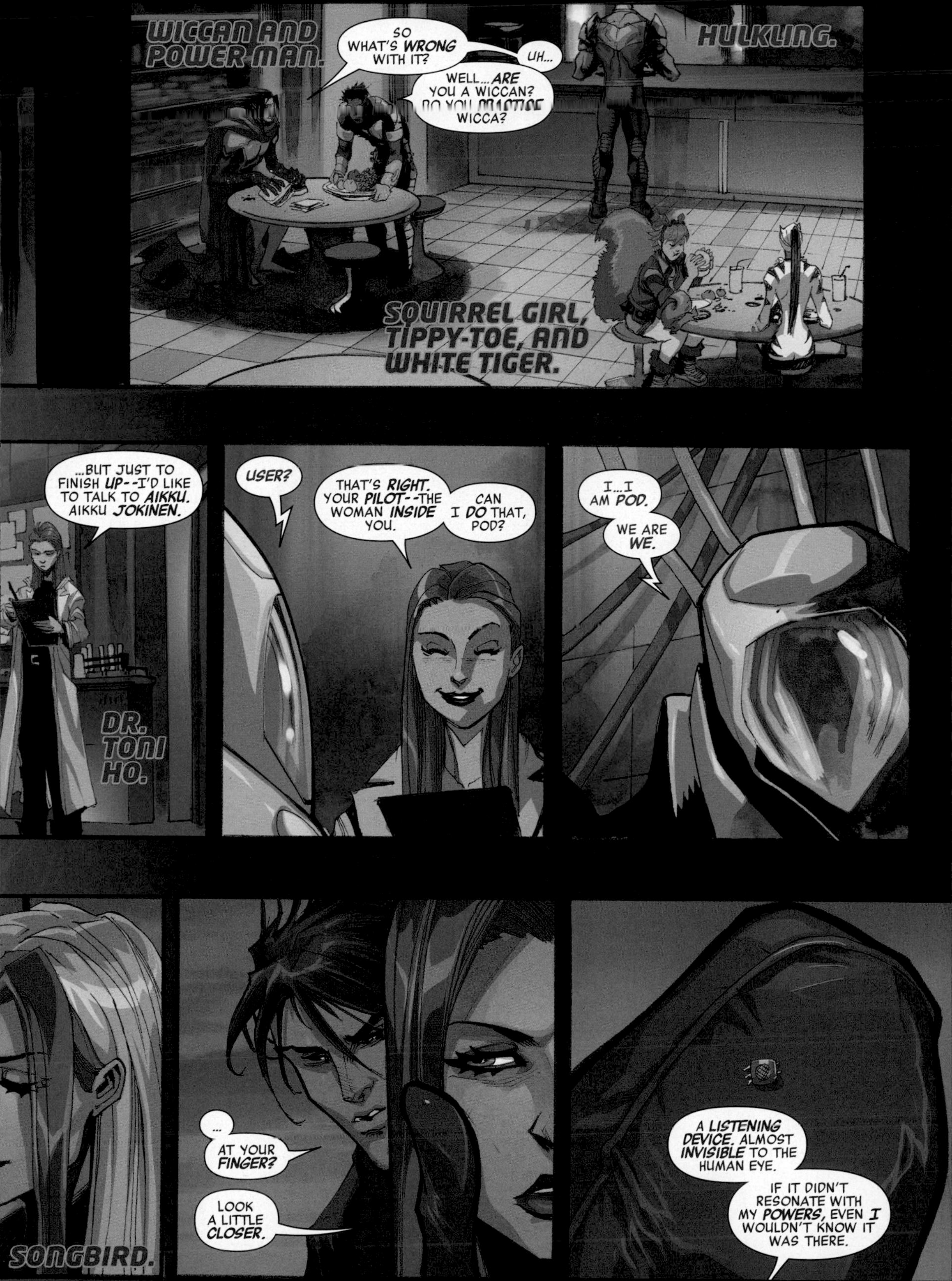
WICCAN AND POWER MAN.
SO WHAT'S WRONG WITH IT?
UH...
WELL...ARE YOU A WICCAN? DO YOU PRACTICE WICCA?
HULKLING.
SQUIRREL GIRL, TIPPY-TOE, AND WHITE TIGER.
...BUT JUST TO FINISH UP--I'D LIKE TO TALK TO AIKKU. AIKKU JOKINEN.
DR. TONI HO.
USER?
THAT'S RIGHT. YOUR PILOT--THE WOMAN INSIDE YOU.
CAN I DO THAT, POD?
I...I AM POD.
WE ARE WE.
SONGBIRD.
...
AT YOUR FINGER?
LOOK A LITTLE CLOSER.
A LISTENING DEVICE. ALMOST INVISIBLE TO THE HUMAN EYE.
IF IT DIDN'T RESONATE WITH MY POWERS, EVEN I WOULDN'T KNOW IT WAS THERE.

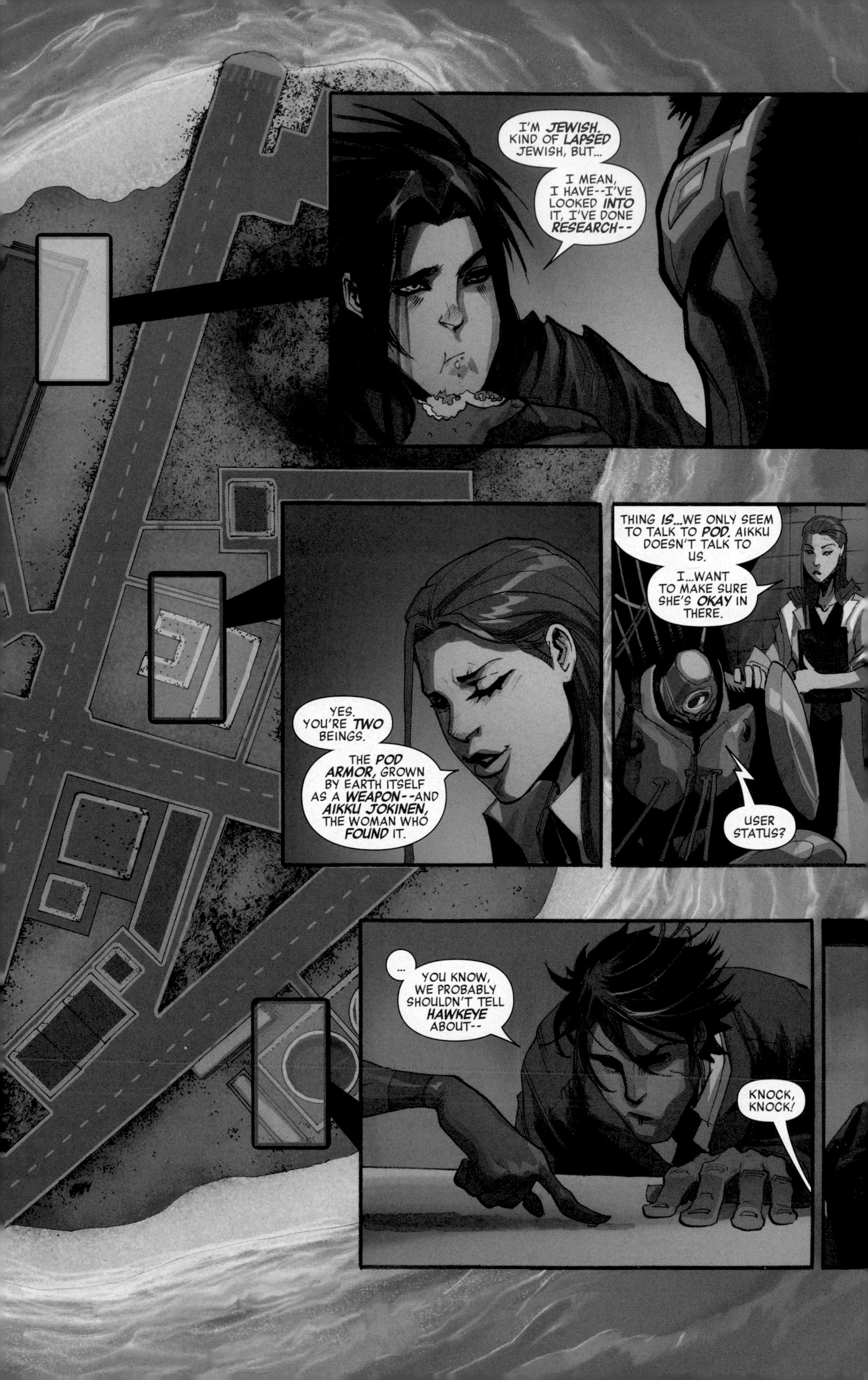
I'M JEWISH. KIND OF LAPSED JEWISH, BUT...
I MEAN, I HAVE--I'VE LOOKED INTO IT, I'VE DONE RESEARCH--
YES. YOU'RE TWO BEINGS.
THE POD ARMOR, GROWN BY EARTH ITSELF AS A WEAPON--AND AIKKU JOKINEN, THE WOMAN WHO FOUND IT.
THING IS...WE ONLY SEEM TO TALK TO POD. AIKKU DOESN'T TALK TO US.
I...WANT TO MAKE SURE SHE'S OKAY IN THERE.
USER STATUS?
...
YOU KNOW, WE PROBABLY SHOULDN'T TELL HAWKEYE ABOUT--
KNOCK, KNOCK!

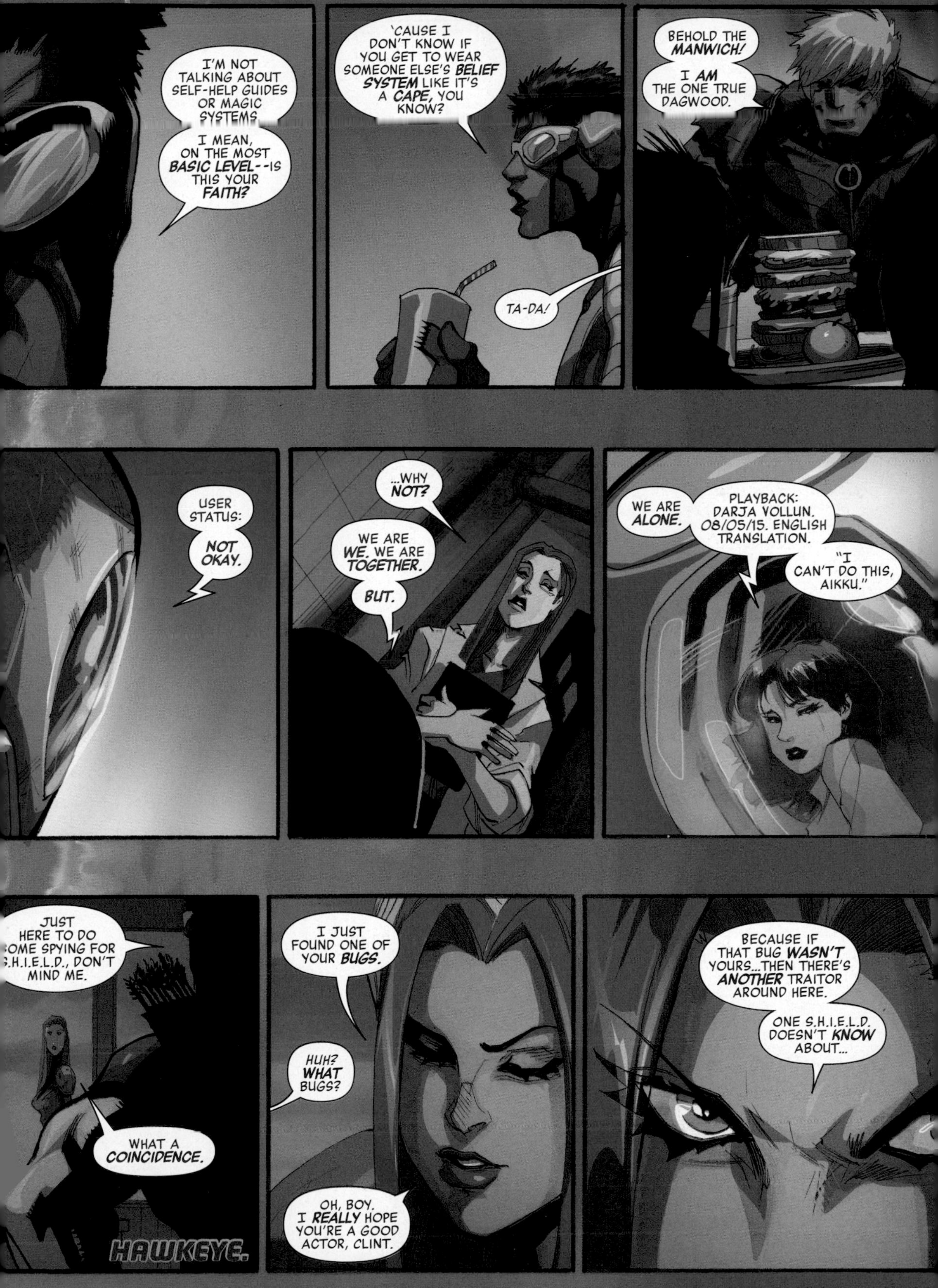

I'M NOT TALKING ABOUT SELF-HELP GUIDES OR MAGIC SYSTEMS
I MEAN, ON THE MOST BASIC LEVEL--IS THIS YOUR FAITH?
'CAUSE I DON'T KNOW IF YOU GET TO WEAR SOMEONE ELSE'S BELIEF SYSTEM LIKE IT'S A CAPE, YOU KNOW?
TA-DA!
BEHOLD THE MANWICH!
I AM THE ONE TRUE DAGWOOD.
USER STATUS:
NOT OKAY.
...WHY NOT?
WE ARE WE. WE ARE TOGETHER.
BUT.
WE ARE ALONE.
PLAYBACK: DARJA VOLLUN. 08/05/15. ENGLISH TRANSLATION.
"I CAN'T DO THIS, AIKKU."
JUST HERE TO DO SOME SPYING FOR S.H.I.E.L.D., DON'T MIND ME.
WHAT A COINCIDENCE.
HAWKEYE.
I JUST FOUND ONE OF YOUR BUGS.
HUH? WHAT BUGS?
OH, BOY. I REALLY HOPE YOU'RE A GOOD ACTOR, CLINT.
BECAUSE IF THAT BUG WASN'T YOURS...THEN THERE'S ANOTHER TRAITOR AROUND HERE.
ONE S.H.I.E.L.D. DOESN'T KNOW ABOUT...

THAT'S INSANE--

WE'RE IN A.I.M. NOW. I HAVE A DUTY TO FOOD SCIENCE.

SO WHAT ARE YOU GUYS TALKING ABOUT?

WELL, I WAS JUST SAYING BILLY'S HERO NAME IS A LITTLE--

SHA-WHOOM

HOLD THAT THOUGHT.

"I--I JUST CAN'T. I CAN'T. YOU'RE SOME--SOME ALIEN THING NOW, YOU'RE NOT HUMAN, AND--"

"--AND I DON'T LOVE YOU ANYMORE."

"I'M SORRY."

ALONE.

NOT OKAY.

NOT OKAY.

AIKKU... I...

SHA-WHOOM

OR MAYBE S.H.I.E.L.D. JUST DIDN'T BOTHER TELLING ME.

I MEAN, YOU'D THINK YEARS OF SERVICE WOULD COUNT FOR SOMETHING--

NOT EVERYTHING IS ABOUT YOU, CLINT--

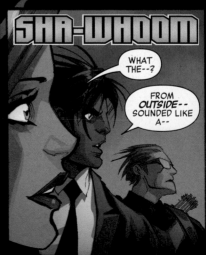

SHA-WHOOM

WHAT THE--?

FROM OUTSIDE-- SOUNDED LIKE A--

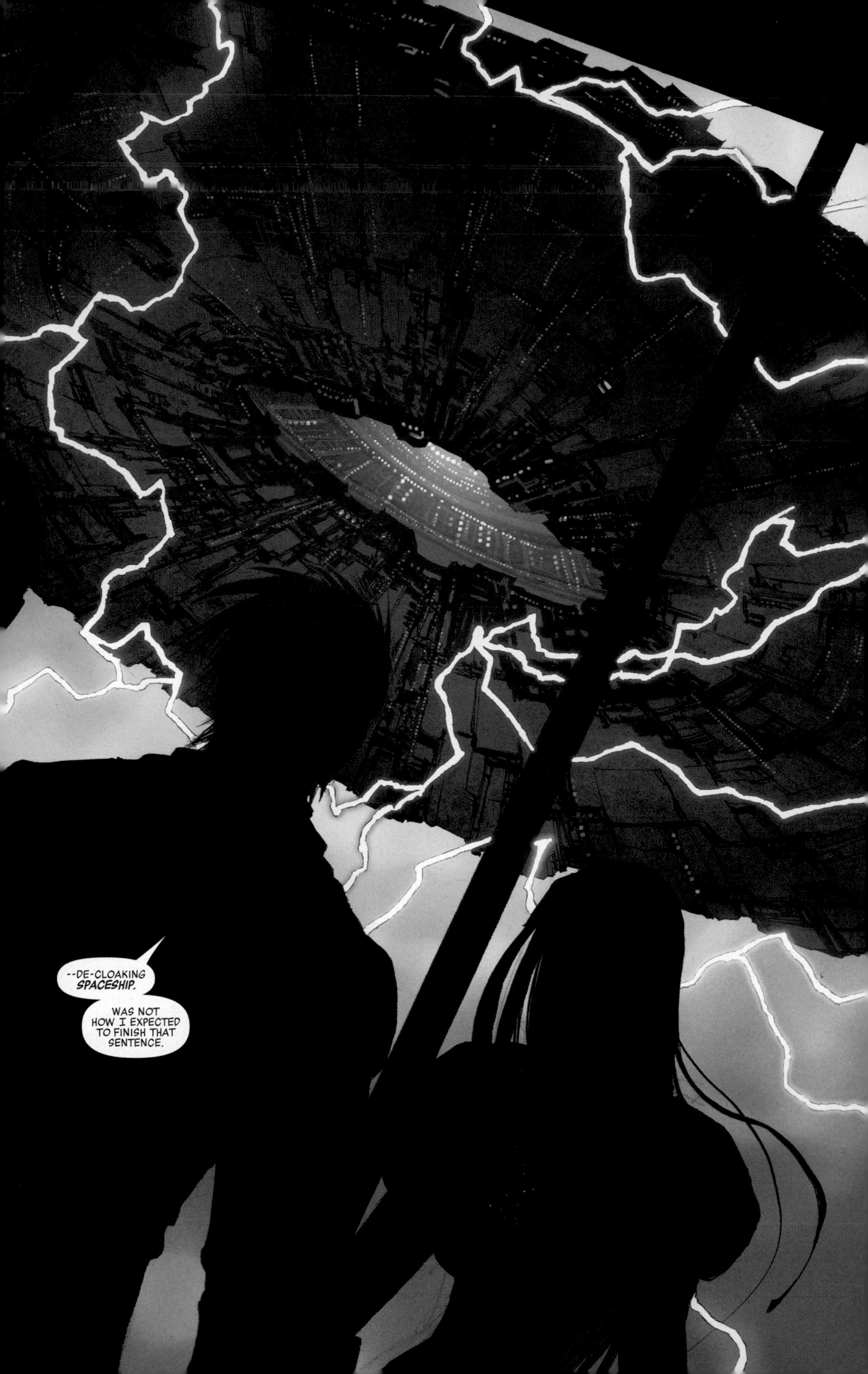
--DE-CLOAKING SPACESHIP.
WAS NOT HOW I EXPECTED TO FINISH THAT SENTENCE.

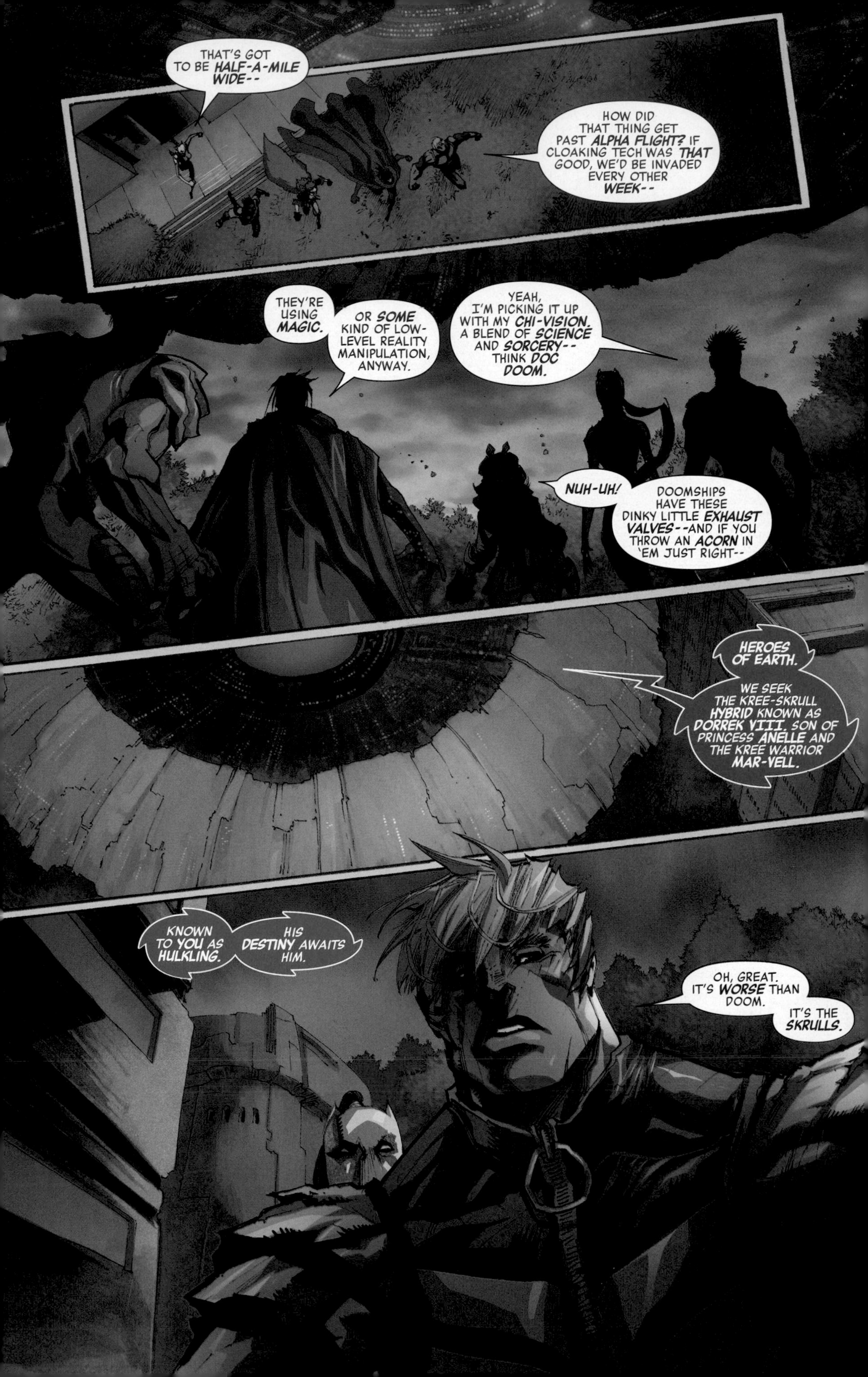
THAT'S GOT TO BE HALF-A-MILE WIDE--
HOW DID THAT THING GET PAST ALPHA FLIGHT? IF CLOAKING TECH WAS THAT GOOD, WE'D BE INVADED EVERY OTHER WEEK--
THEY'RE USING MAGIC.
OR SOME KIND OF LOW-LEVEL REALITY MANIPULATION, ANYWAY.
YEAH, I'M PICKING IT UP WITH MY CHI-VISION. A BLEND OF SCIENCE AND SORCERY--THINK DOC DOOM.
NUH-UH!
DOOMSHIPS HAVE THESE DINKY LITTLE EXHAUST VALVES--AND IF YOU THROW AN ACORN IN 'EM JUST RIGHT--
HEROES OF EARTH.
WE SEEK THE KREE-SKRULL HYBRID KNOWN AS DORREK VIII, SON OF PRINCESS ANELLE AND THE KREE WARRIOR MAR-VELL.
KNOWN TO YOU AS HULKLING.
HIS DESTINY AWAITS HIM.
OH, GREAT. IT'S WORSE THAN DOOM.
IT'S THE SKRULLS.

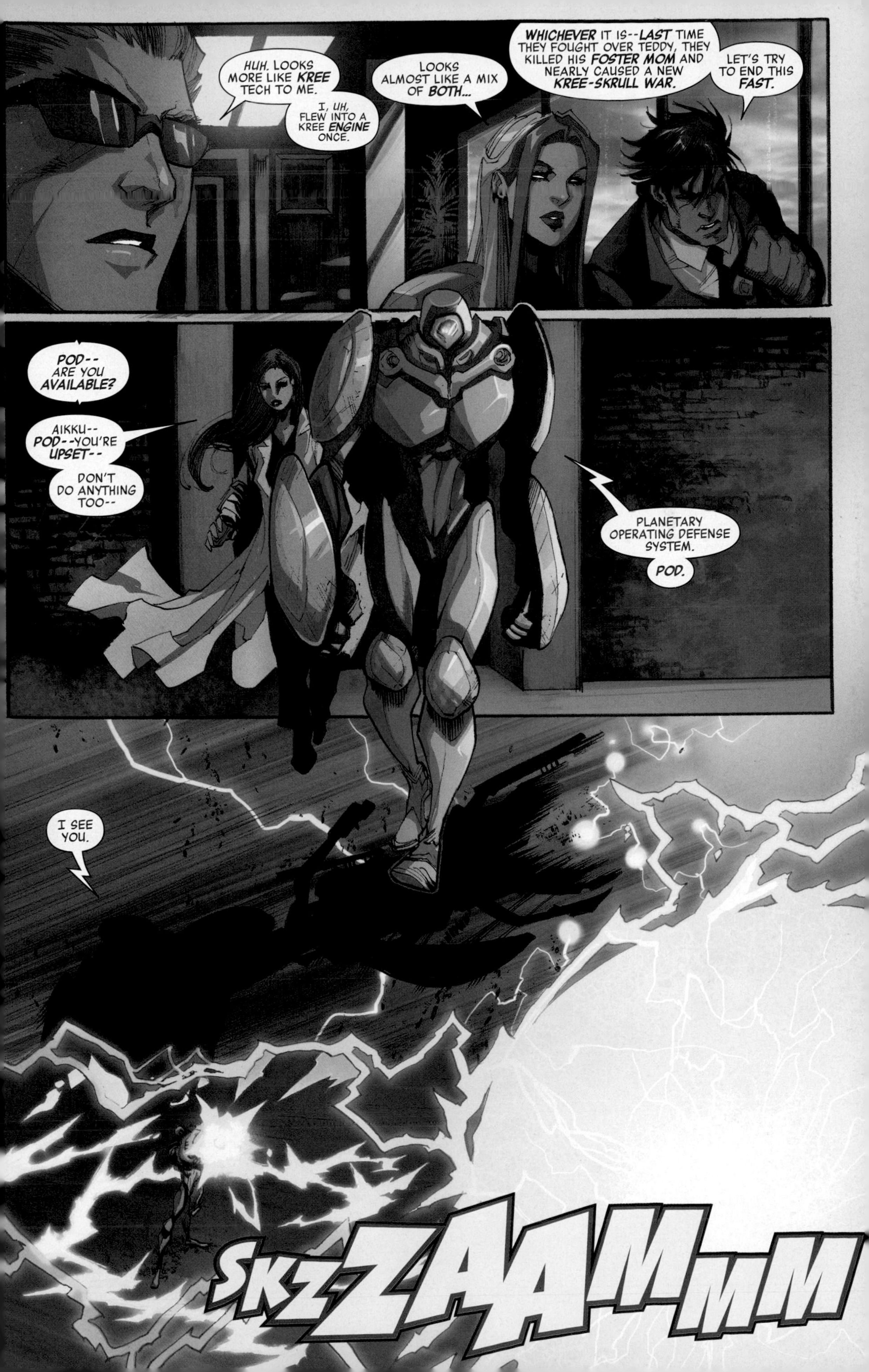
HUH. LOOKS MORE LIKE KREE TECH TO ME.
I, UH, FLEW INTO A KREE ENGINE ONCE.
LOOKS ALMOST LIKE A MIX OF BOTH...
WHICHEVER IT IS--LAST TIME THEY FOUGHT OVER TEDDY, THEY KILLED HIS FOSTER MOM AND NEARLY CAUSED A NEW KREE-SKRULL WAR.
LET'S TRY TO END THIS FAST.
POD-- ARE YOU AVAILABLE?
AIKKU-- POD--YOU'RE UPSET--
DON'T DO ANYTHING TOO--
PLANETARY OPERATING DEFENSE SYSTEM.
POD.
I SEE YOU.
SKZZAAMMMM

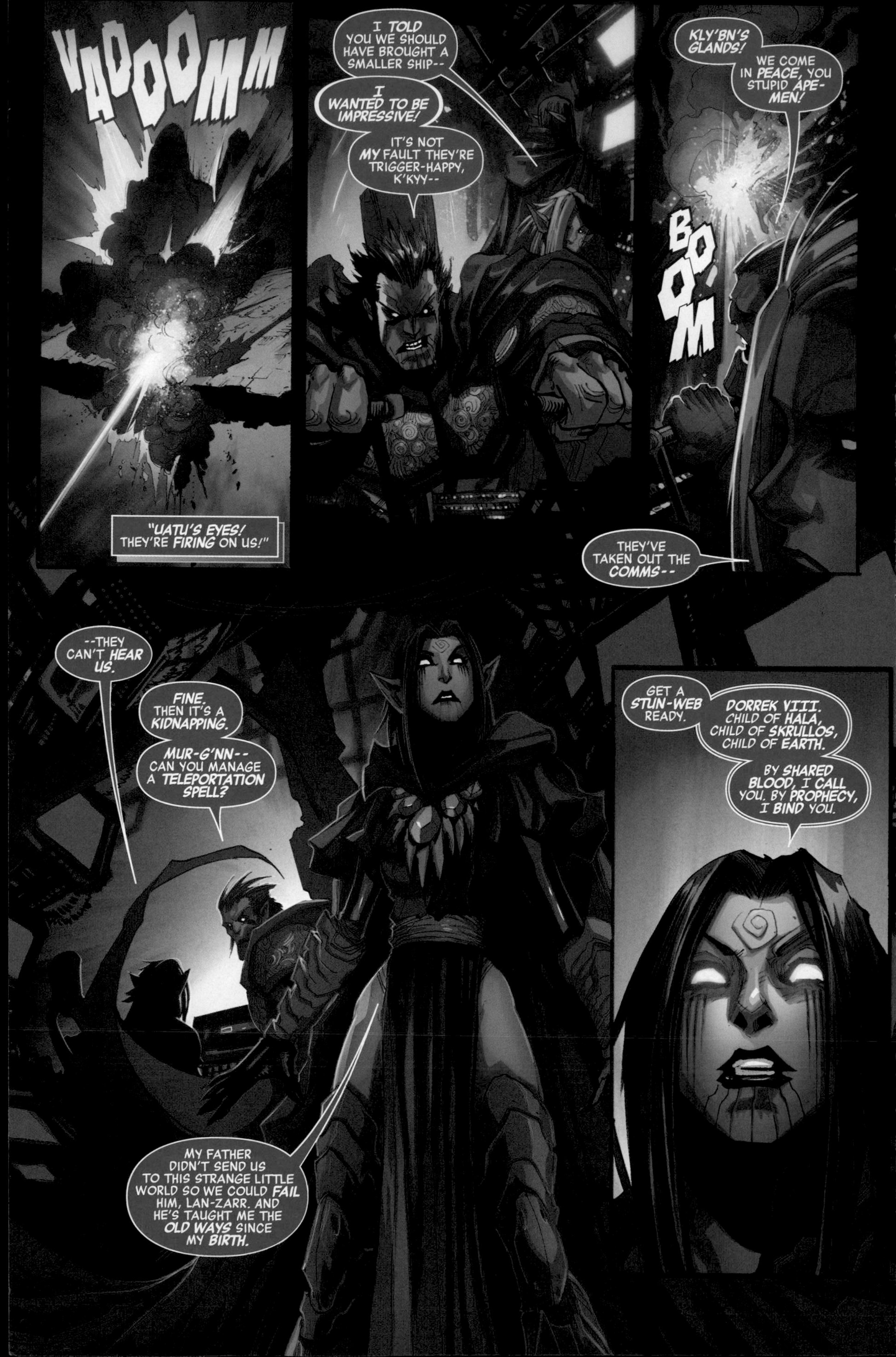
VADOOMM
"UATU'S EYES! THEY'RE FIRING ON US!"
I TOLD YOU WE SHOULD HAVE BROUGHT A SMALLER SHIP--
I WANTED TO BE IMPRESSIVE!
IT'S NOT MY FAULT THEY'RE TRIGGER-HAPPY, K'KYY--
KLY'BN'S GLANDS!
WE COME IN PEACE, YOU STUPID APE-MEN!
BOOM
THEY'VE TAKEN OUT THE COMMS--
--THEY CAN'T HEAR US.
FINE. THEN IT'S A KIDNAPPING.
MUR-G'NN-- CAN YOU MANAGE A TELEPORTATION SPELL?
MY FATHER DIDN'T SEND US TO THIS STRANGE LITTLE WORLD SO WE COULD FAIL HIM, LAN-ZARR. AND HE'S TAUGHT ME THE OLD WAYS SINCE MY BIRTH.
GET A STUN-WEB READY.
DORREK VIII. CHILD OF HALA, CHILD OF SKRULLOS, CHILD OF EARTH.
BY SHARED BLOOD, I CALL YOU. BY PROPHECY, I BIND YOU.

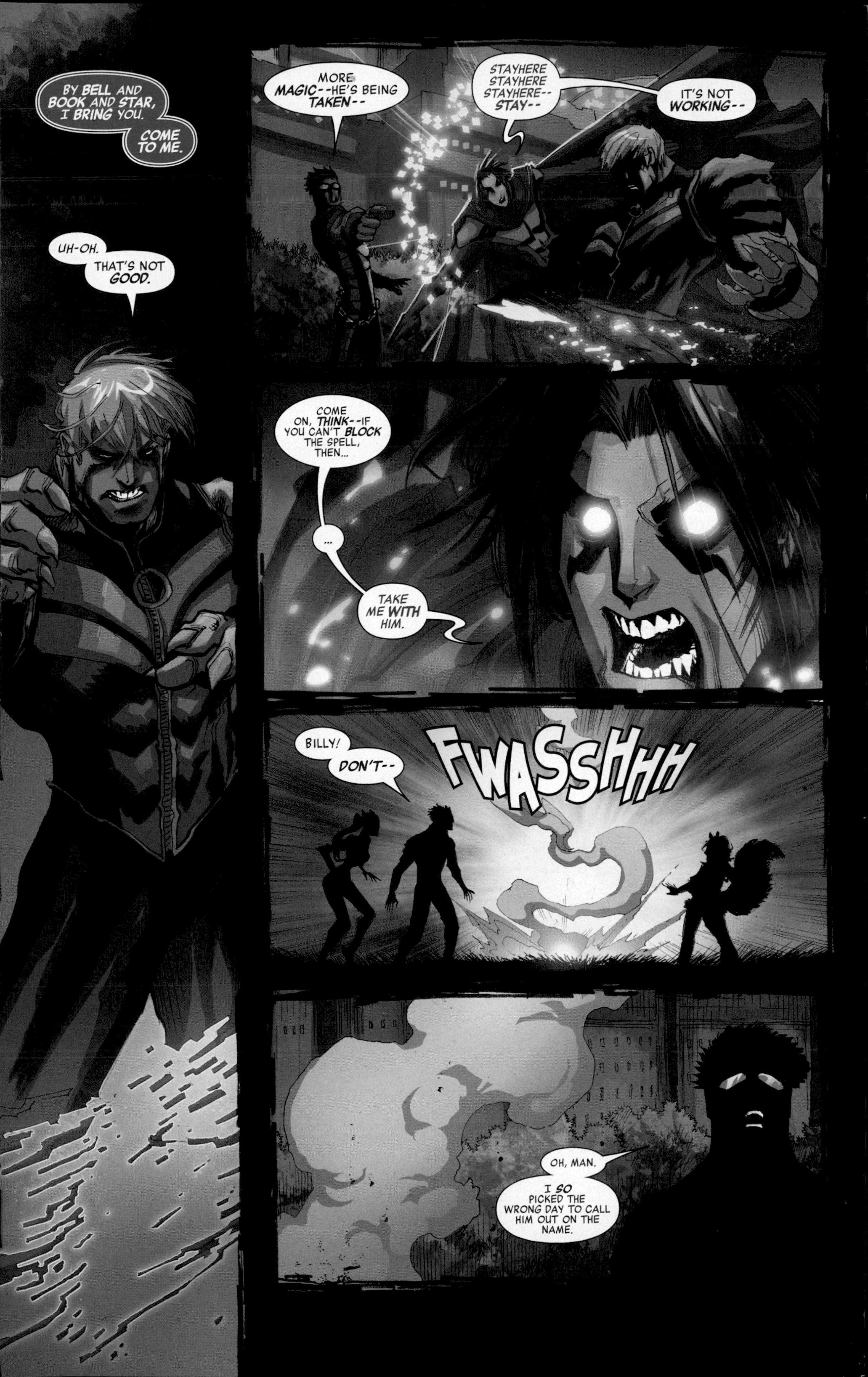
BY BELL AND BOOK AND STAR, I BRING YOU.
COME TO ME.
MORE MAGIC--HE'S BEING TAKEN--
STAYHERE STAYHERE STAYHERE--STAY--
IT'S NOT WORKING--
UH-OH.
THAT'S NOT GOOD.
COME ON, THINK--IF YOU CAN'T BLOCK THE SPELL, THEN...
...
TAKE ME WITH HIM.
BILLY!
DON'T--
FWASSHHH
OH, MAN.
I SO PICKED THE WRONG DAY TO CALL HIM OUT ON THE NAME.

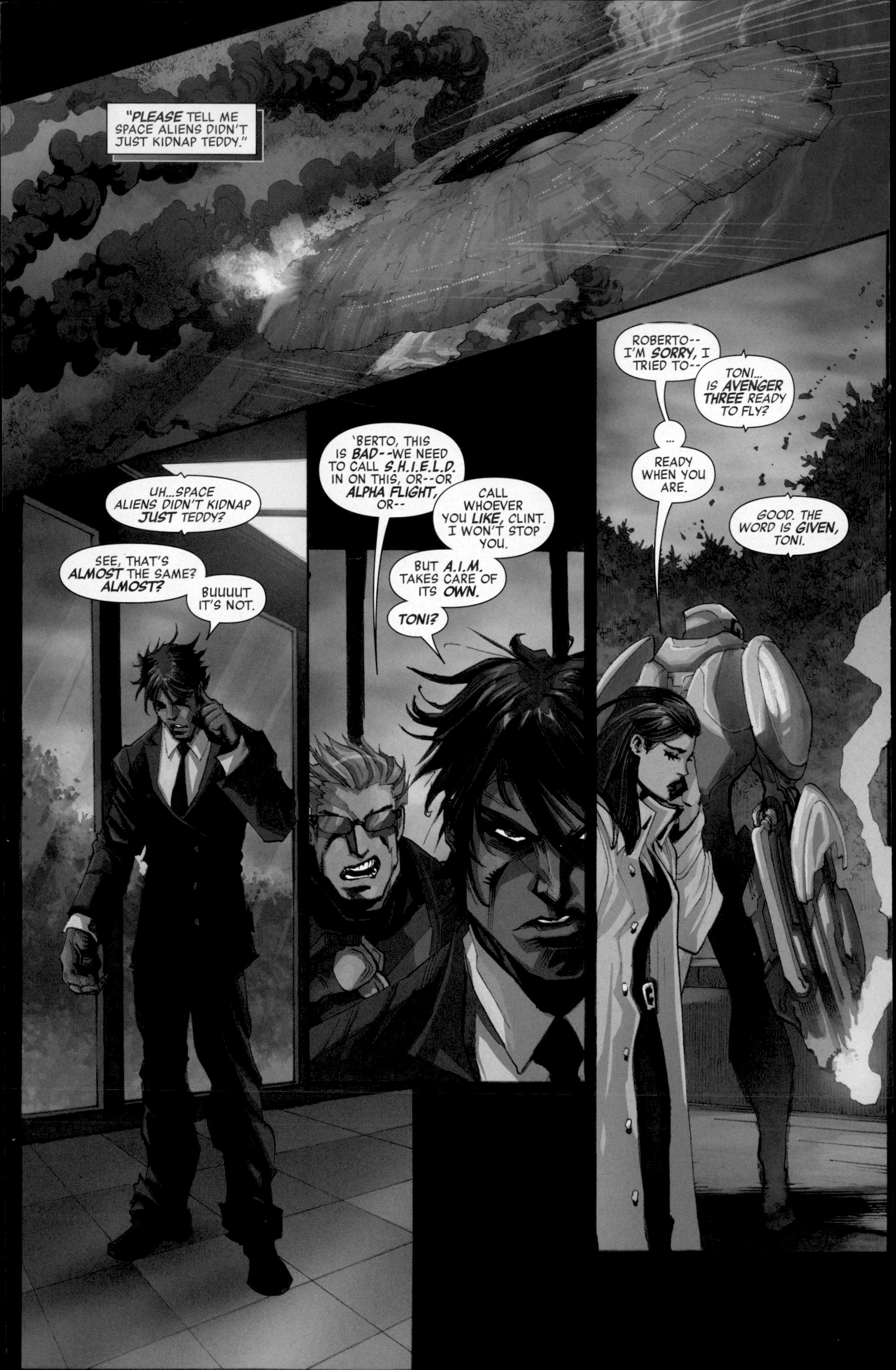
"PLEASE TELL ME SPACE ALIENS DIDN'T JUST KIDNAP TEDDY."
UH...SPACE ALIENS DIDN'T KIDNAP JUST TEDDY?
SEE, THAT'S ALMOST THE SAME? ALMOST?
BUUUUT IT'S NOT.
'BERTO, THIS IS BAD--WE NEED TO CALL S.H.I.E.L.D. IN ON THIS, OR--OR ALPHA FLIGHT, OR--
CALL WHOEVER YOU LIKE, CLINT. I WON'T STOP YOU.
BUT A.I.M. TAKES CARE OF ITS OWN.
TONI?
ROBERTO-- I'M SORRY, I TRIED TO--
TONI... IS AVENGER THREE READY TO FLY?
...
READY WHEN YOU ARE.
GOOD. THE WORD IS GIVEN, TONI.

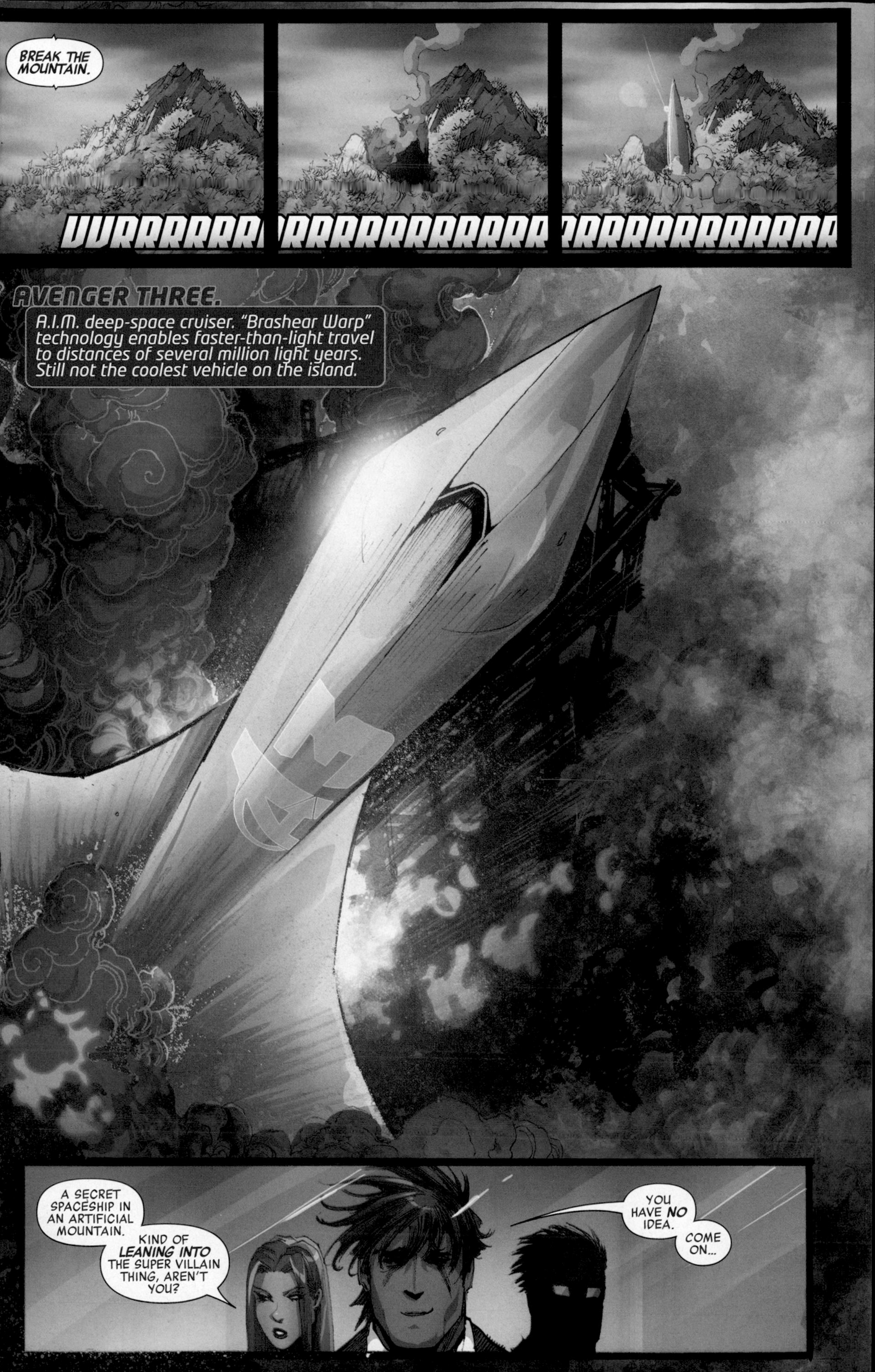
BREAK THE MOUNTAIN.
VVRRRRRRRRRRRRRRRRRRRRRRRRRRRRRRRR
AVENGER THREE.
A.I.M. deep-space cruiser. "Brashear Warp" technology enables faster-than-light travel to distances of several million light years. Still not the coolest vehicle on the island.
A SECRET SPACESHIP IN AN ARTIFICIAL MOUNTAIN.
KIND OF LEANING INTO THE SUPER VILLAIN THING, AREN'T YOU?
YOU HAVE NO IDEA.
COME ON...

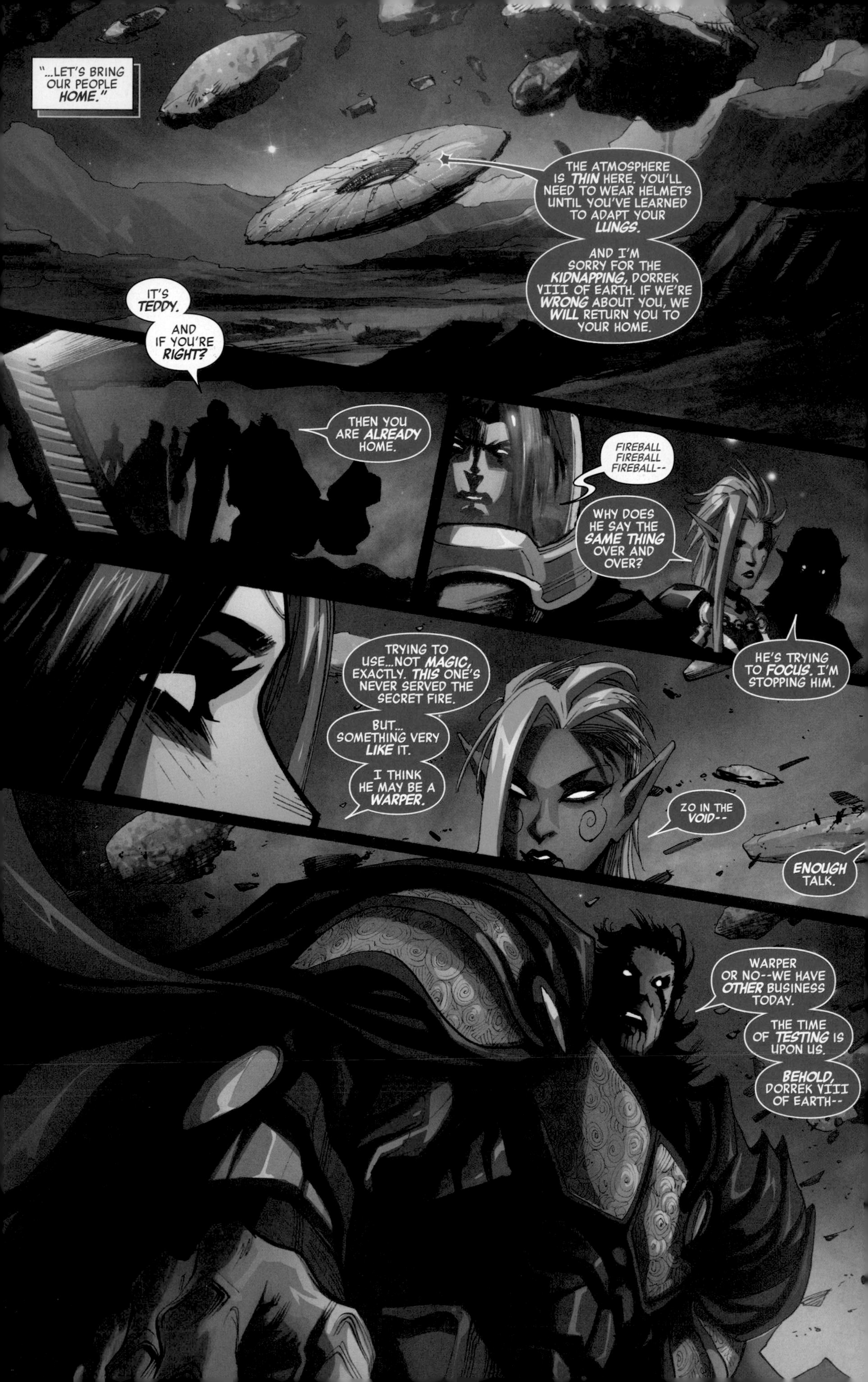
"...LET'S BRING OUR PEOPLE HOME."
THE ATMOSPHERE IS THIN HERE. YOU'LL NEED TO WEAR HELMETS UNTIL YOU'VE LEARNED TO ADAPT YOUR LUNGS.
AND I'M SORRY FOR THE KIDNAPPING, DORREK VIII OF EARTH. IF WE'RE WRONG ABOUT YOU, WE WILL RETURN YOU TO YOUR HOME.
IT'S TEDDY.
AND IF YOU'RE RIGHT?
THEN YOU ARE ALREADY HOME.
FIREBALL FIREBALL FIREBALL--
WHY DOES HE SAY THE SAME THING OVER AND OVER?
HE'S TRYING TO FOCUS. I'M STOPPING HIM.
TRYING TO USE...NOT MAGIC, EXACTLY. THIS ONE'S NEVER SERVED THE SECRET FIRE.
BUT... SOMETHING VERY LIKE IT.
I THINK HE MAY BE A WARPER.
ZO IN THE VOID--
ENOUGH TALK.
WARPER OR NO--WE HAVE OTHER BUSINESS TODAY.
THE TIME OF TESTING IS UPON US.
BEHOLD, DORREK VIII OF EARTH--

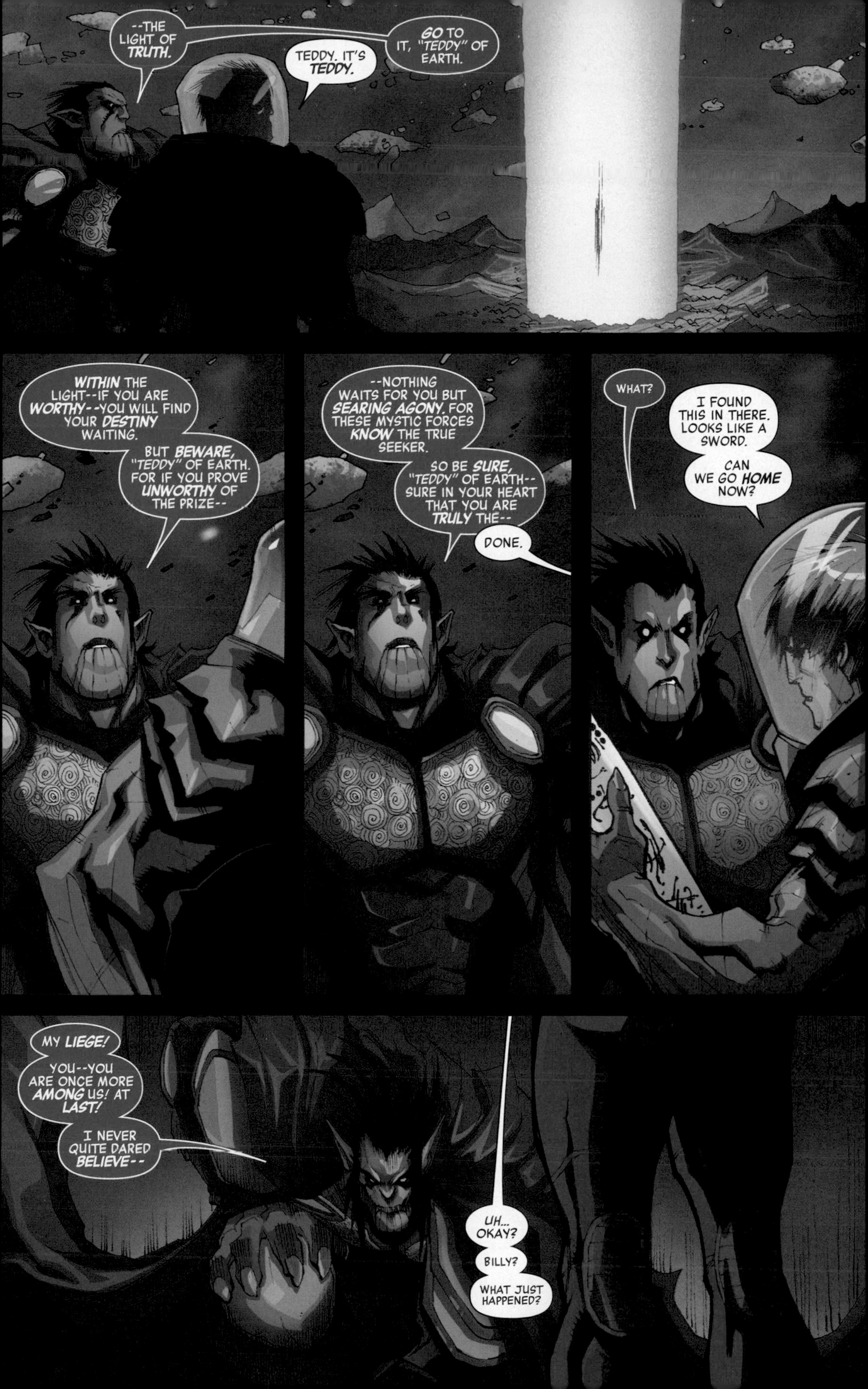
--THE LIGHT OF TRUTH.
TEDDY. IT'S TEDDY.
GO TO IT, "TEDDY" OF EARTH.
WITHIN THE LIGHT--IF YOU ARE WORTHY--YOU WILL FIND YOUR DESTINY WAITING.
BUT BEWARE, "TEDDY" OF EARTH. FOR IF YOU PROVE UNWORTHY OF THE PRIZE--
--NOTHING WAITS FOR YOU BUT SEARING AGONY. FOR THESE MYSTIC FORCES KNOW THE TRUE SEEKER.
SO BE SURE, "TEDDY" OF EARTH--SURE IN YOUR HEART THAT YOU ARE TRULY THE--
DONE.
WHAT?
I FOUND THIS IN THERE. LOOKS LIKE A SWORD.
CAN WE GO HOME NOW?
MY LIEGE!
YOU--YOU ARE ONCE MORE AMONG US! AT LAST!
I NEVER QUITE DARED BELIEVE--
UH... OKAY?
BILLY?
WHAT JUST HAPPENED?

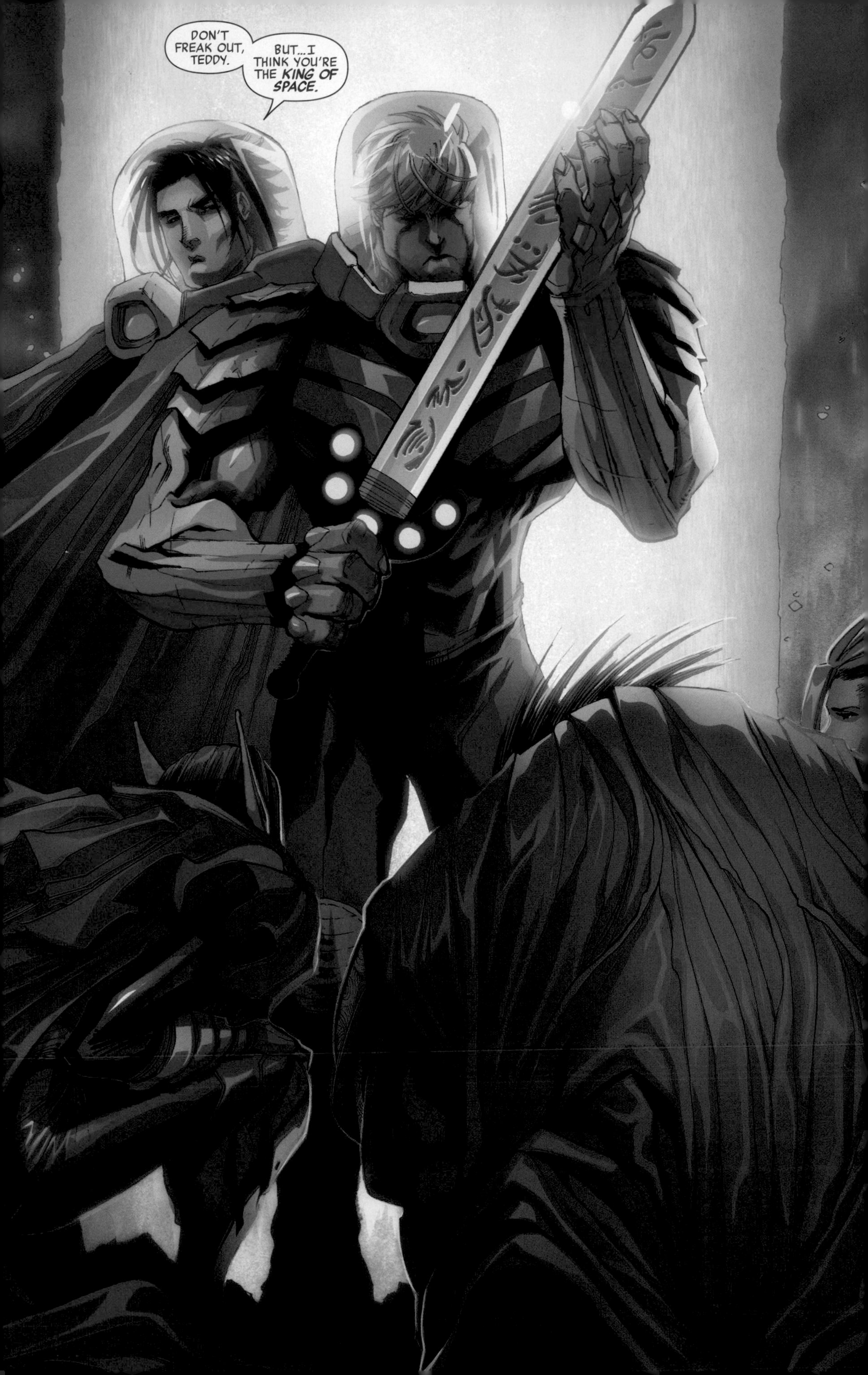
DON'T FREAK OUT, TEDDY.
BUT...I THINK YOU'RE THE KING OF SPACE.

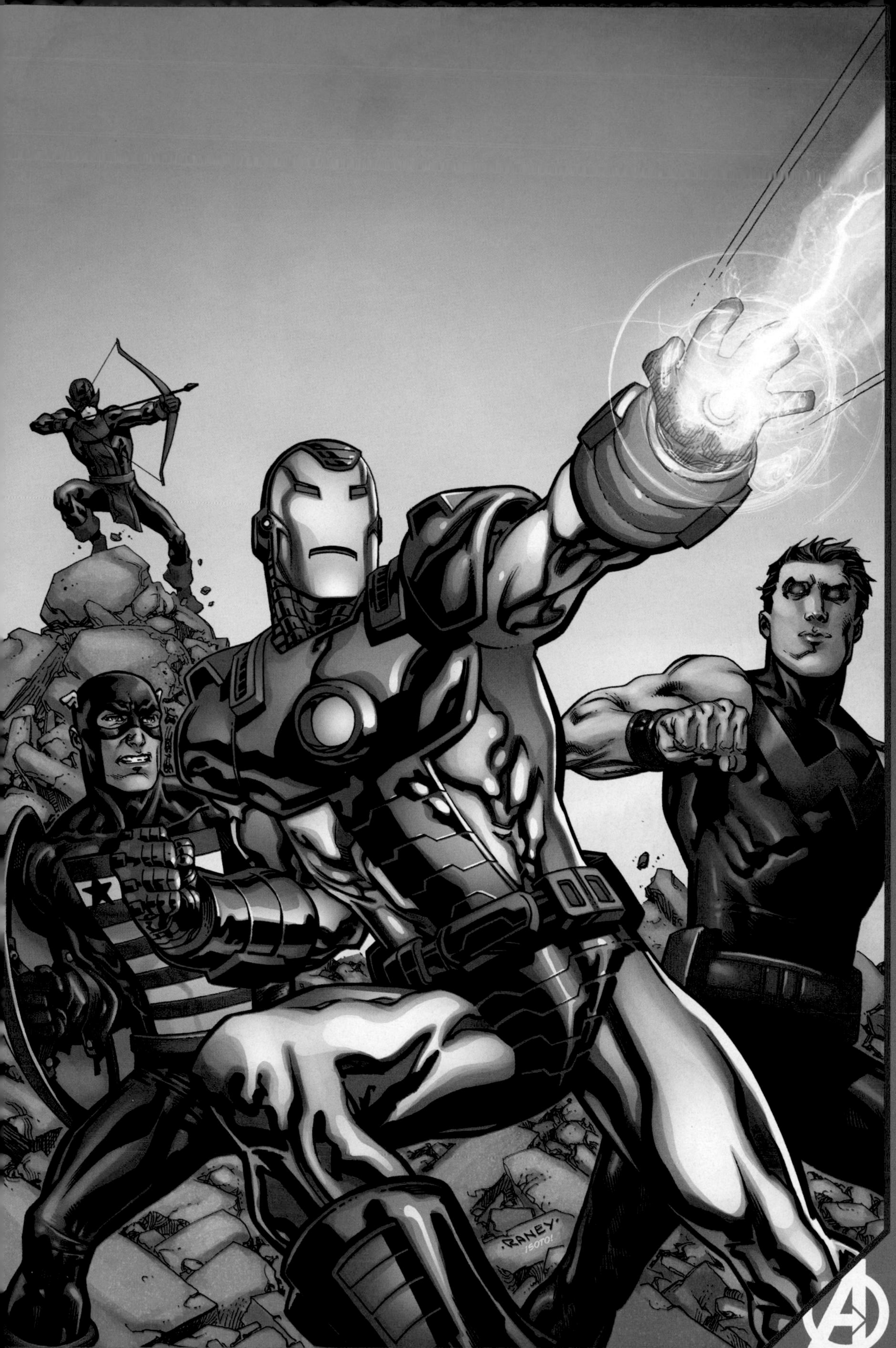
RANEY
¡SOTO!

#4 MARVEL '92 VARIANT BY **TOM RANEY** & **CHRIS SOTOMAYOR**

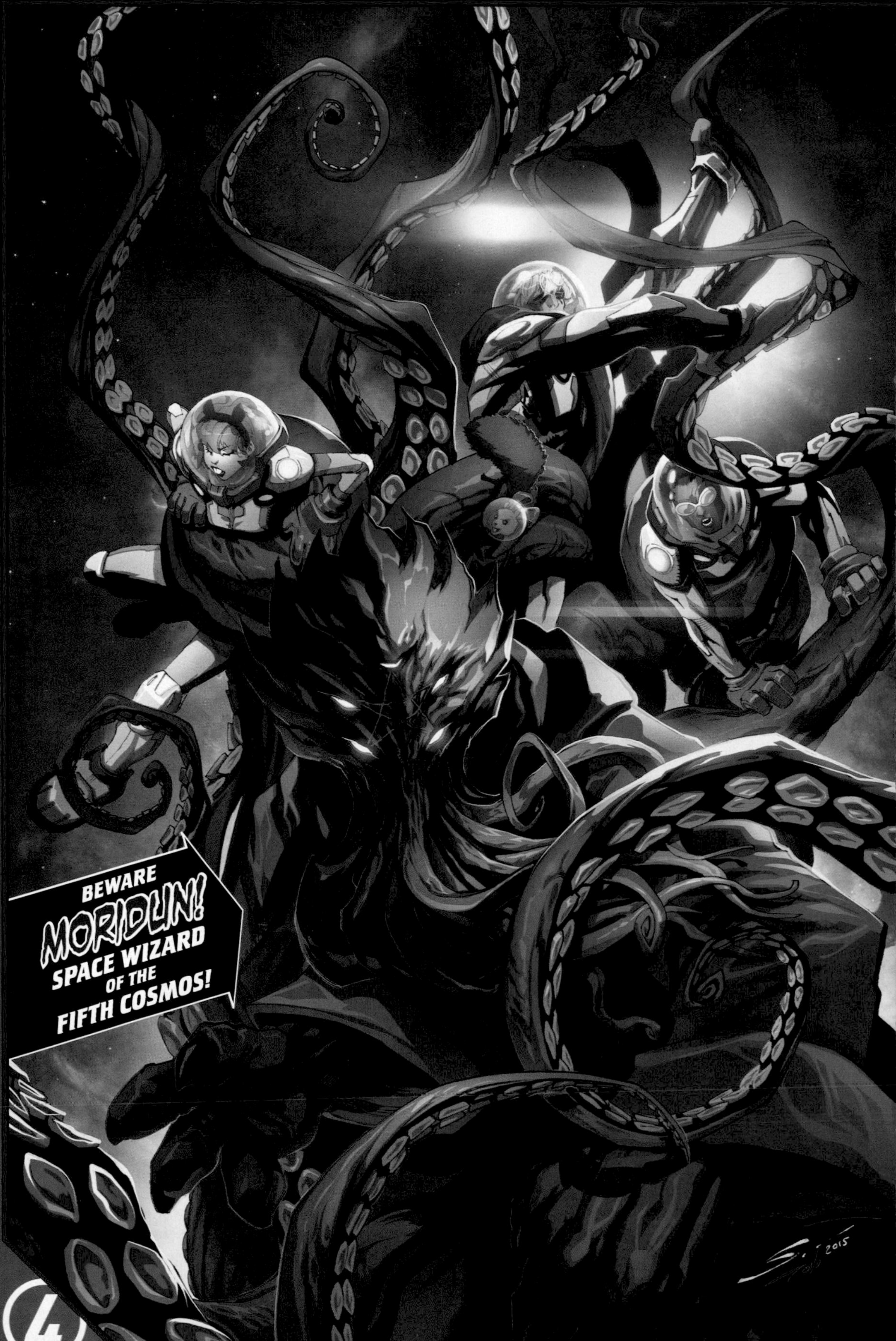
BEWARE
MORIDUN!
SPACE WIZARD
OF THE
FIFTH COSMOS!

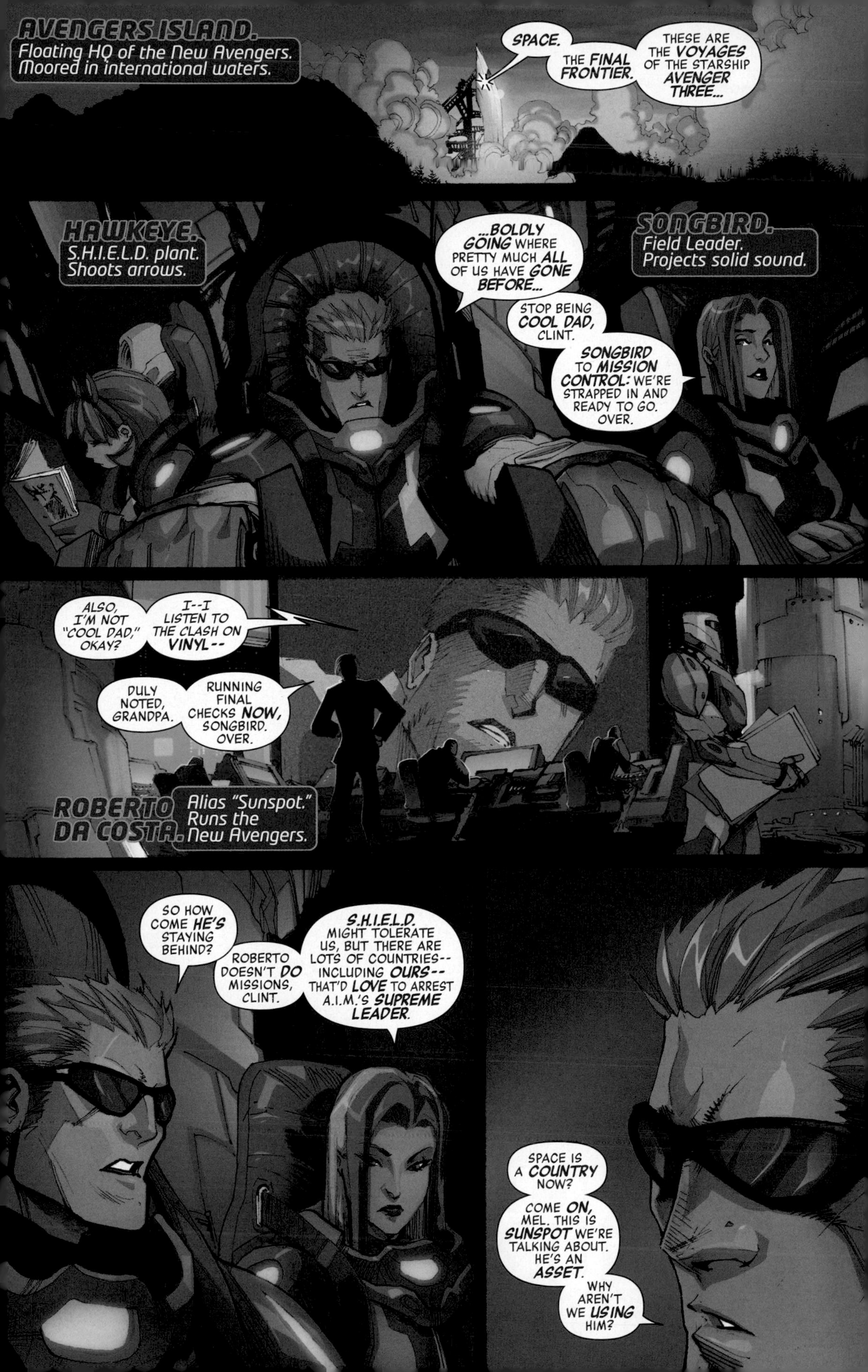
AVENGERS ISLAND.
Floating HQ of the New Avengers. Moored in international waters.
SPACE.
THE FINAL FRONTIER.
THESE ARE THE VOYAGES OF THE STARSHIP AVENGER THREE...
HAWKEYE.
S.H.I.E.L.D. plant. Shoots arrows.
SONGBIRD.
Field Leader. Projects solid sound.
...BOLDLY GOING WHERE PRETTY MUCH ALL OF US HAVE GONE BEFORE...
STOP BEING COOL DAD, CLINT.
SONGBIRD TO MISSION CONTROL: WE'RE STRAPPED IN AND READY TO GO. OVER.
ALSO, I'M NOT "COOL DAD," OKAY?
I--I LISTEN TO THE CLASH ON VINYL--
DULY NOTED, GRANDPA.
RUNNING FINAL CHECKS NOW, SONGBIRD. OVER.
ROBERTO DA COSTA.
Alias "Sunspot." Runs the New Avengers.
SO HOW COME HE'S STAYING BEHIND?
ROBERTO DOESN'T DO MISSIONS, CLINT.
S.H.I.E.L.D. MIGHT TOLERATE US, BUT THERE ARE LOTS OF COUNTRIES--INCLUDING OURS--THAT'D LOVE TO ARREST A.I.M.'S SUPREME LEADER.
SPACE IS A COUNTRY NOW?
COME ON, MEL. THIS IS SUNSPOT WE'RE TALKING ABOUT. HE'S AN ASSET.
WHY AREN'T WE USING HIM?

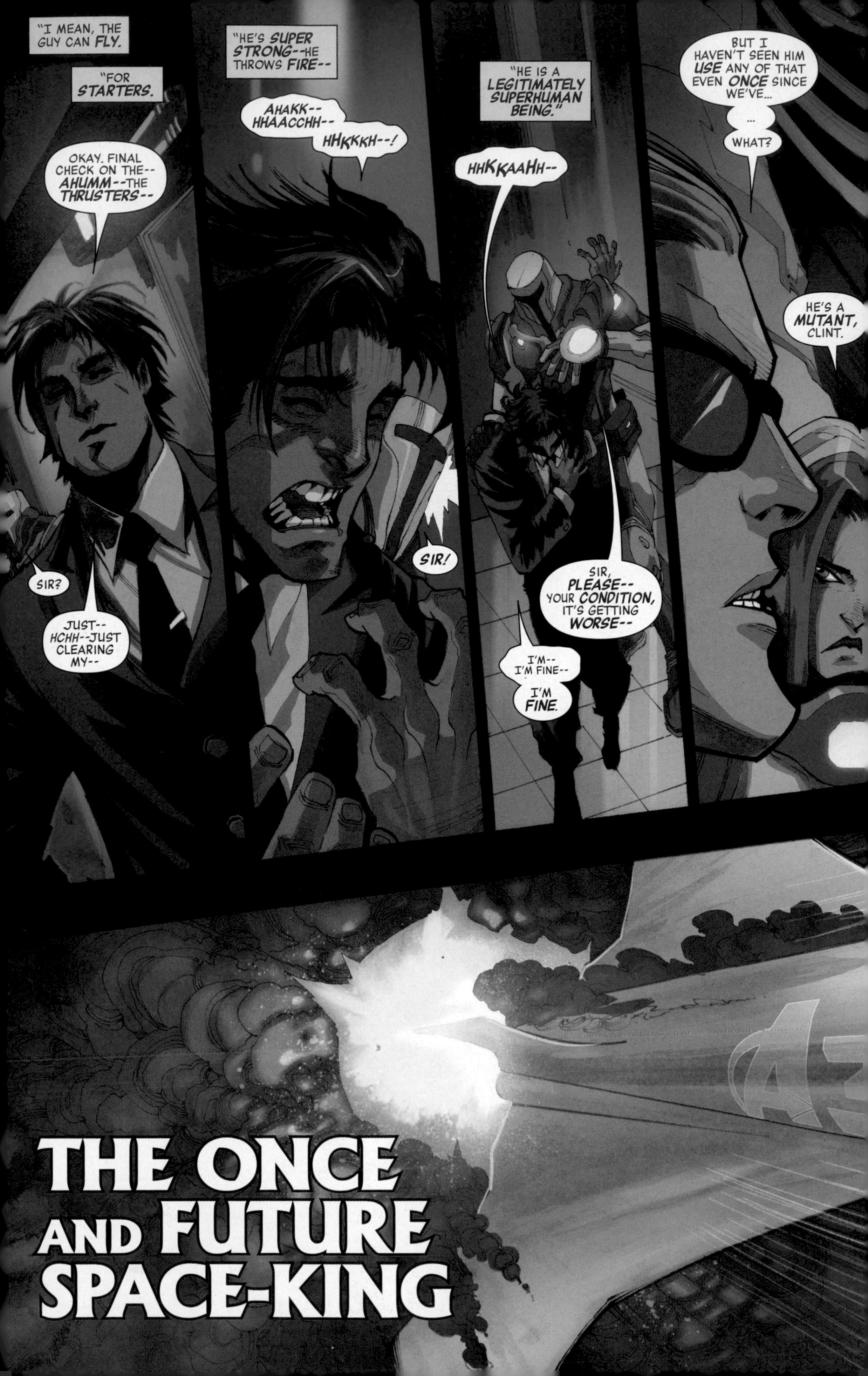
"I MEAN, THE GUY CAN FLY.
"FOR STARTERS.
OKAY. FINAL CHECK ON THE-- AHUMM--THE THRUSTERS--
SIR?
JUST-- HCHH--JUST CLEARING MY--
"HE'S SUPER STRONG--HE THROWS FIRE--
AHAKK-- HHAACCHH--
HHKKKH--!
SIR!
"HE IS A LEGITIMATELY SUPERHUMAN BEING."
HHKKAAHH--
SIR, PLEASE-- YOUR CONDITION, IT'S GETTING WORSE--
I'M-- I'M FINE--
I'M FINE.
BUT I HAVEN'T SEEN HIM USE ANY OF THAT EVEN ONCE SINCE WE'VE...
...
WHAT?
HE'S A MUTANT, CLINT.
THE ONCE AND FUTURE SPACE-KING

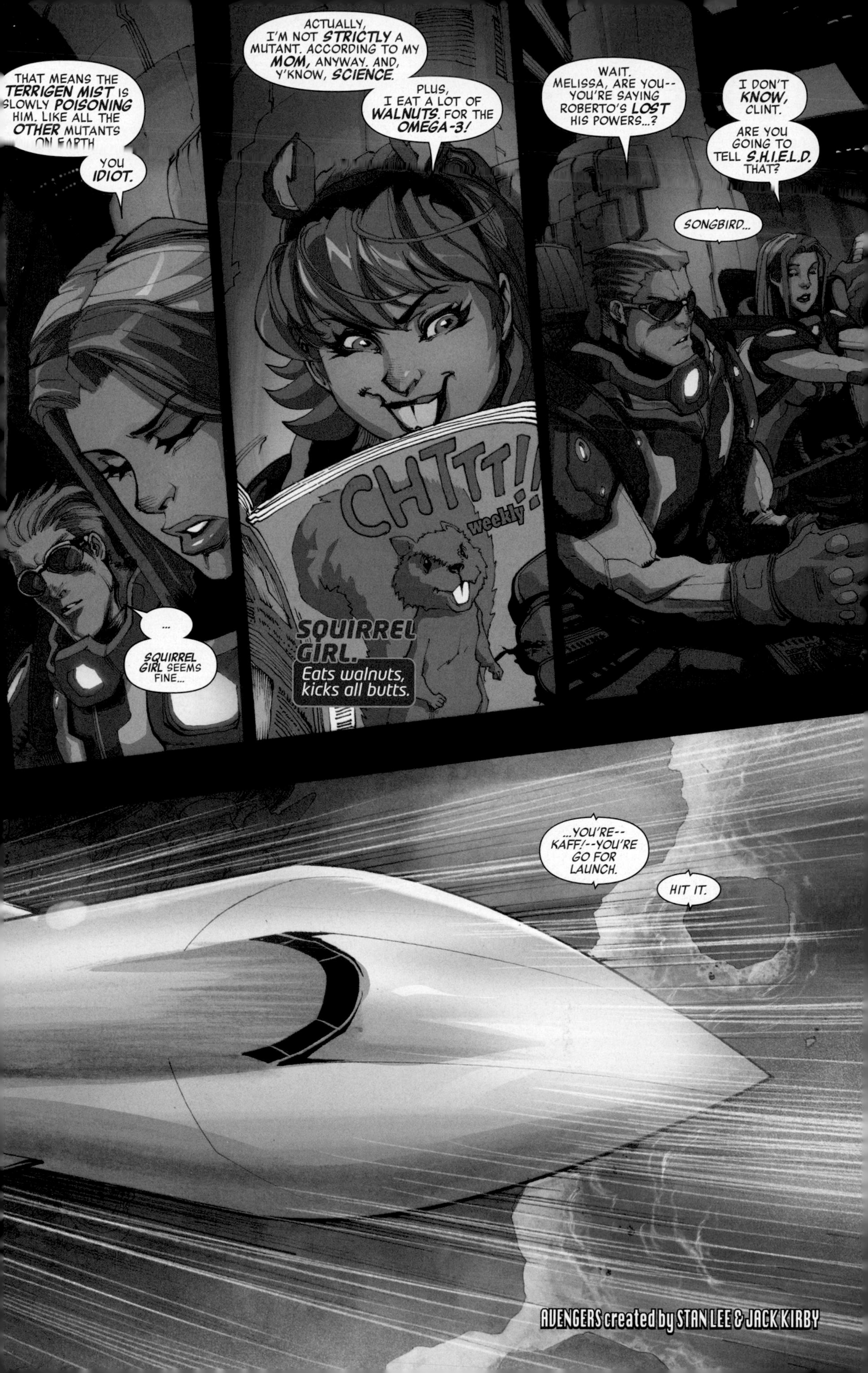

THAT MEANS THE TERRIGEN MIST IS SLOWLY POISONING HIM. LIKE ALL THE OTHER MUTANTS ON EARTH.
YOU IDIOT.
...
SQUIRREL GIRL SEEMS FINE...
ACTUALLY, I'M NOT STRICTLY A MUTANT. ACCORDING TO MY MOM, ANYWAY. AND, Y'KNOW, SCIENCE.
PLUS, I EAT A LOT OF WALNUTS. FOR THE OMEGA-3!
CHTTT!!
weekly
SQUIRREL GIRL.
Eats walnuts, kicks all butts.
WAIT. MELISSA, ARE YOU-- YOU'RE SAYING ROBERTO'S LOST HIS POWERS...?
I DON'T KNOW, CLINT.
ARE YOU GOING TO TELL S.H.I.E.L.D. THAT?
SONGBIRD...
...YOU'RE-- KAFF!--YOU'RE GO FOR LAUNCH.
HIT IT.
AVENGERS created by STAN LEE & JACK KIRBY

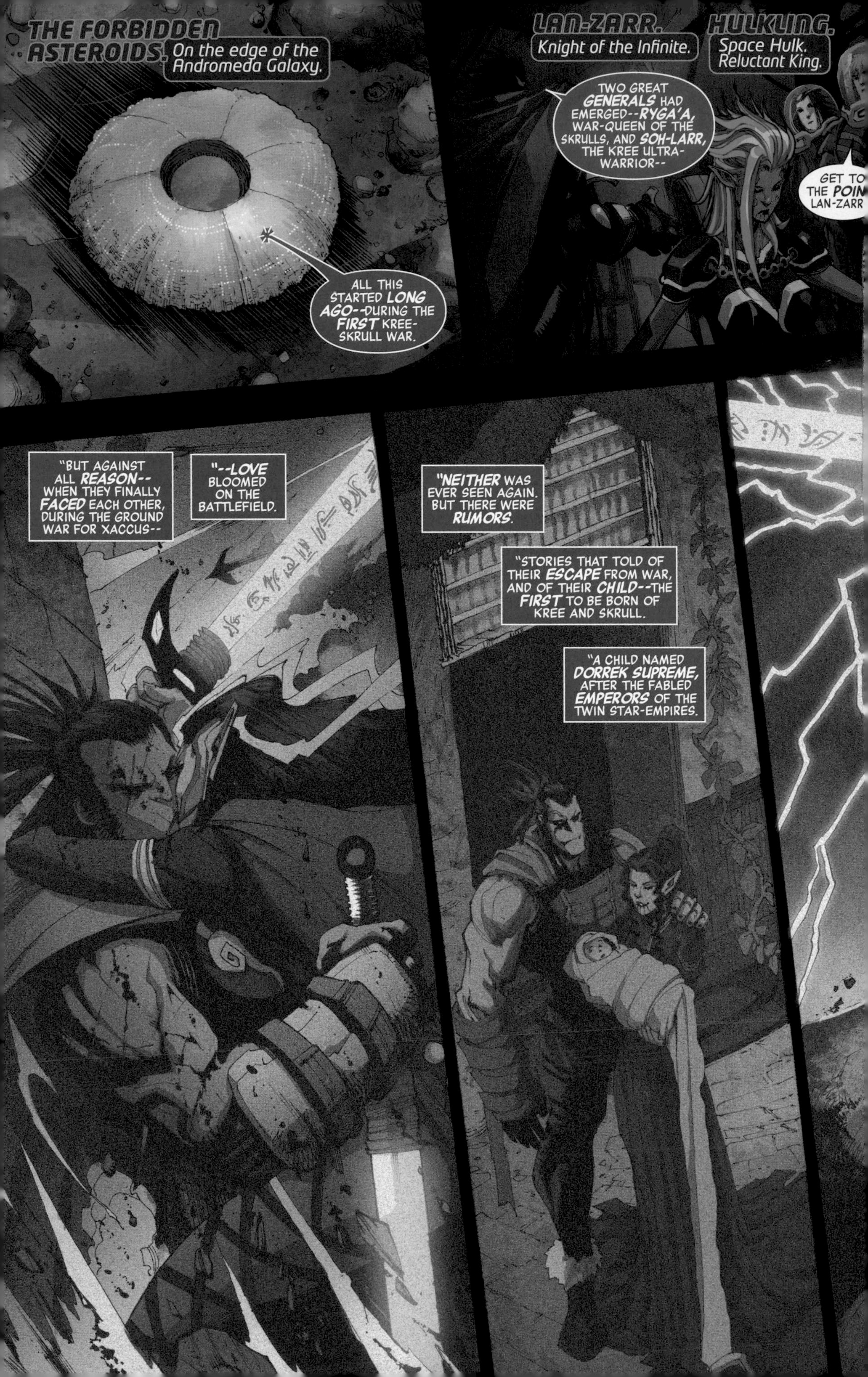
THE FORBIDDEN ASTEROIDS. On the edge of the Andromeda Galaxy.
ALL THIS STARTED LONG AGO--DURING THE FIRST KREE-SKRULL WAR.
LAN-ZARR. Knight of the Infinite.
HULKLING. Space Hulk. Reluctant King.
TWO GREAT GENERALS HAD EMERGED--RYGA'A, WAR-QUEEN OF THE SKRULLS, AND SOH-LARR, THE KREE ULTRA-WARRIOR--
GET TO THE POIN LAN-ZARR
"BUT AGAINST ALL REASON--WHEN THEY FINALLY FACED EACH OTHER, DURING THE GROUND WAR FOR XACCUS--
"--LOVE BLOOMED ON THE BATTLEFIELD.
"NEITHER WAS EVER SEEN AGAIN. BUT THERE WERE RUMORS.
"STORIES THAT TOLD OF THEIR ESCAPE FROM WAR, AND OF THEIR CHILD--THE FIRST TO BE BORN OF KREE AND SKRULL.
"A CHILD NAMED DORREK SUPREME, AFTER THE FABLED EMPERORS OF THE TWIN STAR-EMPIRES.

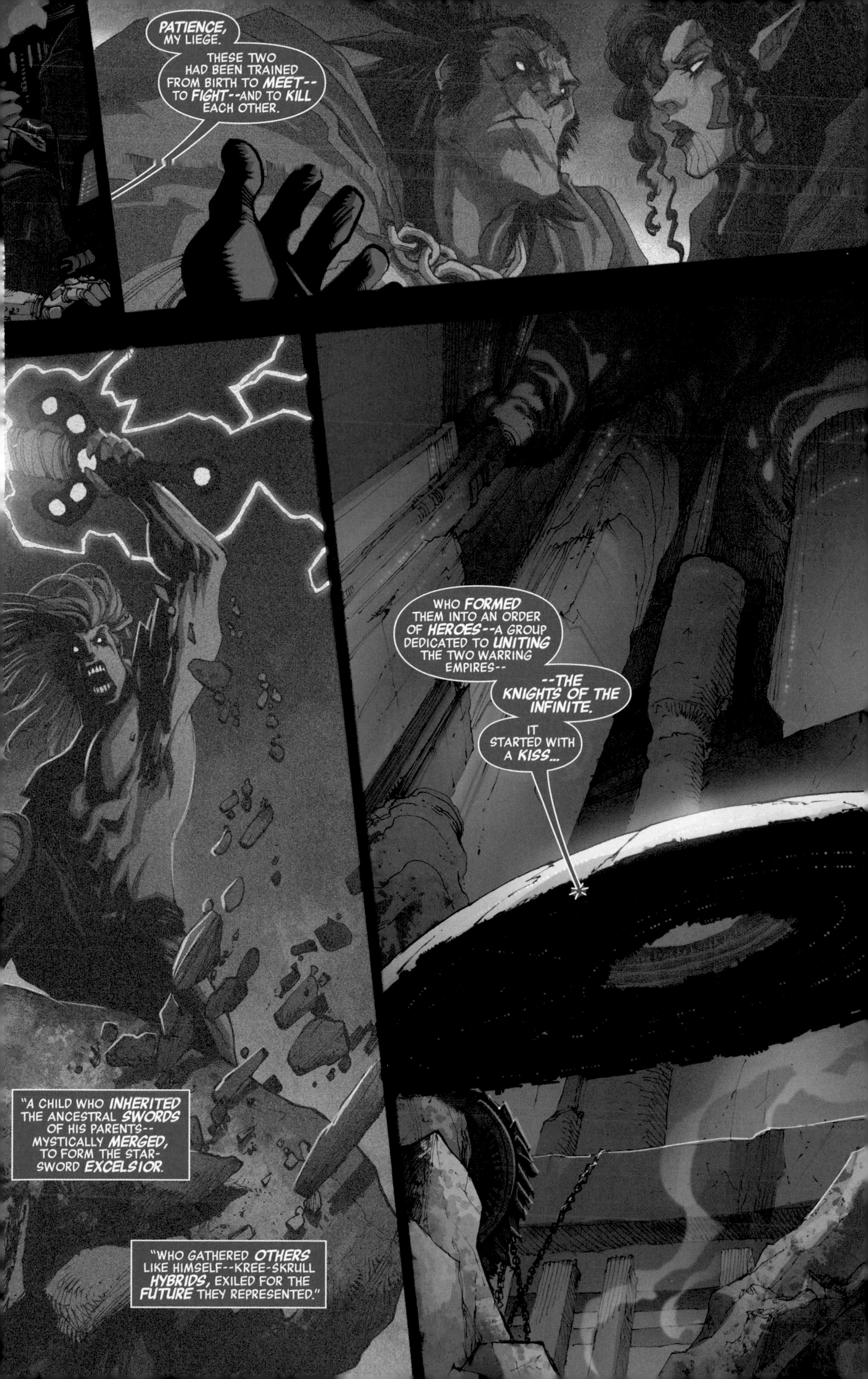
PATIENCE, MY LIEGE.
THESE TWO HAD BEEN TRAINED FROM BIRTH TO MEET--TO FIGHT--AND TO KILL EACH OTHER.
"A CHILD WHO INHERITED THE ANCESTRAL SWORDS OF HIS PARENTS--MYSTICALLY MERGED, TO FORM THE STAR-SWORD EXCELSIOR.
"WHO GATHERED OTHERS LIKE HIMSELF--KREE-SKRULL HYBRIDS, EXILED FOR THE FUTURE THEY REPRESENTED."
WHO FORMED THEM INTO AN ORDER OF HEROES--A GROUP DEDICATED TO UNITING THE TWO WARRING EMPIRES--
--THE KNIGHTS OF THE INFINITE.
IT STARTED WITH A KISS...

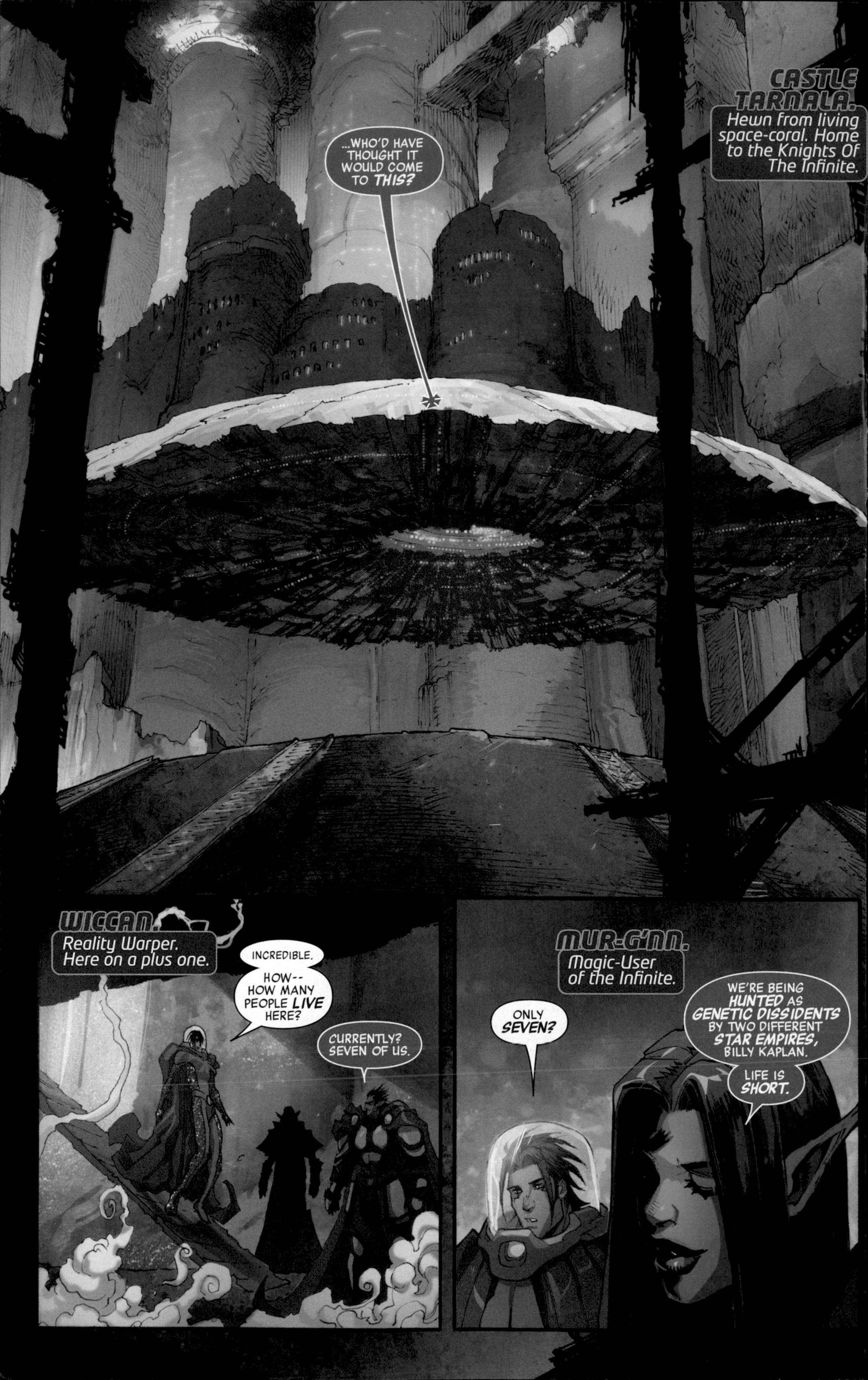
CASTLE TARNALA.
Hewn from living space-coral. Home to the Knights Of The Infinite.
...WHO'D HAVE THOUGHT IT WOULD COME TO THIS?
WICCAN.
Reality Warper. Here on a plus one.
INCREDIBLE.
HOW-- HOW MANY PEOPLE LIVE HERE?
CURRENTLY? SEVEN OF US.
MUR-G'NN.
Magic-User of the Infinite.
ONLY SEVEN?
WE'RE BEING HUNTED AS GENETIC DISSIDENTS BY TWO DIFFERENT STAR EMPIRES, BILLY KAPLAN.
LIFE IS SHORT.

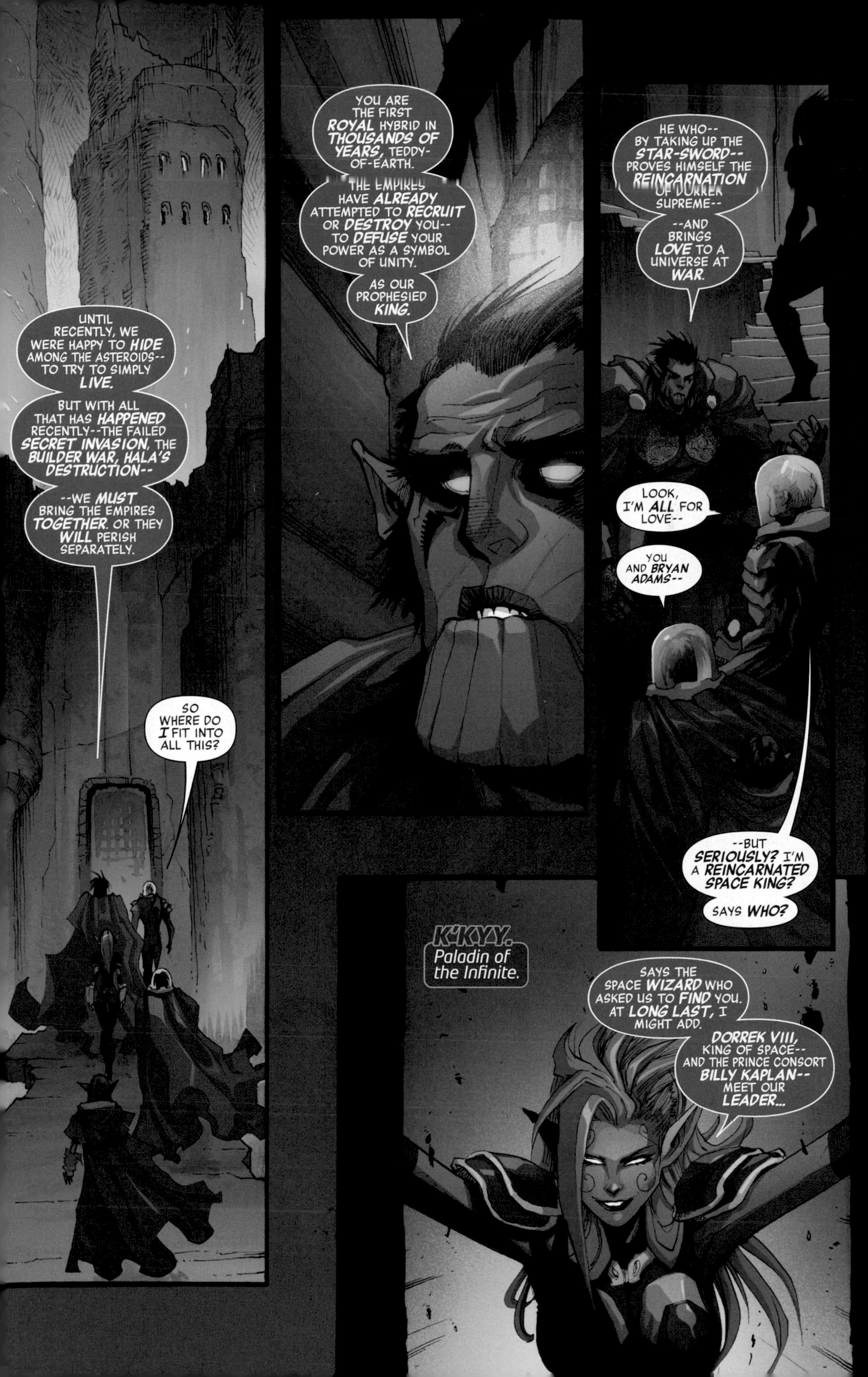

UNTIL RECENTLY, WE WERE HAPPY TO HIDE AMONG THE ASTEROIDS--TO TRY TO SIMPLY LIVE.
BUT WITH ALL THAT HAS HAPPENED RECENTLY--THE FAILED SECRET INVASION, THE BUILDER WAR, HALA'S DESTRUCTION--
--WE MUST BRING THE EMPIRES TOGETHER. OR THEY WILL PERISH SEPARATELY.
SO WHERE DO I FIT INTO ALL THIS?
YOU ARE THE FIRST ROYAL HYBRID IN THOUSANDS OF YEARS, TEDDY-OF-EARTH.
THE EMPIRES HAVE ALREADY ATTEMPTED TO RECRUIT OR DESTROY YOU--TO DEFUSE YOUR POWER AS A SYMBOL OF UNITY.
AS OUR PROPHESIED KING.
HE WHO--BY TAKING UP THE STAR-SWORD--PROVES HIMSELF THE REINCARNATION OF DORREK SUPREME--
--AND BRINGS LOVE TO A UNIVERSE AT WAR.
LOOK, I'M ALL FOR LOVE--
YOU AND BRYAN ADAMS--
--BUT SERIOUSLY? I'M A REINCARNATED SPACE KING?
SAYS WHO?
K'KYY. Paladin of the Infinite.
SAYS THE SPACE WIZARD WHO ASKED US TO FIND YOU. AT LONG LAST, I MIGHT ADD.
DORREK VIII, KING OF SPACE--AND THE PRINCE CONSORT BILLY KAPLAN--MEET OUR LEADER...

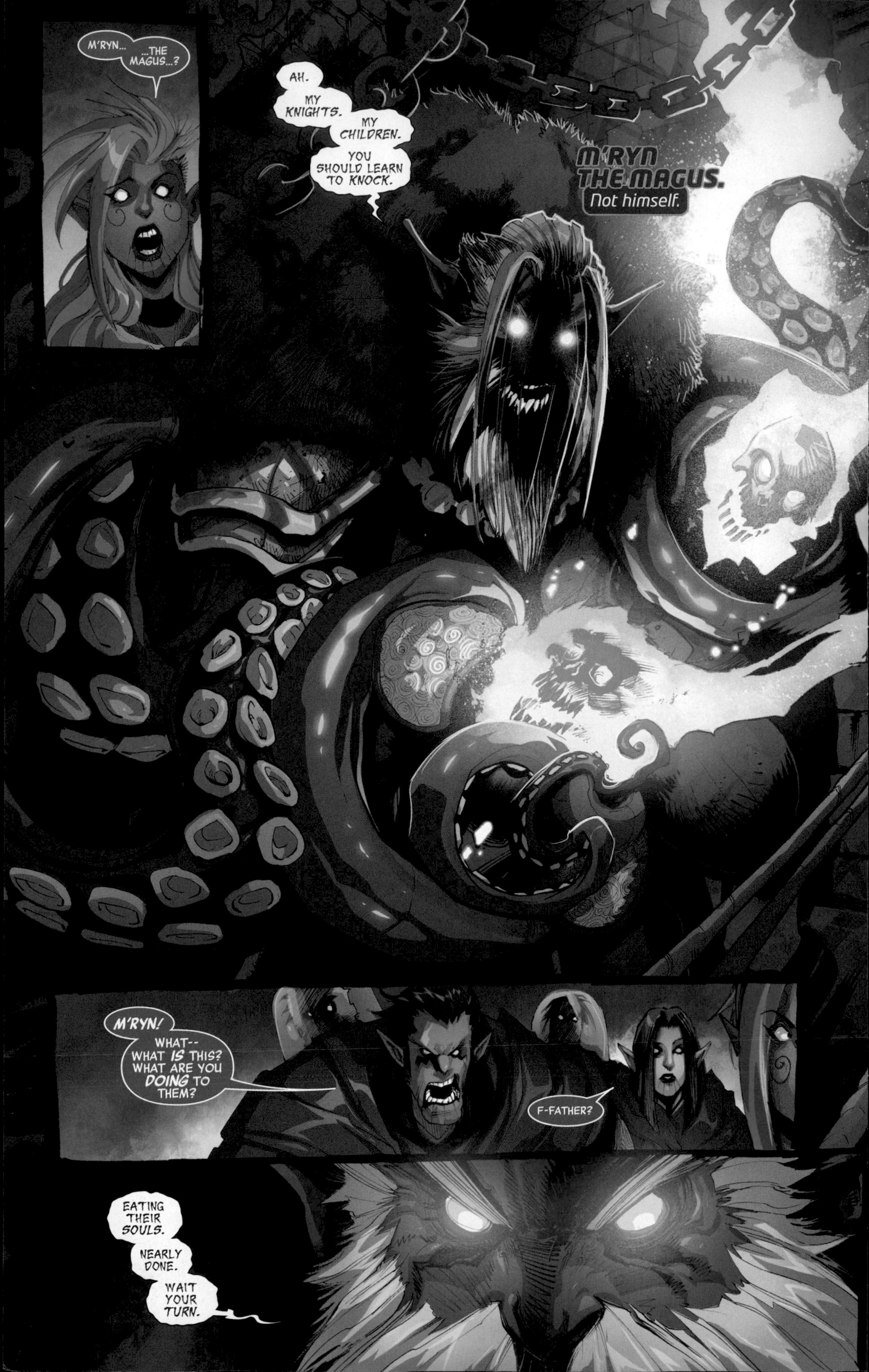
M'RYN... ...THE MAGUS...?
AH.
MY KNIGHTS.
MY CHILDREN.
YOU SHOULD LEARN TO KNOCK.
M'RYN THE MAGUS.
Not himself.
M'RYN!
WHAT-- WHAT IS THIS? WHAT ARE YOU DOING TO THEM?
F-FATHER?
EATING THEIR SOULS.
NEARLY DONE.
WAIT YOUR TURN.

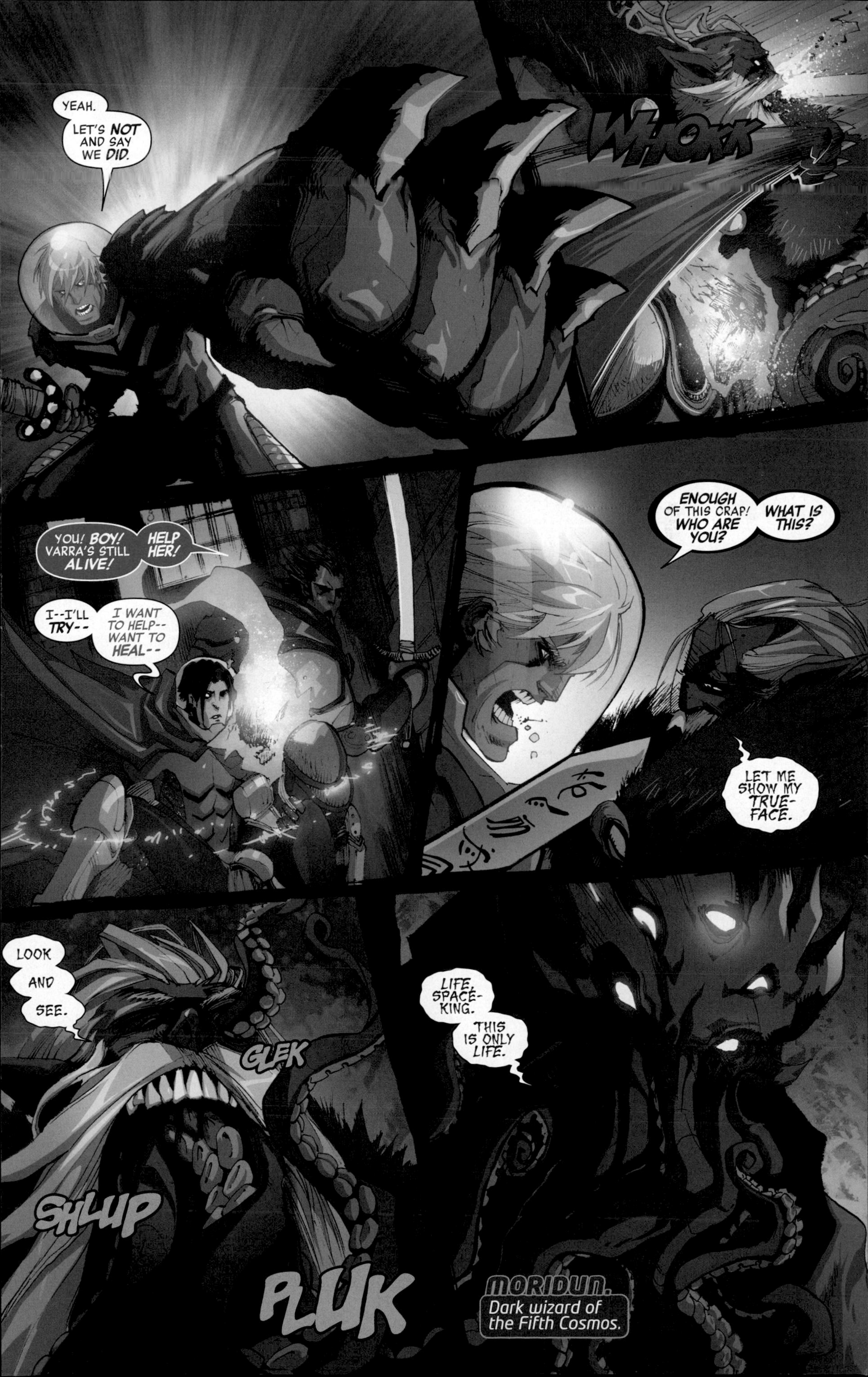
YEAH.
LET'S NOT AND SAY WE DID.
WHOKK
YOU! BOY! VARRA'S STILL ALIVE!
HELP HER!
I--I'LL TRY--
I WANT TO HELP-- WANT TO HEAL--
ENOUGH OF THIS CRAP! WHO ARE YOU?
WHAT IS THIS?
LET ME SHOW MY TRUE-FACE.
LOOK
AND
SEE.
GLEK
LIFE, SPACE-KING.
THIS IS ONLY LIFE.
SHLUP
PLUK
MORIDUN.
Dark wizard of the Fifth Cosmos.

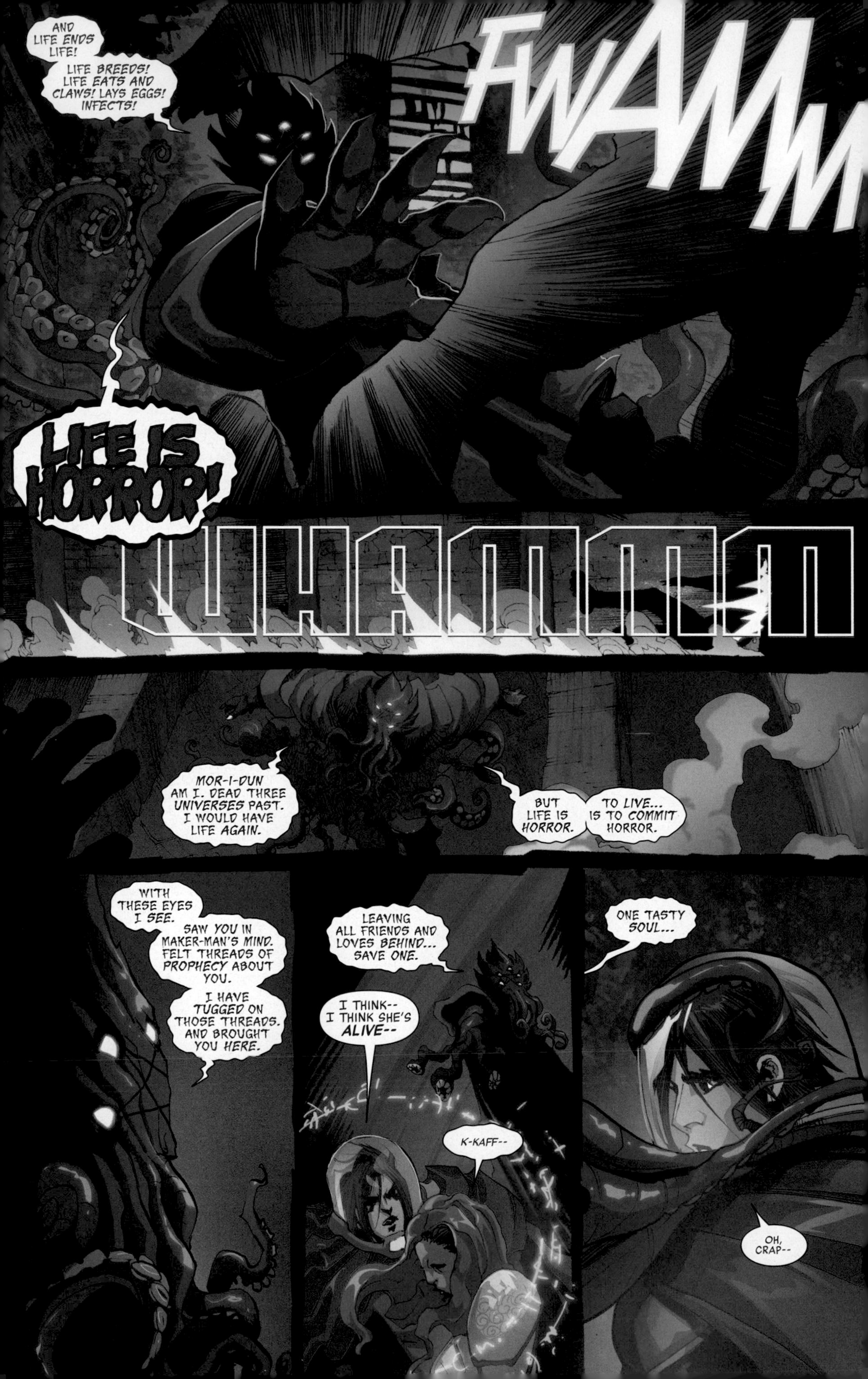
AND LIFE ENDS LIFE!
LIFE BREEDS! LIFE EATS AND CLAWS! LAYS EGGS! INFECTS!
FWAMMM
LIFE IS HORROR!
WHAMMM
MOR-I-DUN AM I. DEAD THREE UNIVERSES PAST. I WOULD HAVE LIFE AGAIN.
BUT LIFE IS HORROR.
TO LIVE... IS TO COMMIT HORROR.
WITH THESE EYES I SEE.
SAW YOU IN MAKER-MAN'S MIND. FELT THREADS OF PROPHECY ABOUT YOU.
I HAVE TUGGED ON THOSE THREADS. AND BROUGHT YOU HERE.
LEAVING ALL FRIENDS AND LOVES BEHIND... SAVE ONE.
I THINK-- I THINK SHE'S ALIVE--
K-KAFF--
ONE TASTY SOUL...
OH, CRAP--

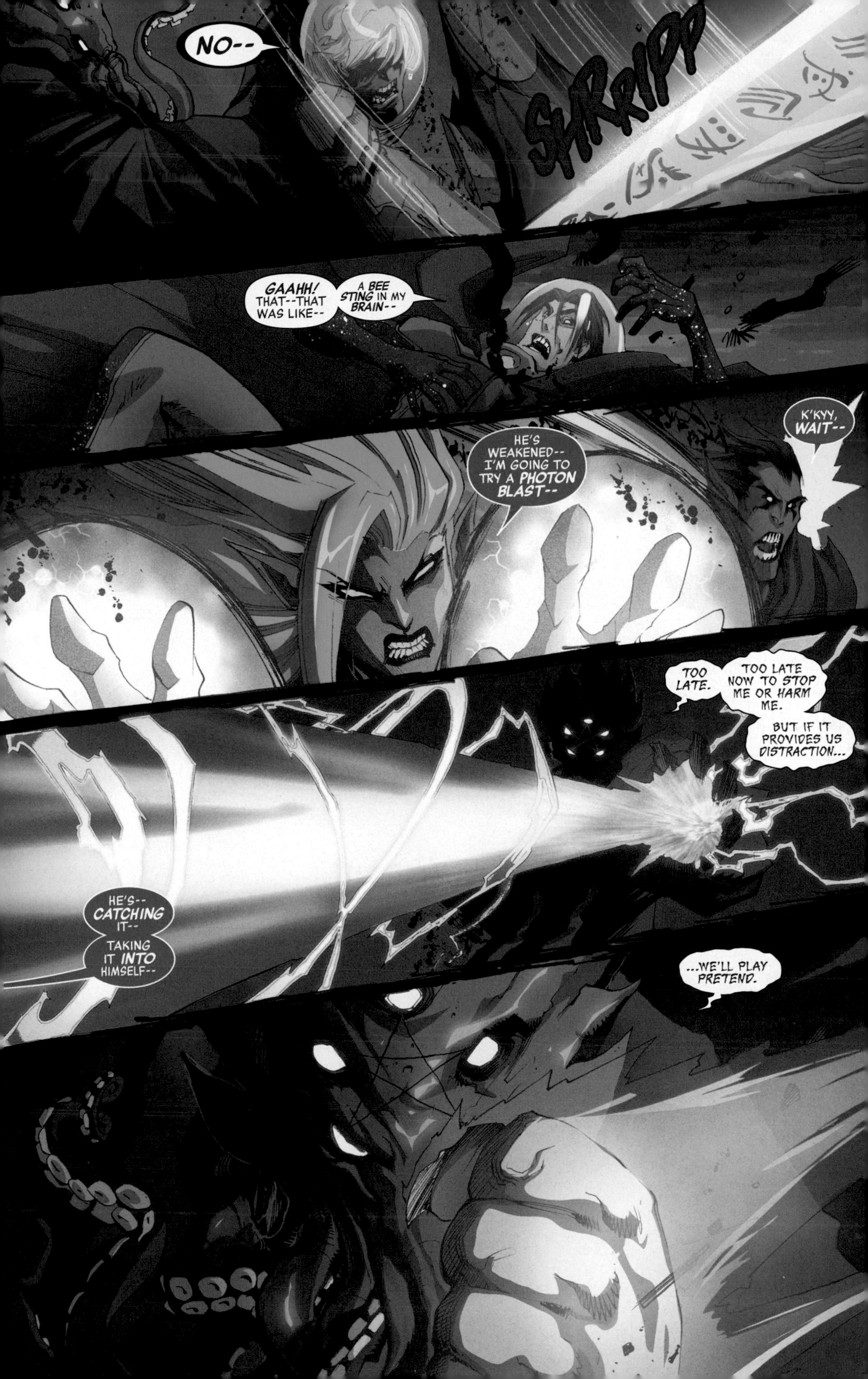
NO--
SHRIPP
GAAHH! THAT--THAT WAS LIKE--
A BEE STING IN MY BRAIN--
K'KYY, WAIT--
HE'S WEAKENED-- I'M GOING TO TRY A PHOTON BLAST--
TOO LATE.
TOO LATE NOW TO STOP ME OR HARM ME.
BUT IF IT PROVIDES US DISTRACTION...
HE'S-- CATCHING IT--
TAKING IT INTO HIMSELF--
...WE'LL PLAY PRETEND.

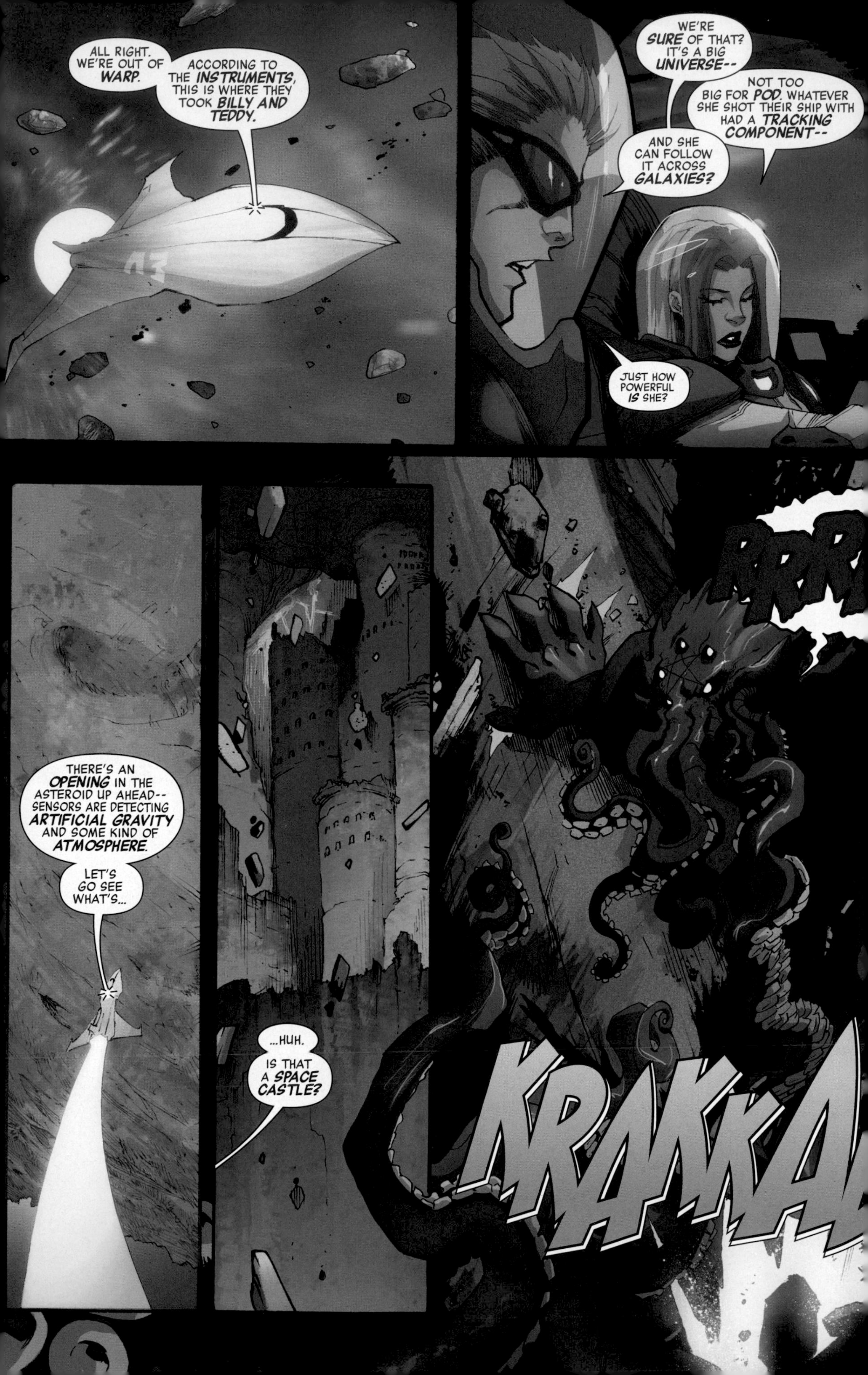
ALL RIGHT. WE'RE OUT OF WARP.
ACCORDING TO THE INSTRUMENTS, THIS IS WHERE THEY TOOK BILLY AND TEDDY.
WE'RE SURE OF THAT? IT'S A BIG UNIVERSE--
NOT TOO BIG FOR POD. WHATEVER SHE SHOT THEIR SHIP WITH HAD A TRACKING COMPONENT--
AND SHE CAN FOLLOW IT ACROSS GALAXIES?
JUST HOW POWERFUL IS SHE?
THERE'S AN OPENING IN THE ASTEROID UP AHEAD-- SENSORS ARE DETECTING ARTIFICIAL GRAVITY AND SOME KIND OF ATMOSPHERE.
LET'S GO SEE WHAT'S...
...HUH.
IS THAT A SPACE CASTLE?
RRRR
KRAKKA

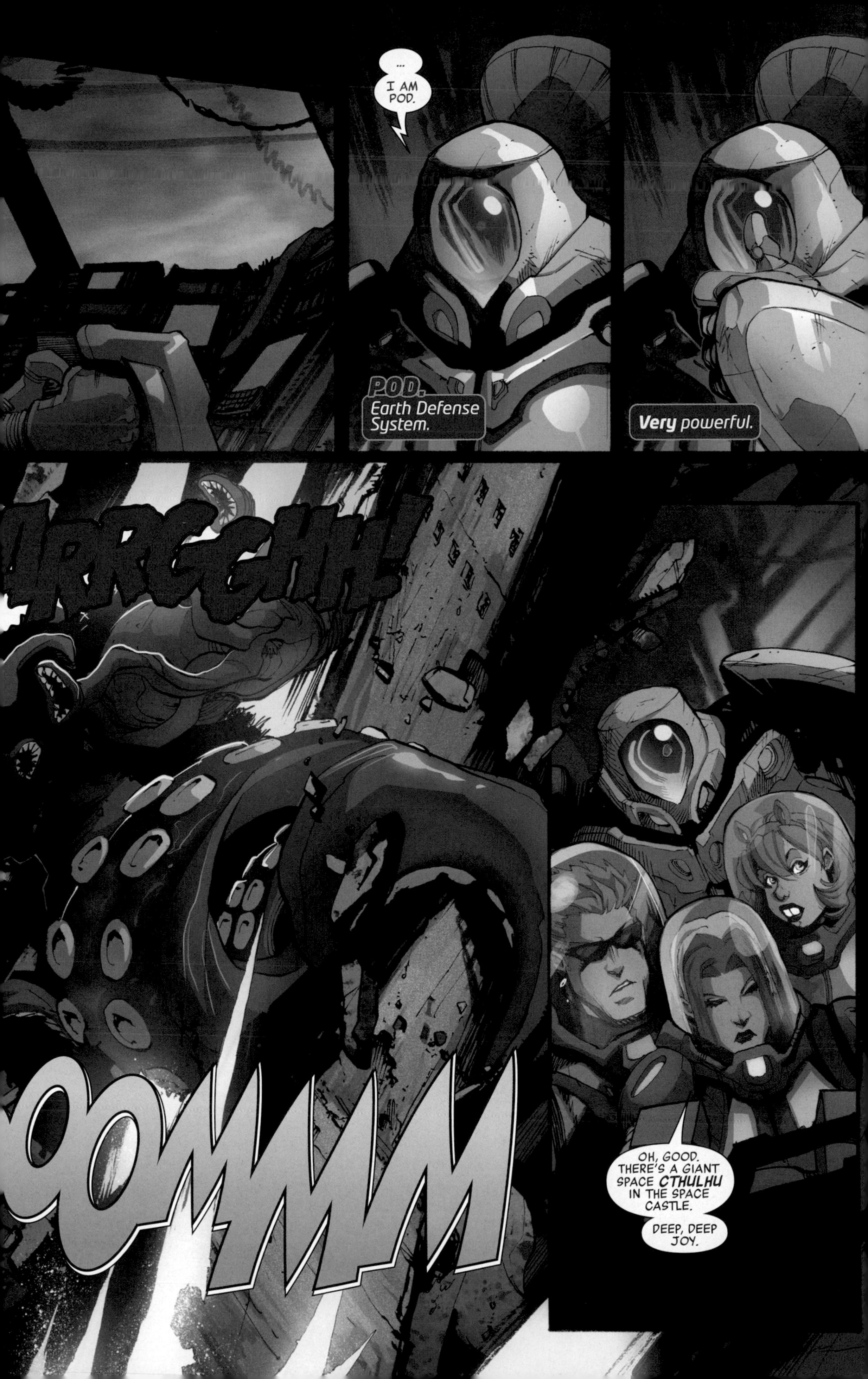
...
I AM POD.
POD.
Earth Defense System.
Very powerful.
OH, GOOD. THERE'S A GIANT SPACE CTHULHU IN THE SPACE CASTLE.
DEEP, DEEP JOY.

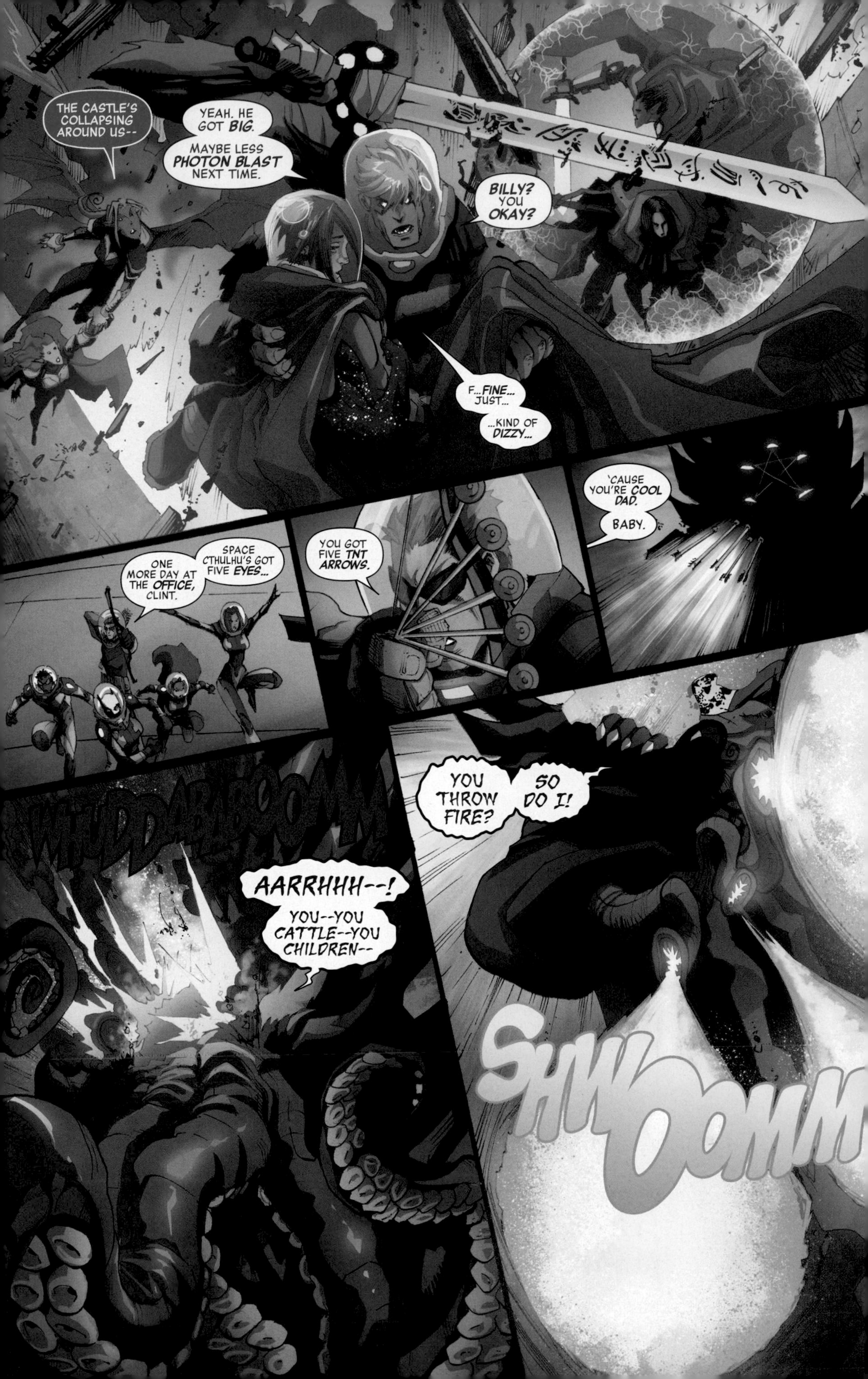
THE CASTLE'S COLLAPSING AROUND US--
YEAH. HE GOT BIG.
MAYBE LESS PHOTON BLAST NEXT TIME.
BILLY? YOU OKAY?
F...FINE... JUST...
...KIND OF DIZZY...
ONE MORE DAY AT THE OFFICE, CLINT.
SPACE CTHULHU'S GOT FIVE EYES...
YOU GOT FIVE TNT ARROWS.
'CAUSE YOU'RE COOL DAD.
BABY.
WUDDABOOMM
AARRHHH--!
YOU--YOU CATTLE--YOU CHILDREN--
YOU THROW FIRE?
SO DO I!
SHWOOMM

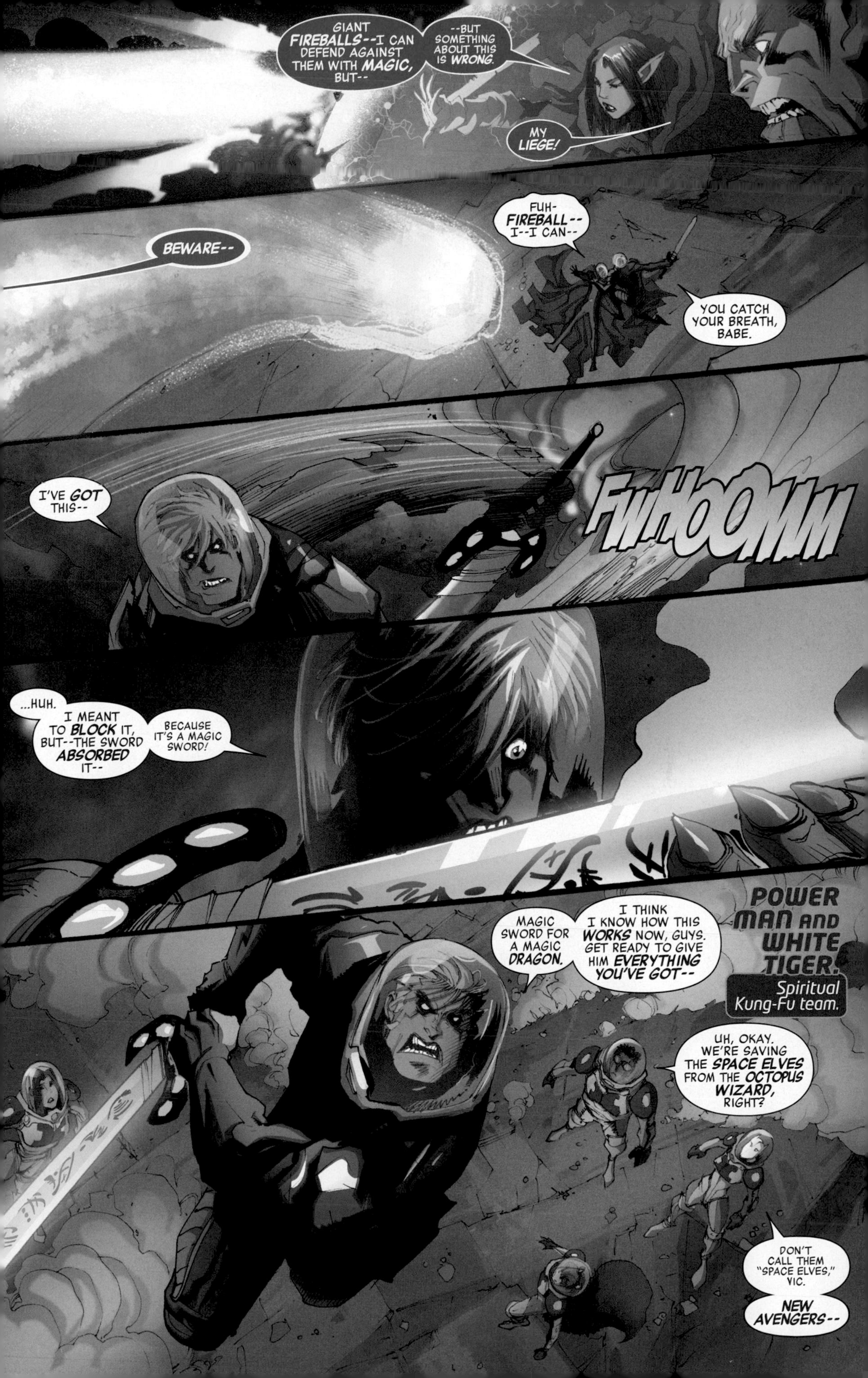

GIANT FIREBALLS--I CAN DEFEND AGAINST THEM WITH MAGIC, BUT--
--BUT SOMETHING ABOUT THIS IS WRONG.
MY LIEGE!
BEWARE--
FUH- FIREBALL-- I--I CAN--
YOU CATCH YOUR BREATH, BABE.
I'VE GOT THIS--
FWHOOMM
...HUH.
I MEANT TO BLOCK IT, BUT--THE SWORD ABSORBED IT--
BECAUSE IT'S A MAGIC SWORD!
MAGIC SWORD FOR A MAGIC DRAGON.
I THINK I KNOW HOW THIS WORKS NOW, GUYS. GET READY TO GIVE HIM EVERYTHING YOU'VE GOT--
POWER MAN AND WHITE TIGER.
Spiritual Kung-Fu team.
UH, OKAY. WE'RE SAVING THE SPACE ELVES FROM THE OCTOPUS WIZARD, RIGHT?
DON'T CALL THEM "SPACE ELVES," VIC.
NEW AVENGERS--

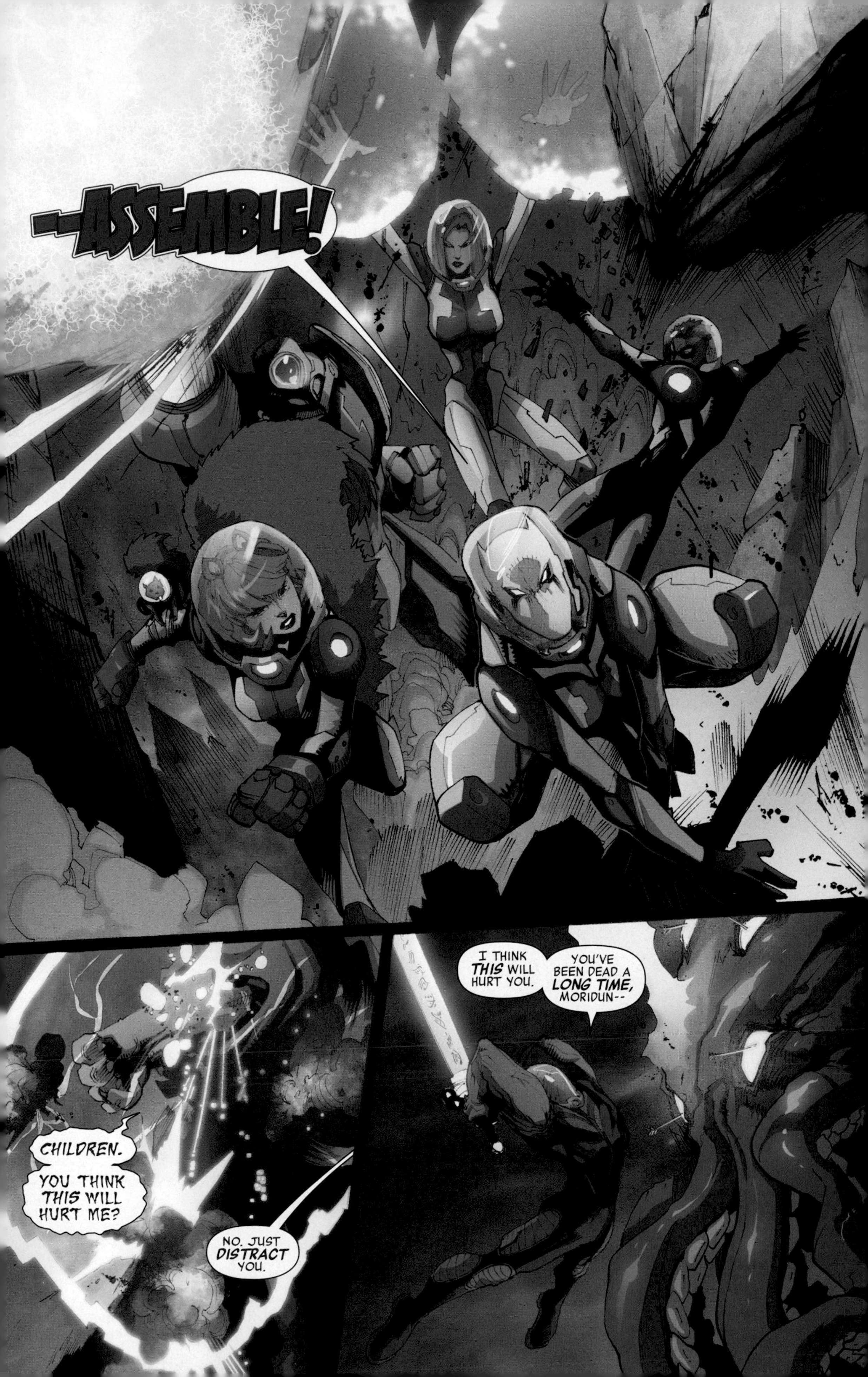
--ASSEMBLE!
CHILDREN.
YOU THINK THIS WILL HURT ME?
NO. JUST DISTRACT YOU.
I THINK THIS WILL HURT YOU.
YOU'VE BEEN DEAD A LONG TIME, MORIDUN--

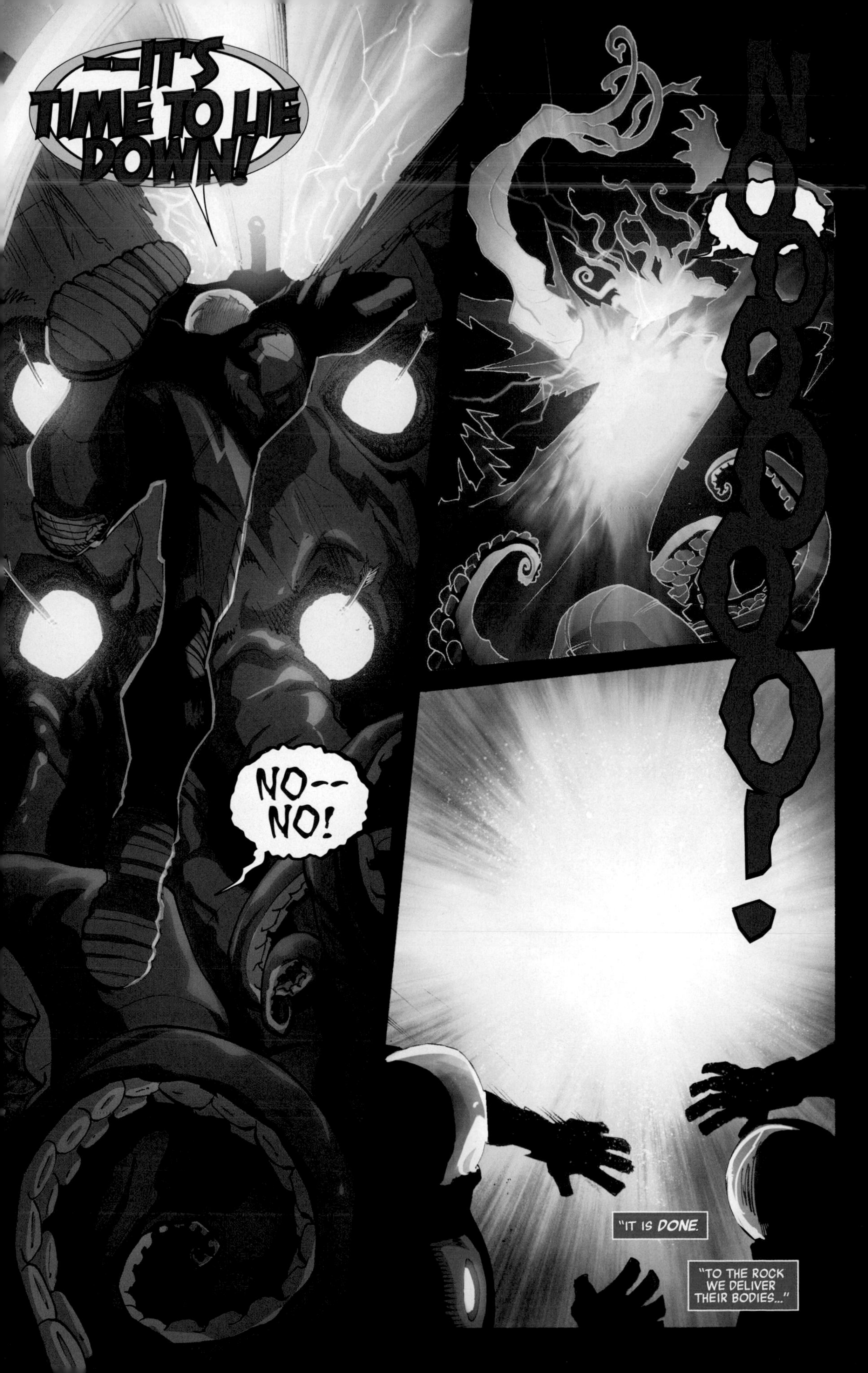
--IT'S TIME TO LIE DOWN!
NO-- NO!
NOOOOOO!
"IT IS DONE.
"TO THE ROCK WE DELIVER THEIR BODIES..."

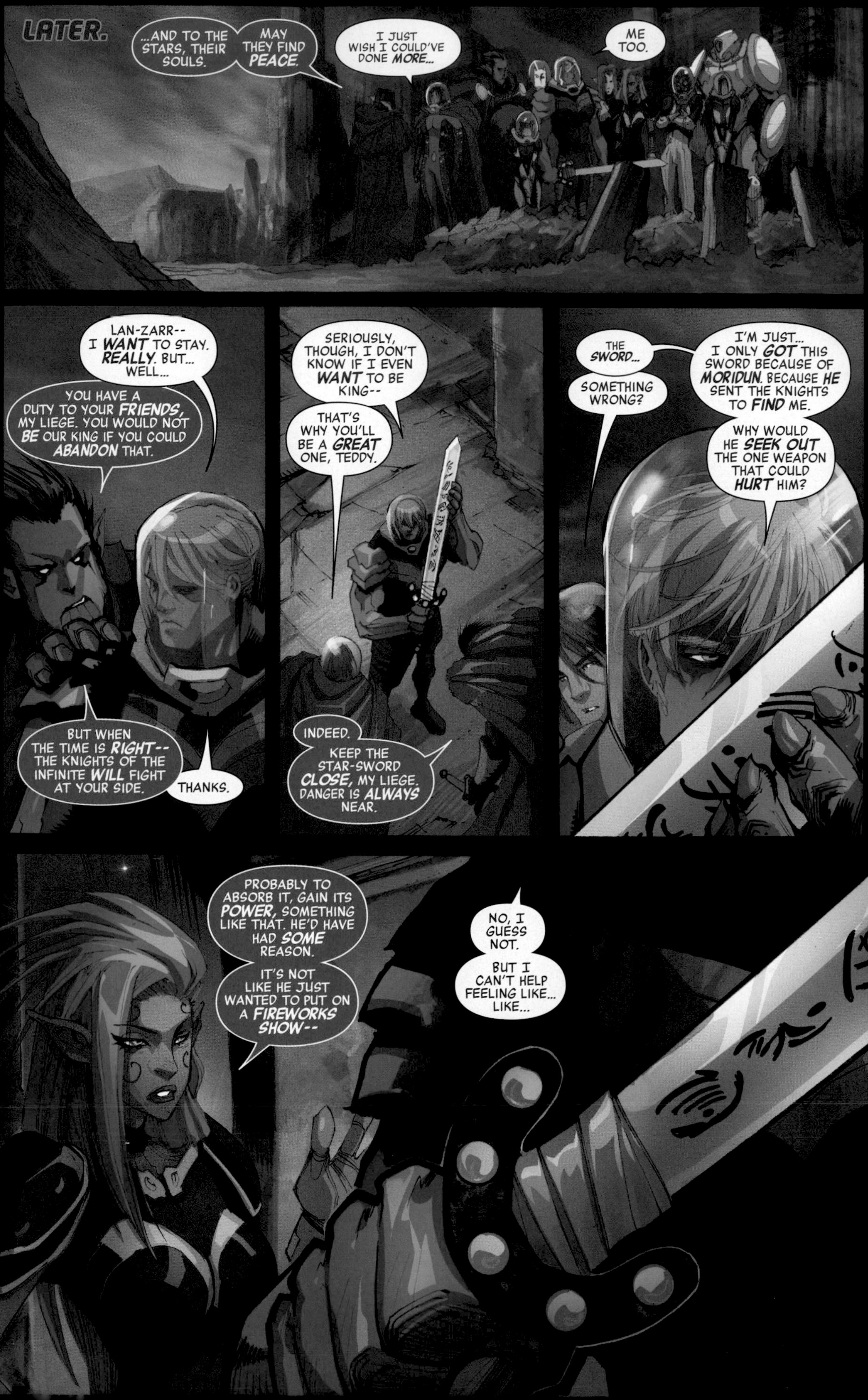
LATER.
...AND TO THE STARS, THEIR SOULS.
MAY THEY FIND PEACE.
I JUST WISH I COULD'VE DONE MORE...
ME TOO.
LAN-ZARR-- I WANT TO STAY. REALLY. BUT... WELL...
YOU HAVE A DUTY TO YOUR FRIENDS, MY LIEGE. YOU WOULD NOT BE OUR KING IF YOU COULD ABANDON THAT.
BUT WHEN THE TIME IS RIGHT-- THE KNIGHTS OF THE INFINITE WILL FIGHT AT YOUR SIDE.
THANKS.
SERIOUSLY, THOUGH, I DON'T KNOW IF I EVEN WANT TO BE KING--
THAT'S WHY YOU'LL BE A GREAT ONE, TEDDY.
INDEED.
KEEP THE STAR-SWORD CLOSE, MY LIEGE. DANGER IS ALWAYS NEAR.
THE SWORD...
SOMETHING WRONG?
I'M JUST... I ONLY GOT THIS SWORD BECAUSE OF MORIDUN. BECAUSE HE SENT THE KNIGHTS TO FIND ME.
WHY WOULD HE SEEK OUT THE ONE WEAPON THAT COULD HURT HIM?
PROBABLY TO ABSORB IT, GAIN ITS POWER, SOMETHING LIKE THAT. HE'D HAVE HAD SOME REASON.
IT'S NOT LIKE HE JUST WANTED TO PUT ON A FIREWORKS SHOW--
NO, I GUESS NOT.
BUT I CAN'T HELP FEELING LIKE... LIKE...

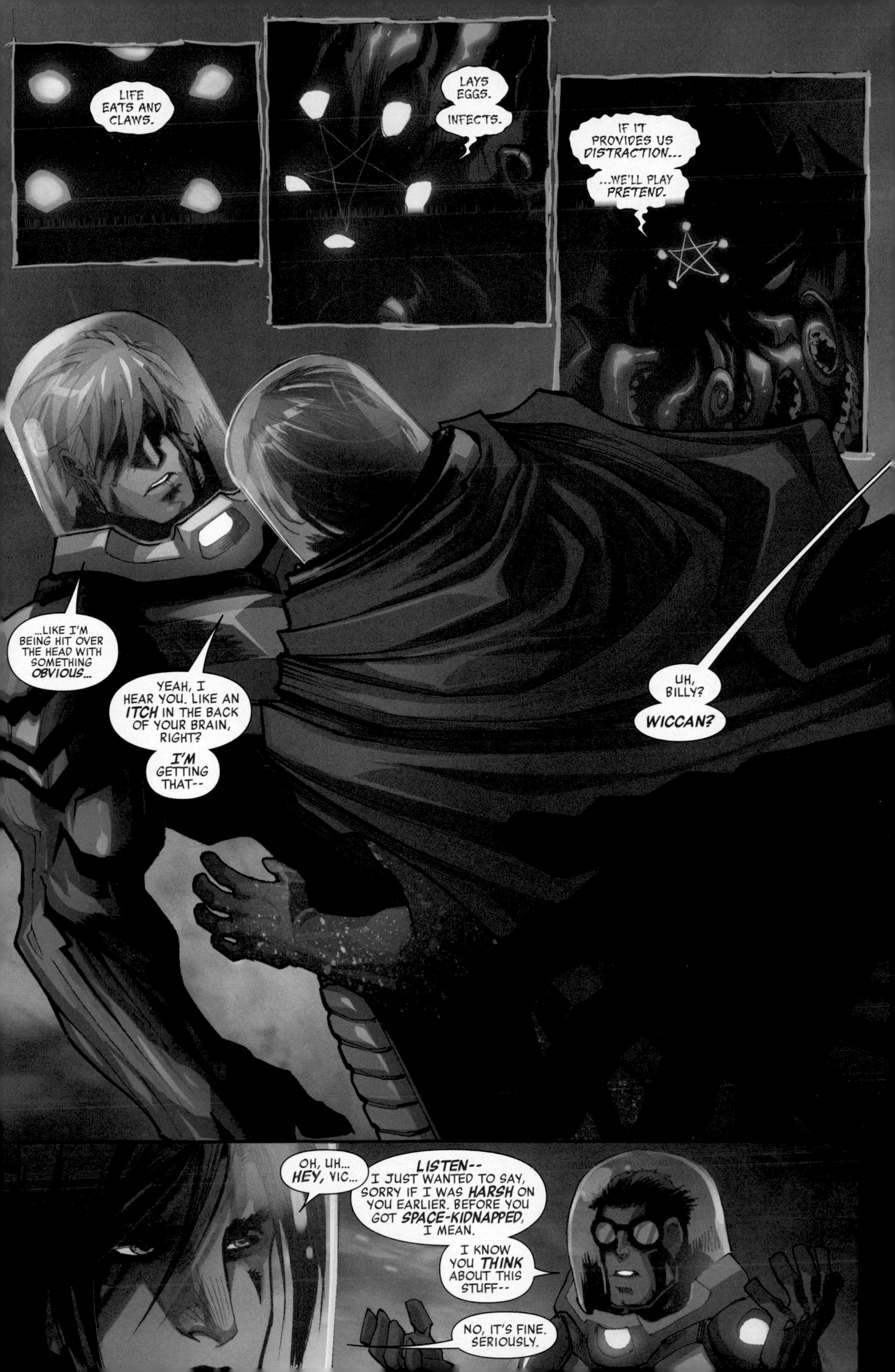
LIFE EATS AND CLAWS.
LAYS EGGS.
INFECTS.
IF IT PROVIDES US DISTRACTION...
...WE'LL PLAY PRETEND.
...LIKE I'M BEING HIT OVER THE HEAD WITH SOMETHING OBVIOUS...
YEAH, I HEAR YOU. LIKE AN ITCH IN THE BACK OF YOUR BRAIN, RIGHT?
I'M GETTING THAT--
UH, BILLY?
WICCAN?
OH, UH... HEY, VIC...
LISTEN-- I JUST WANTED TO SAY, SORRY IF I WAS HARSH ON YOU EARLIER. BEFORE YOU GOT SPACE-KIDNAPPED, I MEAN.
I KNOW YOU THINK ABOUT THIS STUFF--
NO, IT'S FINE. SERIOUSLY.

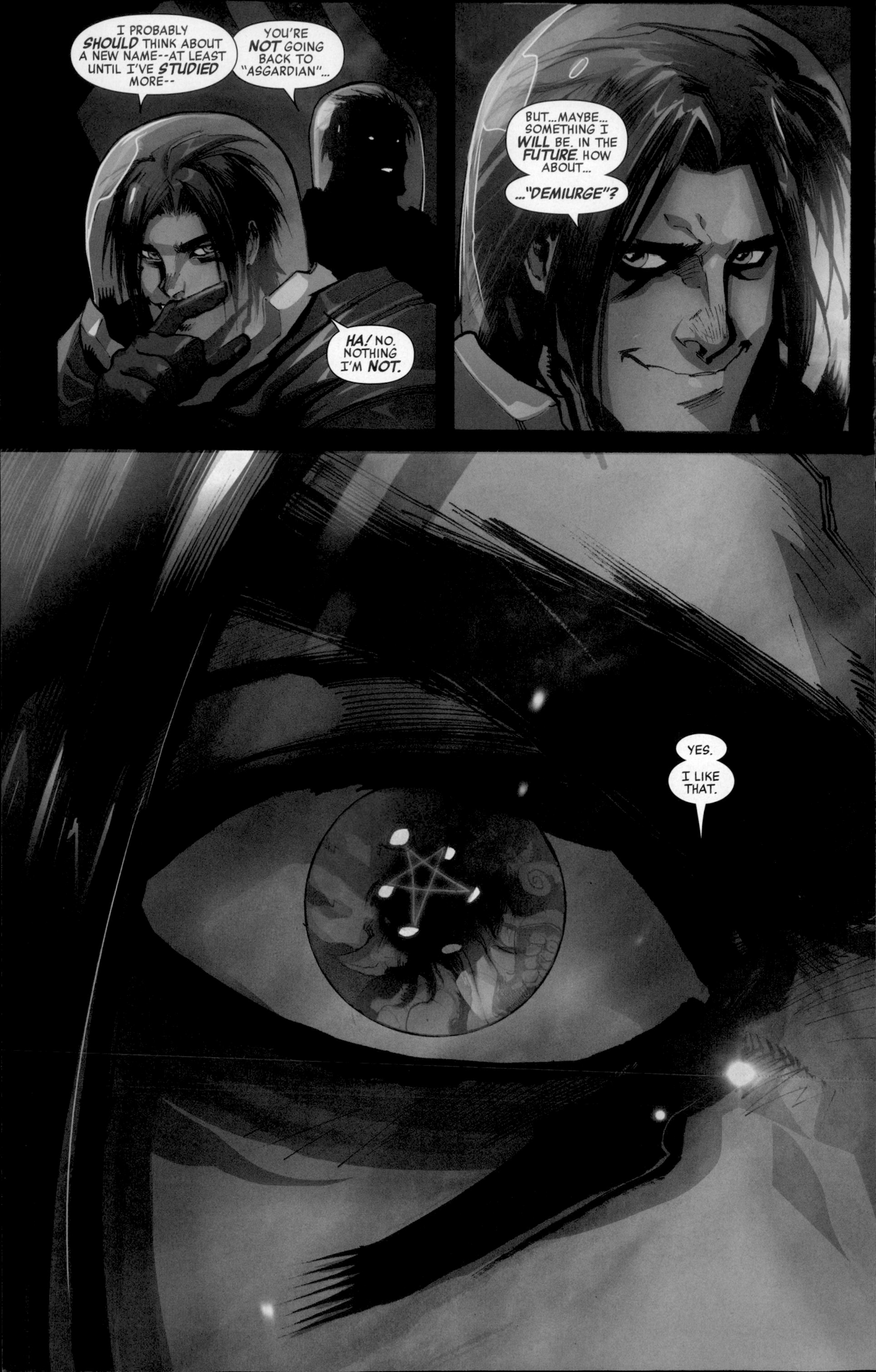
I PROBABLY **SHOULD** THINK ABOUT A NEW NAME--AT LEAST UNTIL I'VE **STUDIED** MORE--
YOU'RE **NOT** GOING BACK TO "ASGARDIAN"...
HA! NO. NOTHING I'M **NOT.**
BUT...MAYBE... SOMETHING I **WILL** BE. IN THE **FUTURE**. HOW ABOUT...
..."**DEMIURGE**"?
YES.
I LIKE THAT.

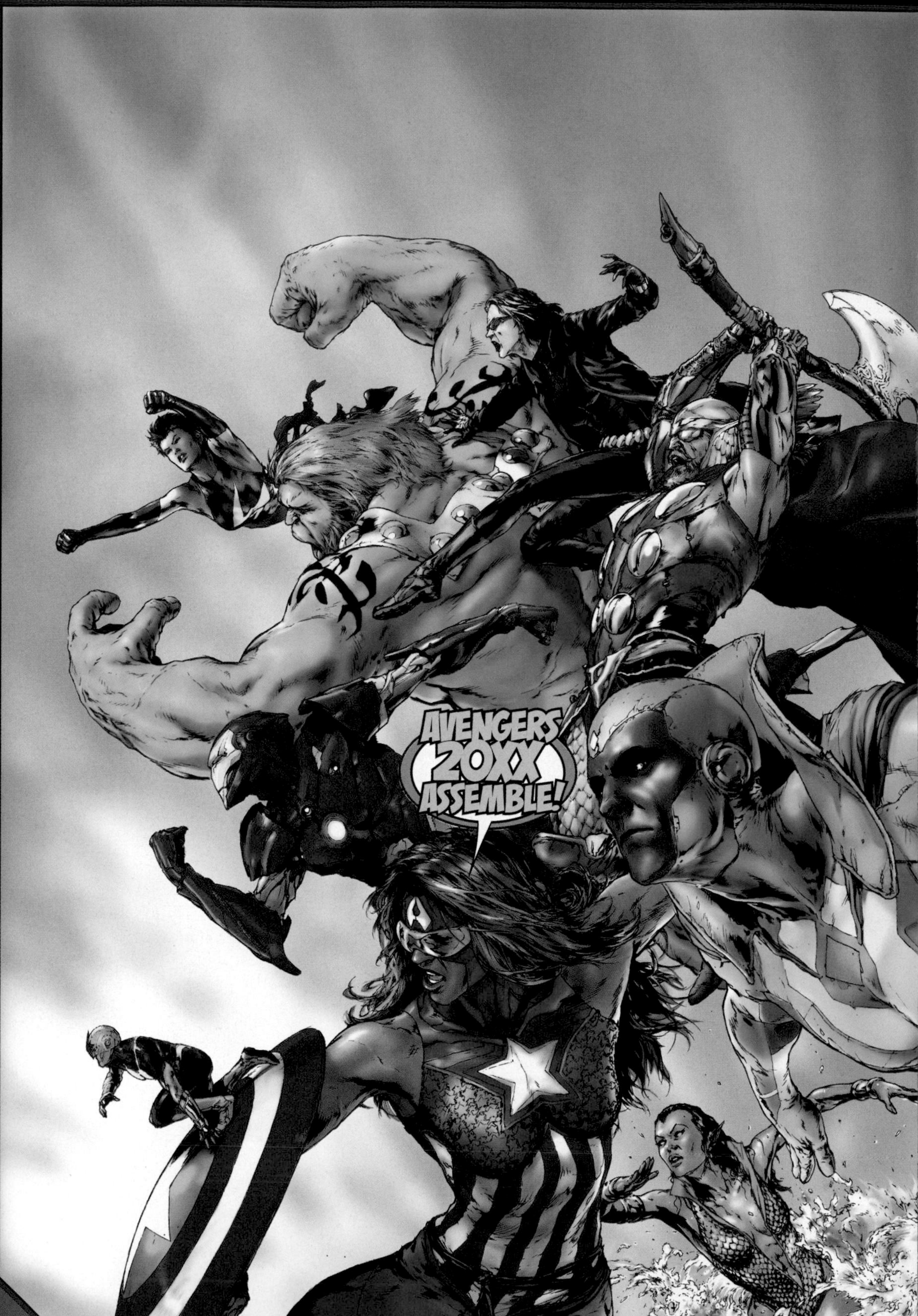
AVENGERS 20XX ASSEMBLE!

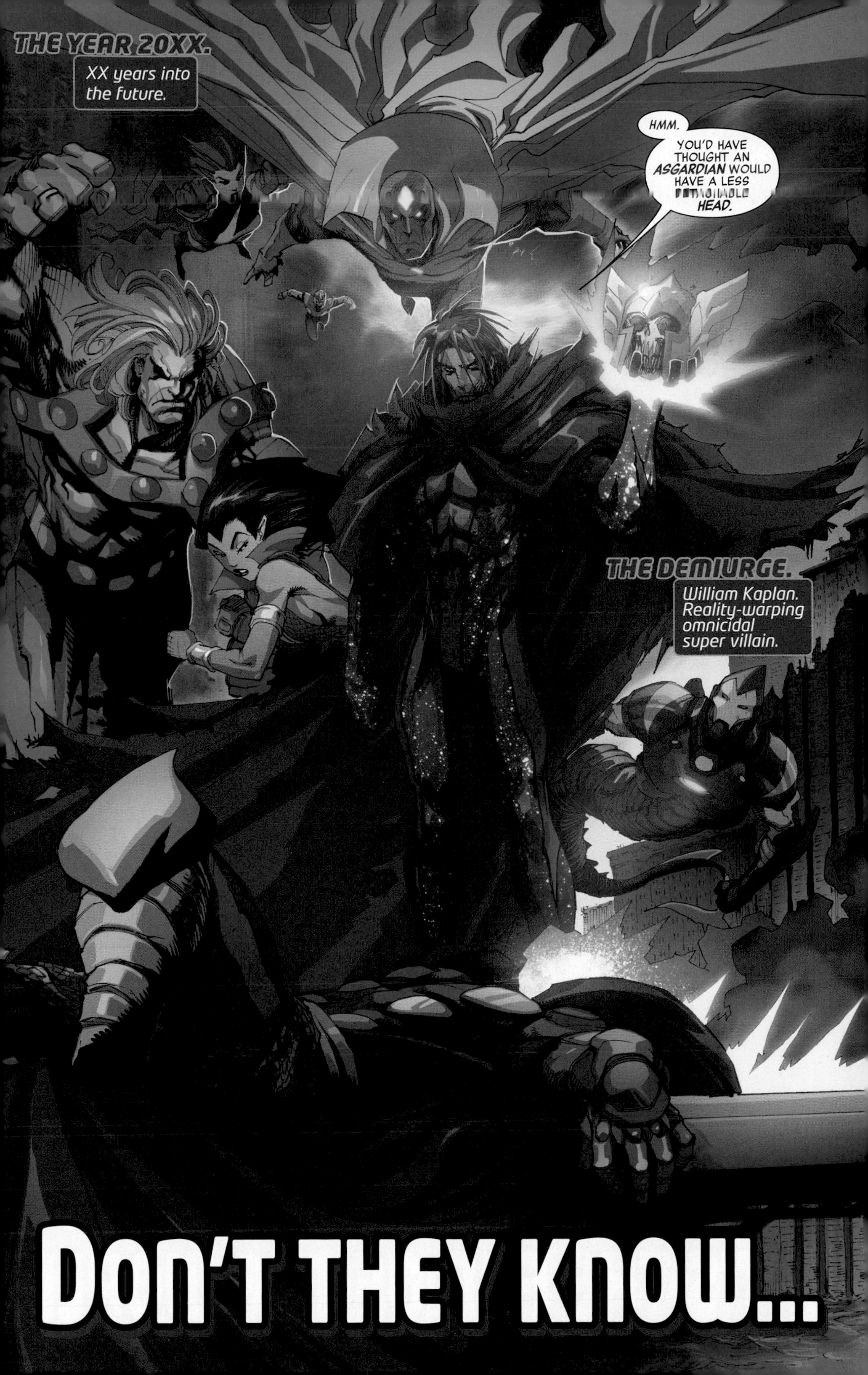
THE YEAR 20XX.
XX years into the future.
HMM.
YOU'D HAVE THOUGHT AN ASGARDIAN WOULD HAVE A LESS
HEAD.
THE DEMIURGE.
William Kaplan. Reality-warping omnicidal super villain.
DON'T THEY KNOW...

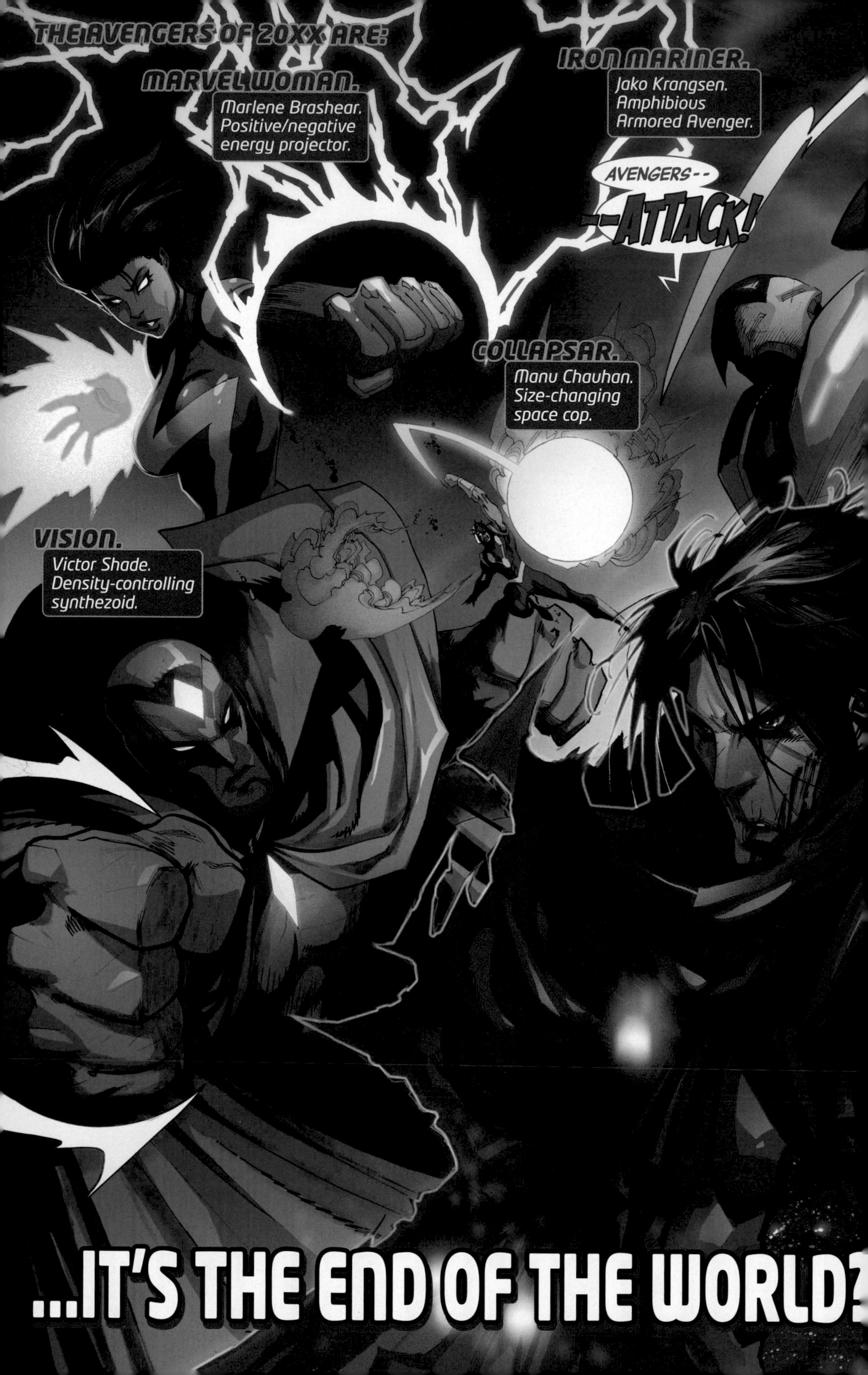
THE AVENGERS OF 20XX ARE:
MARVEL WOMAN.
Marlene Brashear. Positive/negative energy projector.
IRON MARINER.
Jako Krangsen. Amphibious Armored Avenger.
AVENGERS--
--ATTACK!
COLLAPSAR.
Manu Chauhan. Size-changing space cop.
VISION.
Victor Shade. Density-controlling synthezoid.
...IT'S THE END OF THE WORLD?

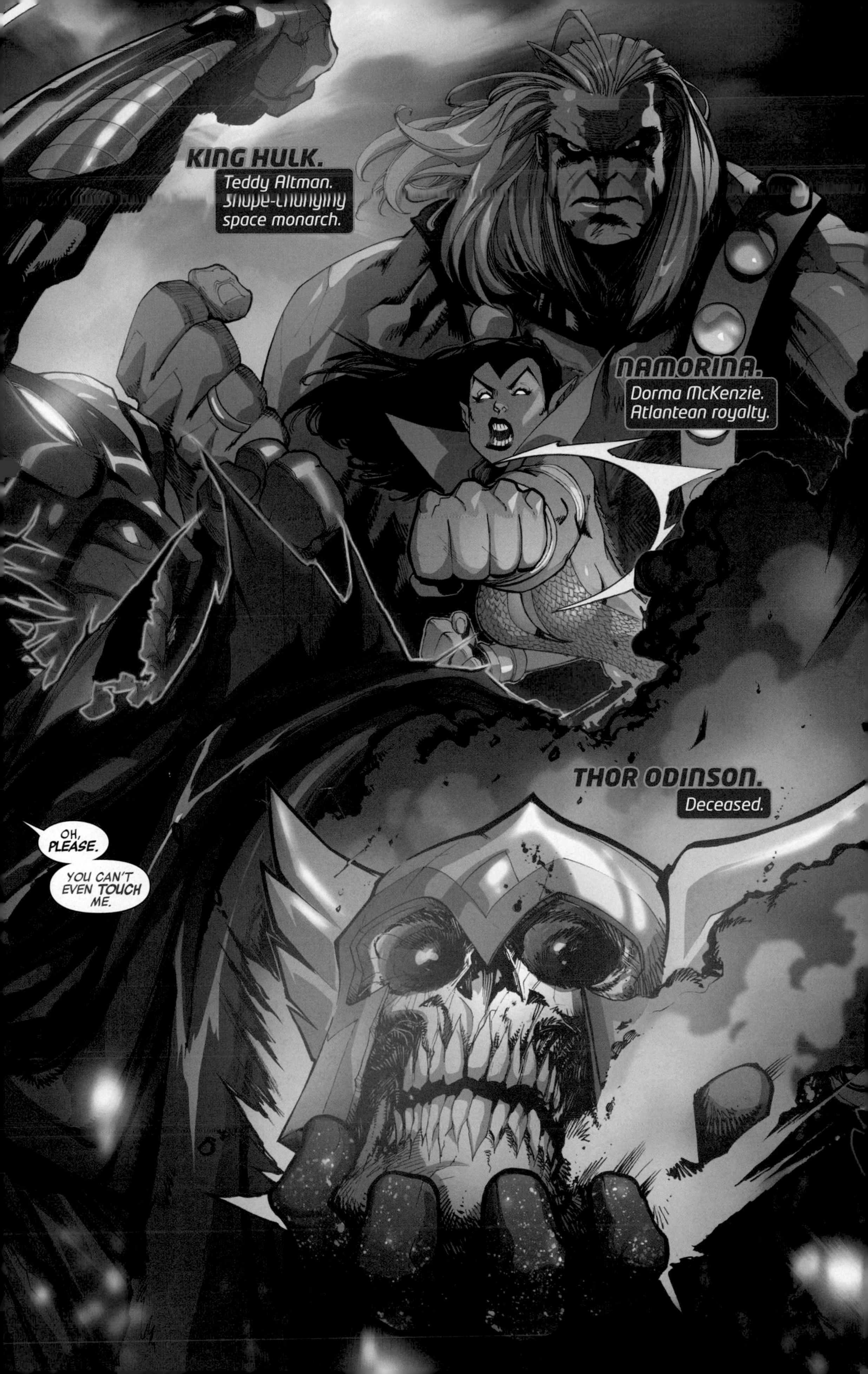
KING HULK.
Teddy Altman. Shape-changing space monarch.
NAMORINA.
Dorma McKenzie. Atlantean royalty.
THOR ODINSON.
Deceased.
OH, PLEASE.
YOU CAN'T EVEN TOUCH ME.

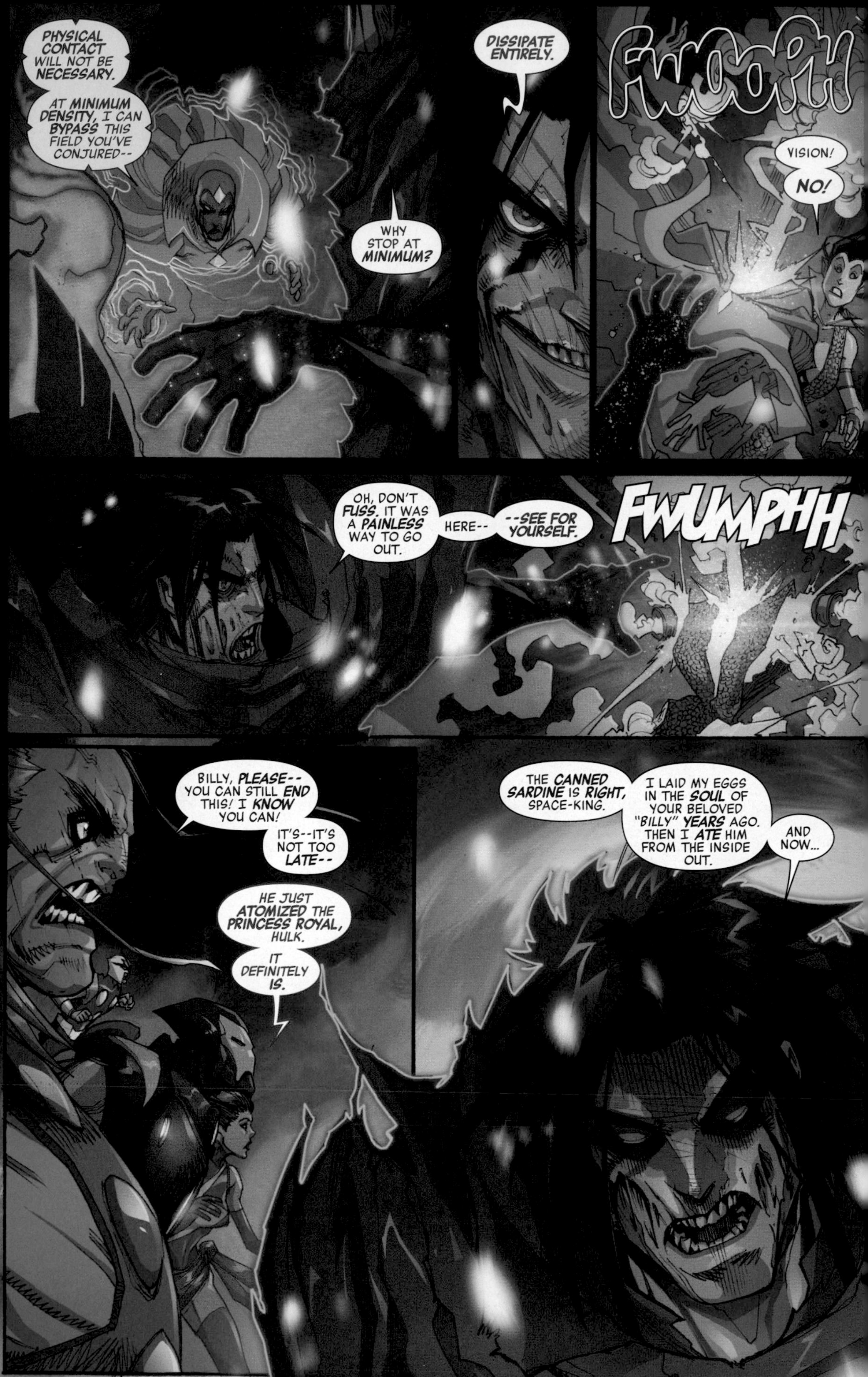
PHYSICAL CONTACT WILL NOT BE NECESSARY.
AT MINIMUM DENSITY, I CAN BYPASS THIS FIELD YOU'VE CONJURED--
WHY STOP AT MINIMUM?
DISSIPATE ENTIRELY.
FWOOPH
VISION!
NO!
OH, DON'T FUSS. IT WAS A PAINLESS WAY TO GO OUT.
HERE--
--SEE FOR YOURSELF.
FWUMPHH
BILLY, PLEASE-- YOU CAN STILL END THIS! I KNOW YOU CAN!
IT'S--IT'S NOT TOO LATE--
HE JUST ATOMIZED THE PRINCESS ROYAL, HULK.
IT DEFINITELY IS.
THE CANNED SARDINE IS RIGHT, SPACE-KING.
I LAID MY EGGS IN THE SOUL OF YOUR BELOVED "BILLY" YEARS AGO. THEN I ATE HIM FROM THE INSIDE OUT.
AND NOW...

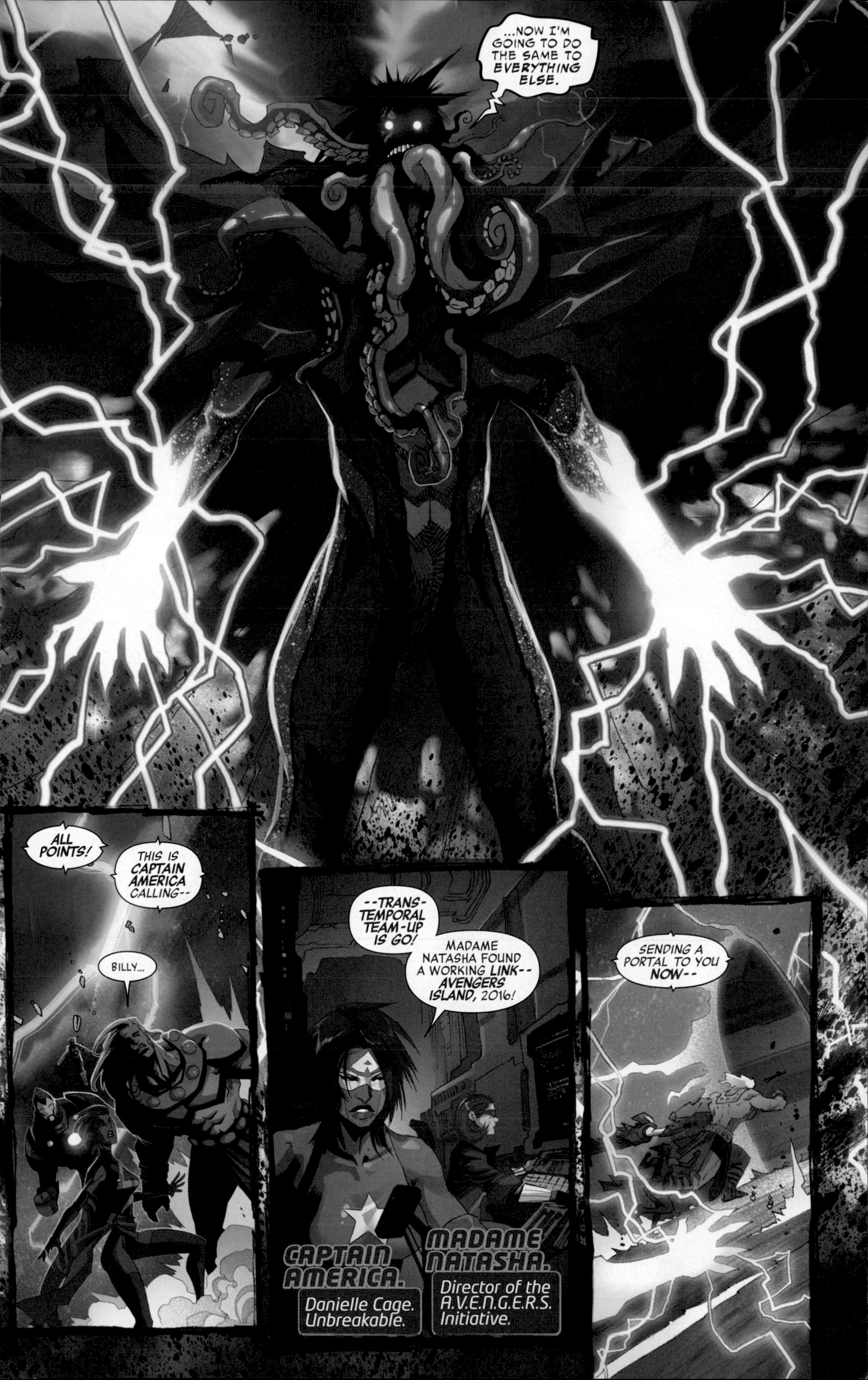
...NOW I'M GOING TO DO THE SAME TO EVERYTHING ELSE.
ALL POINTS!
THIS IS CAPTAIN AMERICA CALLING--
BILLY...
--TRANS-TEMPORAL TEAM-UP IS GO!
MADAME NATASHA FOUND A WORKING LINK--AVENGERS ISLAND, 2016!
CAPTAIN AMERICA.
Danielle Cage. Unbreakable.
MADAME NATASHA.
Director of the A.V.E.N.G.E.R.S. Initiative.
SENDING A PORTAL TO YOU NOW--

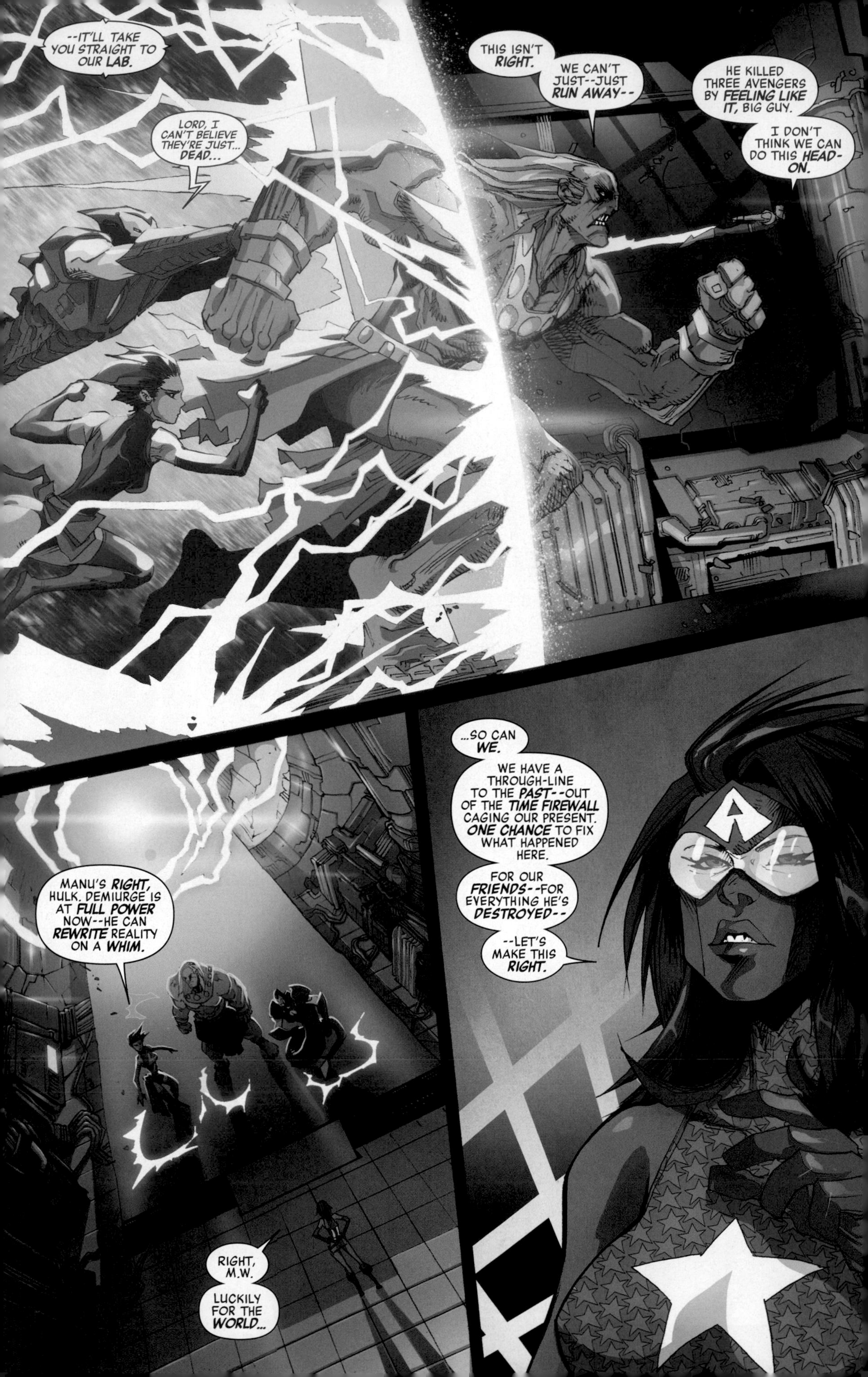
--IT'LL TAKE YOU STRAIGHT TO OUR LAB.
LORD, I CAN'T BELIEVE THEY'RE JUST... DEAD...
THIS ISN'T RIGHT.
WE CAN'T JUST--JUST RUN AWAY--
HE KILLED THREE AVENGERS BY FEELING LIKE IT, BIG GUY.
I DON'T THINK WE CAN DO THIS HEAD-ON.
MANU'S RIGHT, HULK. DEMIURGE IS AT FULL POWER NOW--HE CAN REWRITE REALITY ON A WHIM.
RIGHT, M.W.
LUCKILY FOR THE WORLD...
...SO CAN WE.
WE HAVE A THROUGH-LINE TO THE PAST--OUT OF THE TIME FIREWALL CAGING OUR PRESENT. ONE CHANCE TO FIX WHAT HAPPENED HERE.
FOR OUR FRIENDS--FOR EVERYTHING HE'S DESTROYED--
--LET'S MAKE THIS RIGHT.

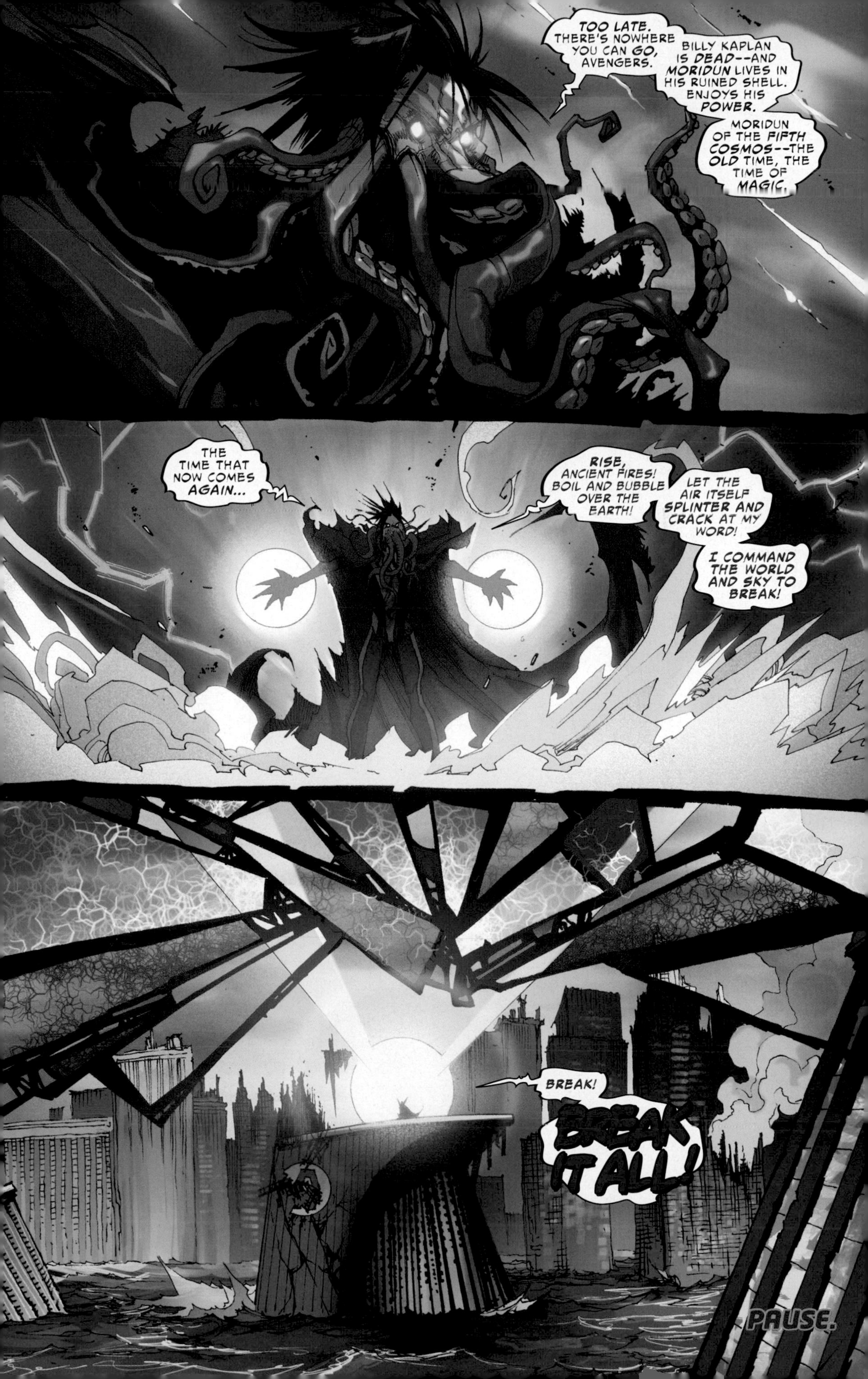
TOO LATE. THERE'S NOWHERE YOU CAN GO, AVENGERS.
BILLY KAPLAN IS DEAD--AND MORIDUN LIVES IN HIS RUINED SHELL. ENJOYS HIS POWER.
MORIDUN OF THE FIFTH COSMOS--THE OLD TIME, THE TIME OF MAGIC.
THE TIME THAT NOW COMES AGAIN...
RISE, ANCIENT FIRES! BOIL AND BUBBLE OVER THE EARTH!
LET THE AIR ITSELF SPLINTER AND CRACK AT MY WORD!
I COMMAND THE WORLD AND SKY TO BREAK!
BREAK!
BREAK IT ALL!
PAUSE.

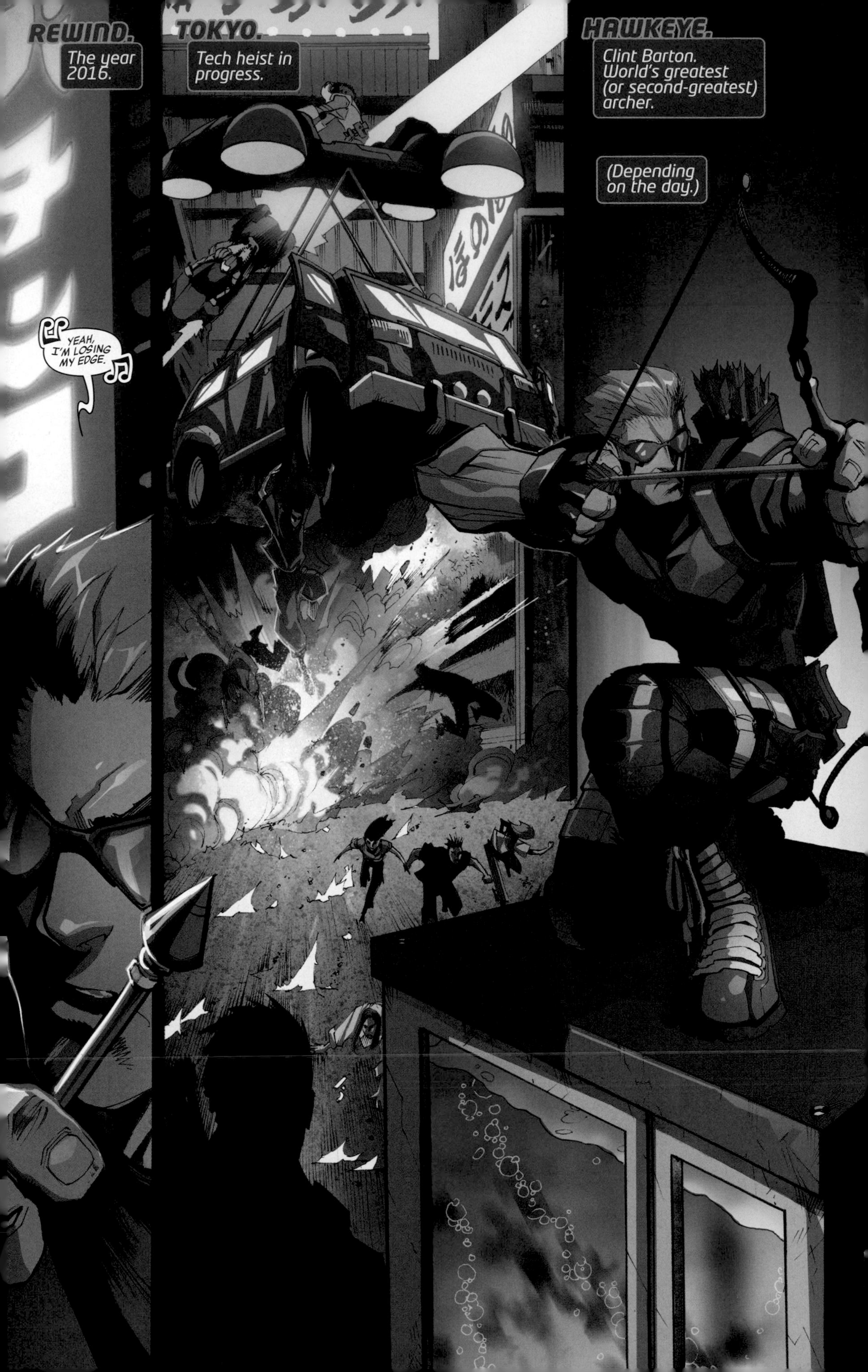
REWIND.
The year 2016.
TOKYO.
Tech heist in progress.
HAWKEYE.
Clint Barton. World's greatest (or second-greatest) archer.
(Depending on the day.)
YEAH, I'M LOSING MY EDGE.

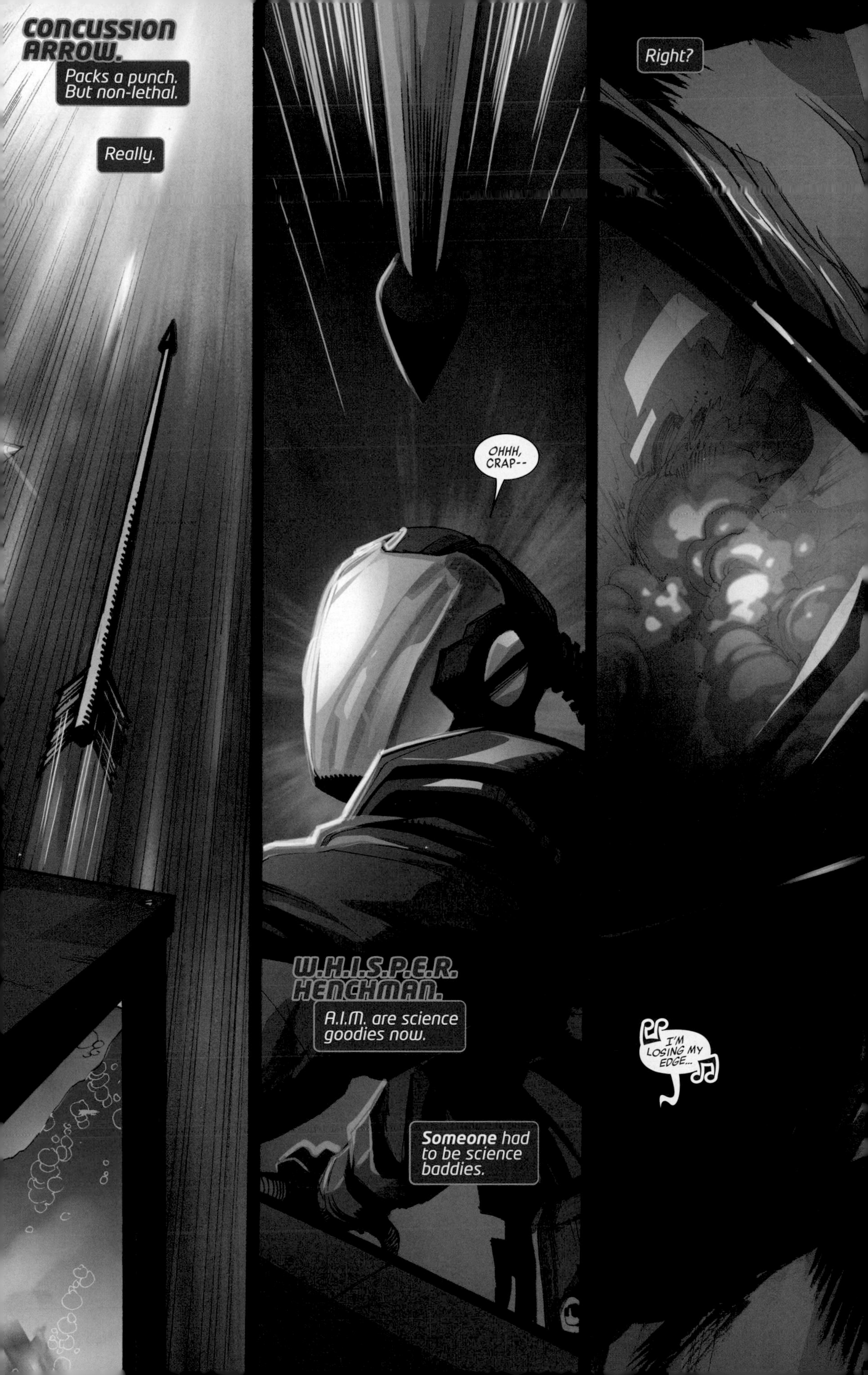

CONCUSSION ARROW.
Packs a punch. But non-lethal.
Really.
OHHH, CRAP--
W.H.I.S.P.E.R. HENCHMAN.
A.I.M. are science goodies now.
Someone had to be science baddies.
Right?
I'M LOSING MY EDGE...

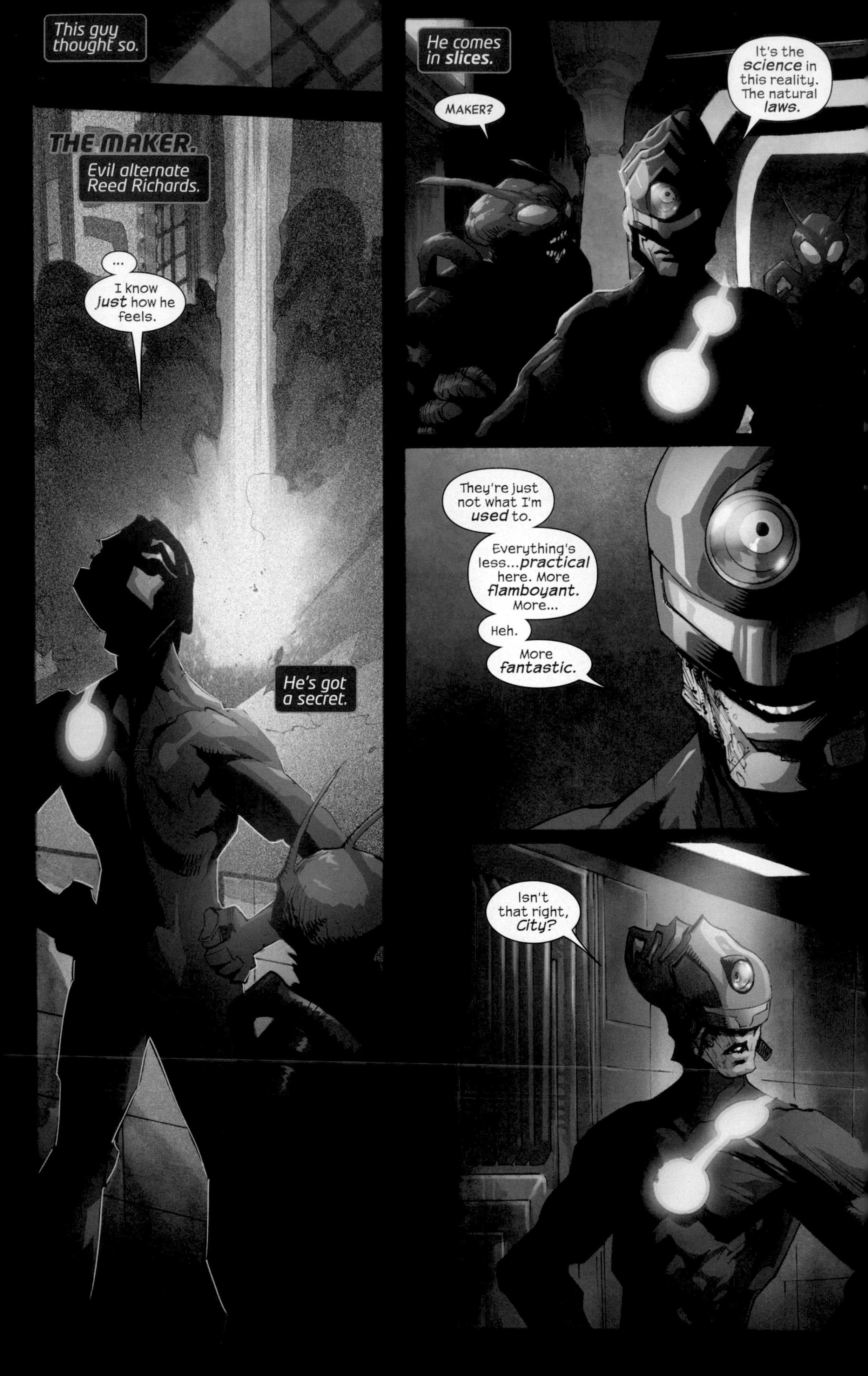

This guy thought so.
THE MAKER.
Evil alternate Reed Richards.
...
I know *just* how he feels.
He's got a secret.
He comes in **slices.**
MAKER?
It's the **science** in this reality. The natural **laws.**
They're just not what I'm *used* to.
Everything's less...***practical*** here. More ***flamboyant.*** More...
Heh.
More ***fantastic.***
Isn't that right, *City?*

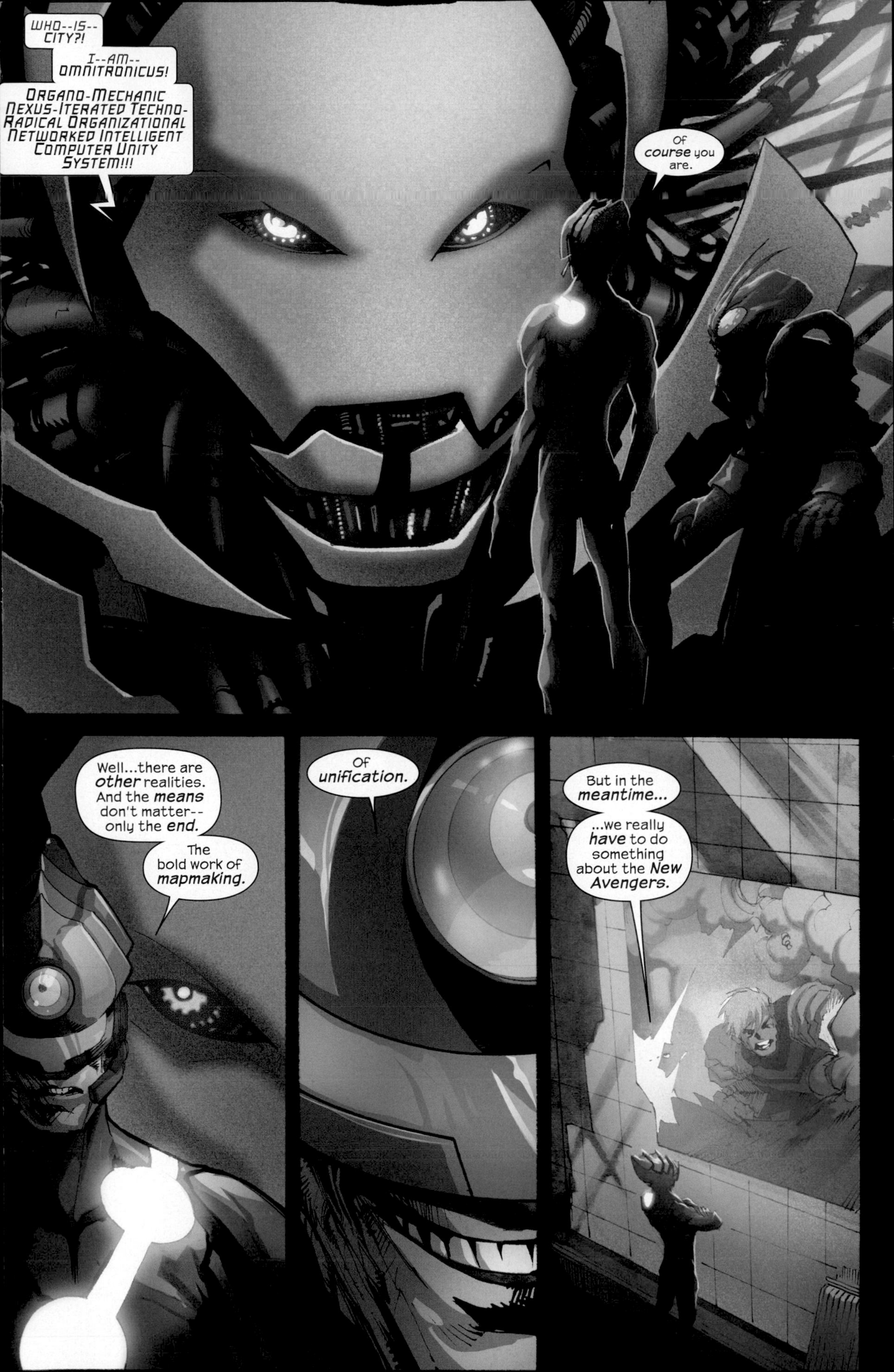
WHO--IS--CITY?!
I--AM--OMNITRONICUS!
ORGANO-MECHANIC NEXUS-ITERATED TECHNO-RADICAL ORGANIZATIONAL NETWORKED INTELLIGENT COMPUTER UNITY SYSTEM!!!
Of course you are.
Well...there are other realities. And the means don't matter--only the end.
The bold work of mapmaking.
Of unification.
But in the meantime...
...we really have to do something about the New Avengers.

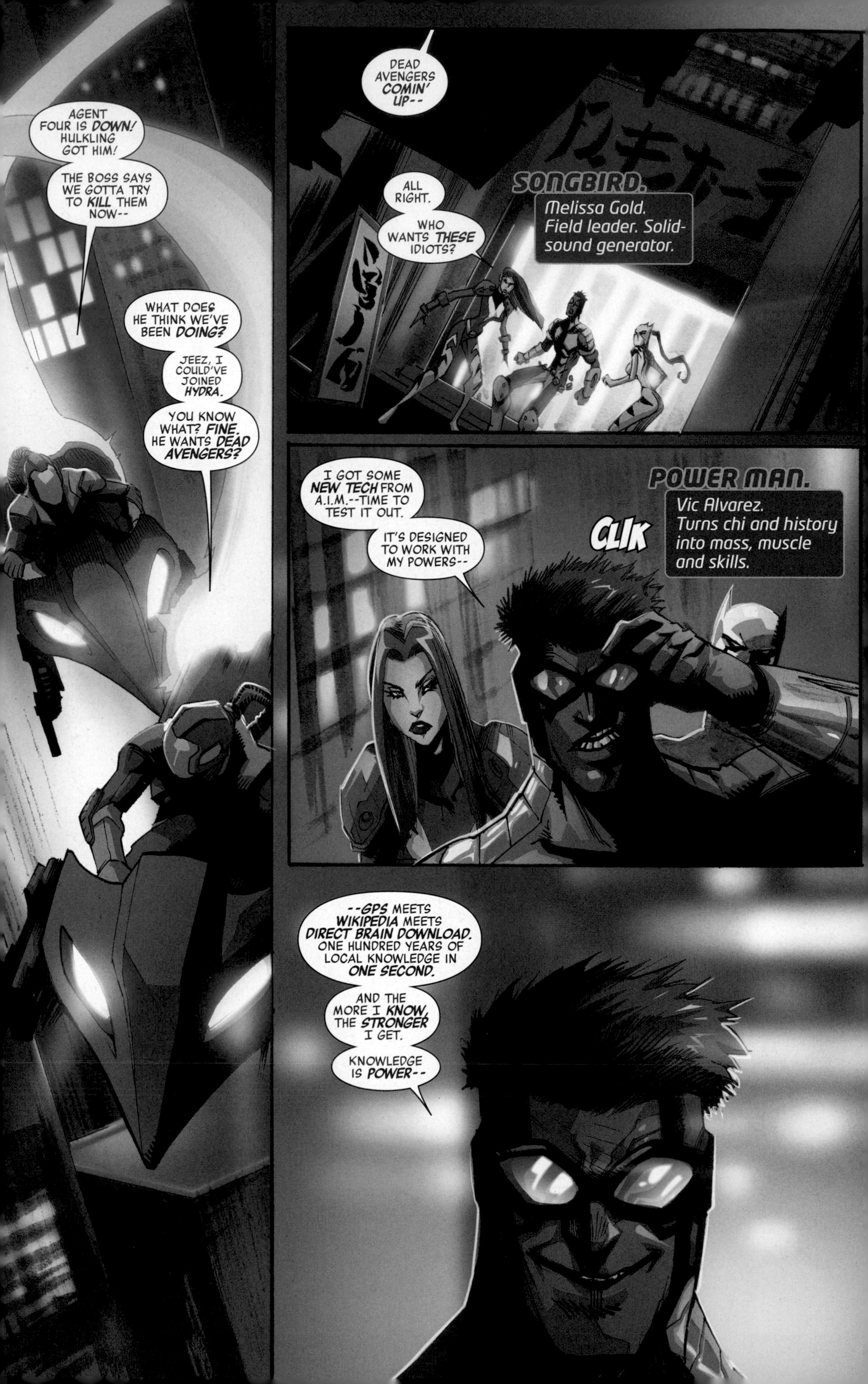

AGENT FOUR IS DOWN! HULKLING GOT HIM!
THE BOSS SAYS WE GOTTA TRY TO KILL THEM NOW--
WHAT DOES HE THINK WE'VE BEEN DOING?
JEEZ, I COULD'VE JOINED HYDRA.
YOU KNOW WHAT? FINE. HE WANTS DEAD AVENGERS?
DEAD AVENGERS COMIN' UP--
ALL RIGHT.
WHO WANTS THESE IDIOTS?
SONGBIRD.
Melissa Gold. Field leader. Solid-sound generator.
I GOT SOME NEW TECH FROM A.I.M.--TIME TO TEST IT OUT.
IT'S DESIGNED TO WORK WITH MY POWERS--
POWER MAN.
Vic Alvarez. Turns chi and history into mass, muscle and skills.
CLIK
--GPS MEETS WIKIPEDIA MEETS DIRECT BRAIN DOWNLOAD. ONE HUNDRED YEARS OF LOCAL KNOWLEDGE IN ONE SECOND.
AND THE MORE I KNOW, THE STRONGER I GET.
KNOWLEDGE IS POWER--

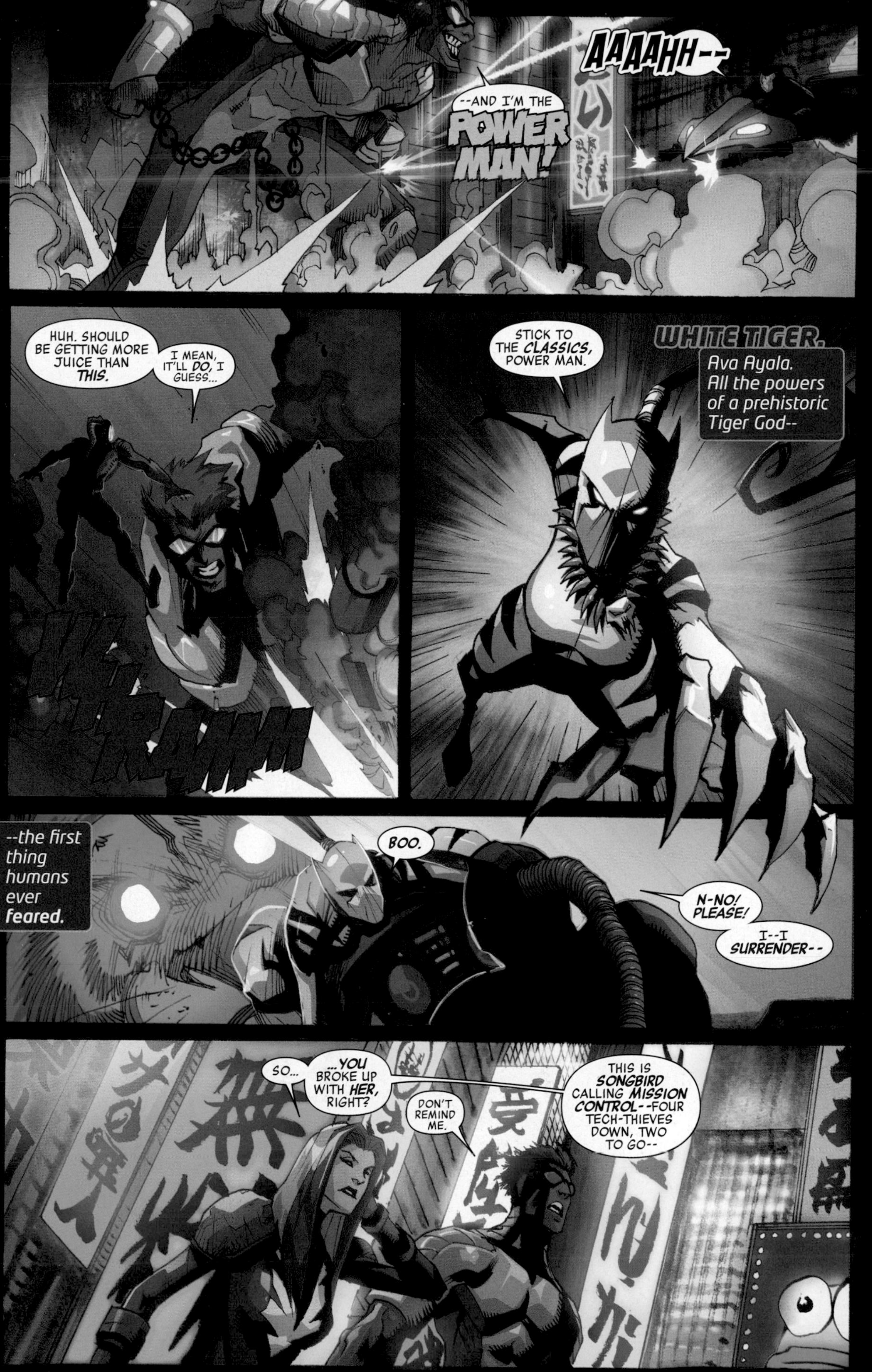

--AND I'M THE
POWER MAN!
AAAAHH--
HUH. SHOULD BE GETTING MORE JUICE THAN THIS.
I MEAN, IT'LL DO, I GUESS...
STICK TO THE CLASSICS, POWER MAN.
WHITE TIGER.
Ava Ayala. All the powers of a prehistoric Tiger God--
--the first thing humans ever feared.
BOO.
N-NO! PLEASE!
I--I SURRENDER--
SO...
...YOU BROKE UP WITH HER, RIGHT?
DON'T REMIND ME.
THIS IS SONGBIRD CALLING MISSION CONTROL--FOUR TECH-THIEVES DOWN, TWO TO GO--

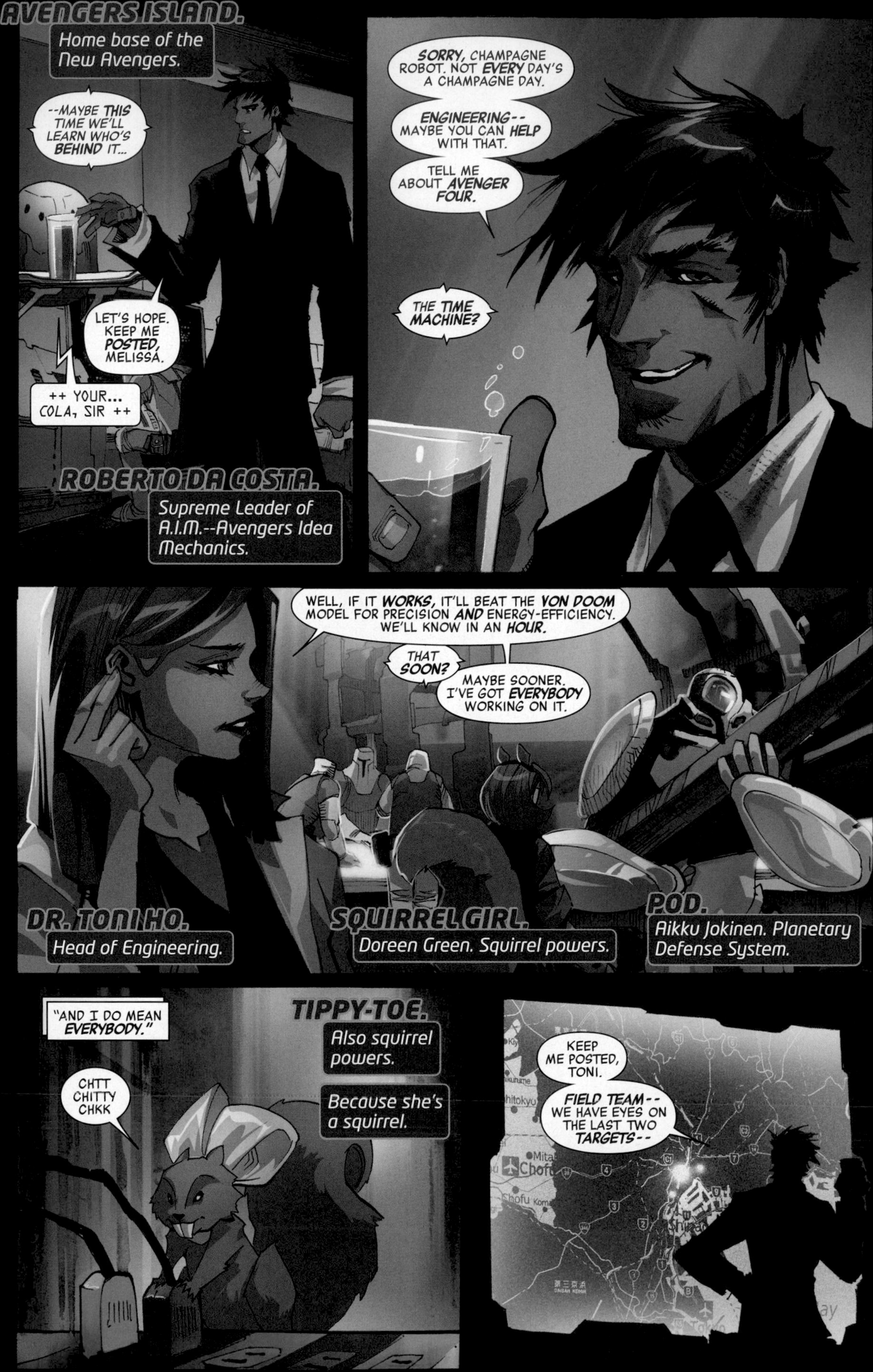
AVENGERS ISLAND.
Home base of the New Avengers.
--MAYBE THIS TIME WE'LL LEARN WHO'S BEHIND IT...
LET'S HOPE. KEEP ME POSTED, MELISSA.
++ YOUR... COLA, SIR ++
ROBERTO DA COSTA.
Supreme Leader of A.I.M.--Avengers Idea Mechanics.
SORRY, CHAMPAGNE ROBOT. NOT EVERY DAY'S A CHAMPAGNE DAY.
ENGINEERING-- MAYBE YOU CAN HELP WITH THAT.
TELL ME ABOUT AVENGER FOUR.
THE TIME MACHINE?
WELL, IF IT WORKS, IT'LL BEAT THE VON DOOM MODEL FOR PRECISION AND ENERGY-EFFICIENCY. WE'LL KNOW IN AN HOUR.
THAT SOON?
MAYBE SOONER. I'VE GOT EVERYBODY WORKING ON IT.
DR. TONI HO.
Head of Engineering.
SQUIRREL GIRL.
Doreen Green. Squirrel powers.
POD.
Aikku Jokinen. Planetary Defense System.
"AND I DO MEAN EVERYBODY."
TIPPY-TOE.
Also squirrel powers.
Because she's a squirrel.
CHTT CHITTY CHKK
KEEP ME POSTED, TONI.
FIELD TEAM-- WE HAVE EYES ON THE LAST TWO TARGETS--

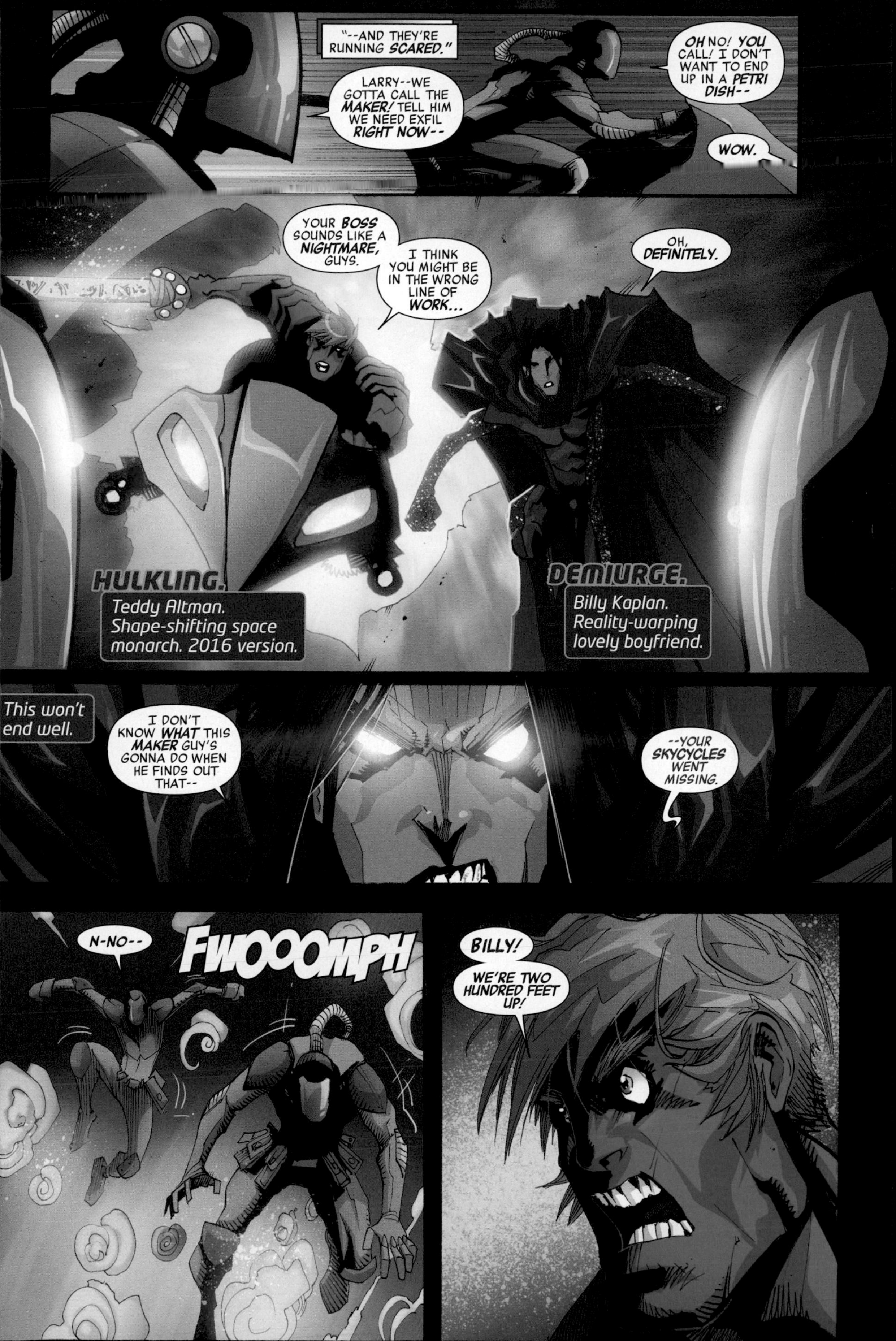
"--AND THEY'RE RUNNING SCARED."
LARRY--WE GOTTA CALL THE MAKER! TELL HIM WE NEED EXFIL RIGHT NOW--
OH NO! YOU CALL! I DON'T WANT TO END UP IN A PETRI DISH--
WOW.
YOUR BOSS SOUNDS LIKE A NIGHTMARE, GUYS.
I THINK YOU MIGHT BE IN THE WRONG LINE OF WORK...
OH, DEFINITELY.
HULKLING.
Teddy Altman. Shape-shifting space monarch. 2016 version.
DEMIURGE.
Billy Kaplan. Reality-warping lovely boyfriend.
This won't end well.
I DON'T KNOW WHAT THIS MAKER GUY'S GONNA DO WHEN HE FINDS OUT THAT--
--YOUR SKYCYCLES WENT MISSING.
N-NO--
FWOOOMPH
BILLY!
WE'RE TWO HUNDRED FEET UP!

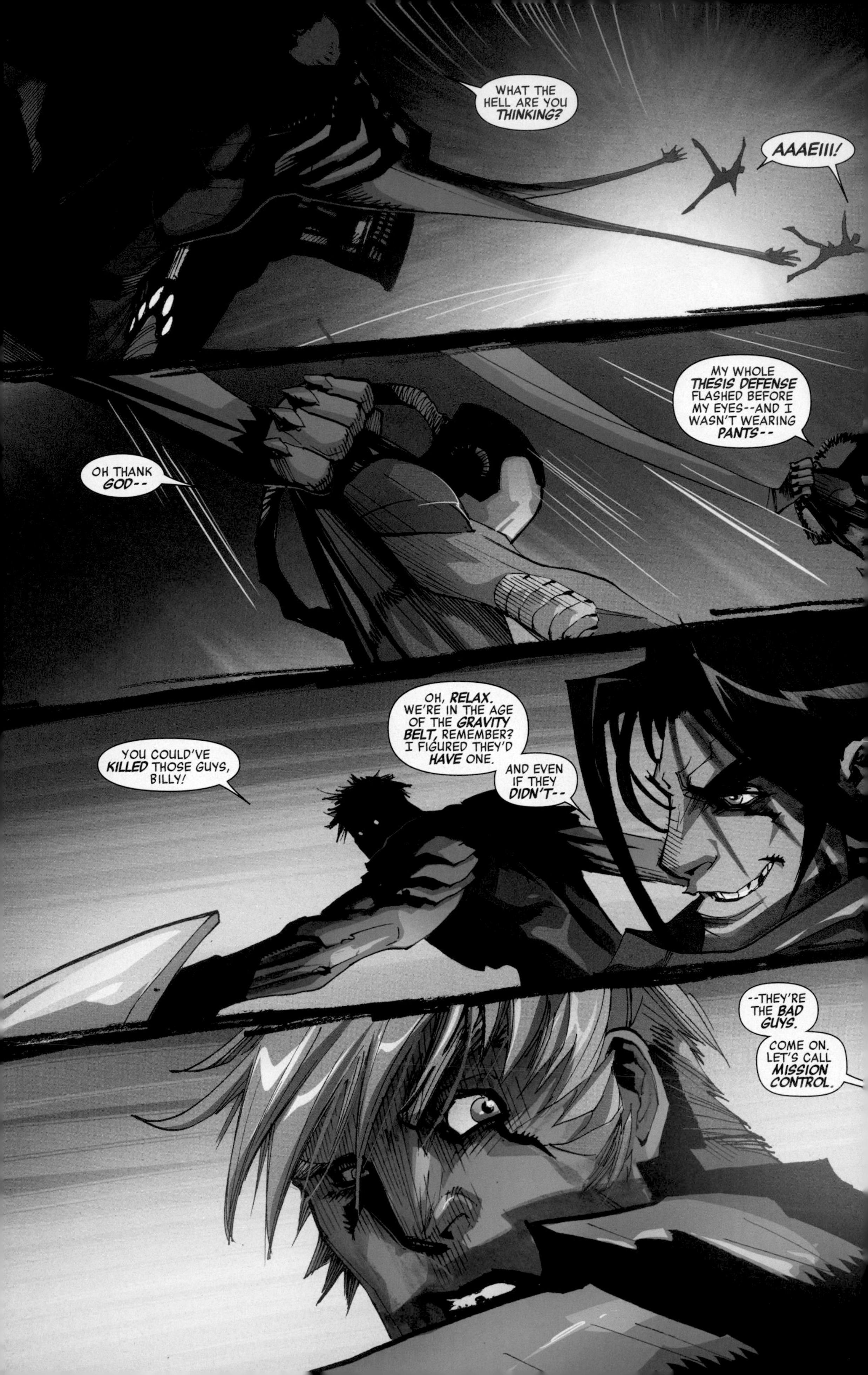
WHAT THE HELL ARE YOU THINKING?
AAAEIII!
MY WHOLE THESIS DEFENSE FLASHED BEFORE MY EYES--AND I WASN'T WEARING PANTS--
OH THANK GOD--
YOU COULD'VE KILLED THOSE GUYS, BILLY!
OH, RELAX. WE'RE IN THE AGE OF THE GRAVITY BELT, REMEMBER? I FIGURED THEY'D HAVE ONE.
AND EVEN IF THEY DIDN'T--
--THEY'RE THE BAD GUYS.
COME ON. LET'S CALL MISSION CONTROL.

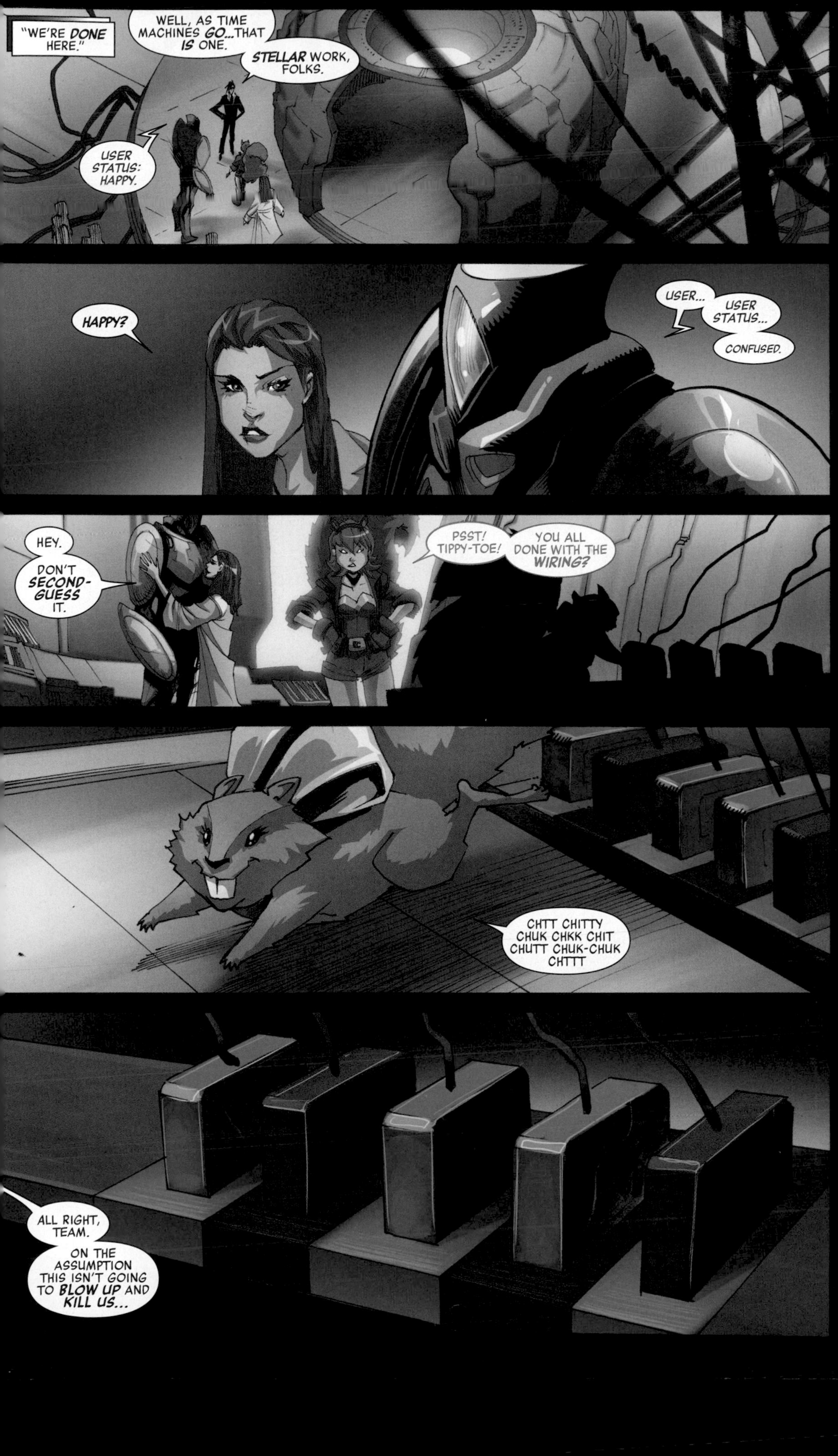
"WE'RE DONE HERE."
WELL, AS TIME MACHINES GO...THAT IS ONE.
STELLAR WORK, FOLKS.
USER STATUS: HAPPY.
HAPPY?
USER...
USER STATUS...
CONFUSED.
HEY.
DON'T SECOND-GUESS IT.
PSST! TIPPY-TOE!
YOU ALL DONE WITH THE WIRING?
CHTT CHITTY CHUK CHKK CHIT CHUTT CHUK-CHUK CHTTT
ALL RIGHT, TEAM.
ON THE ASSUMPTION THIS ISN'T GOING TO BLOW UP AND KILL US...

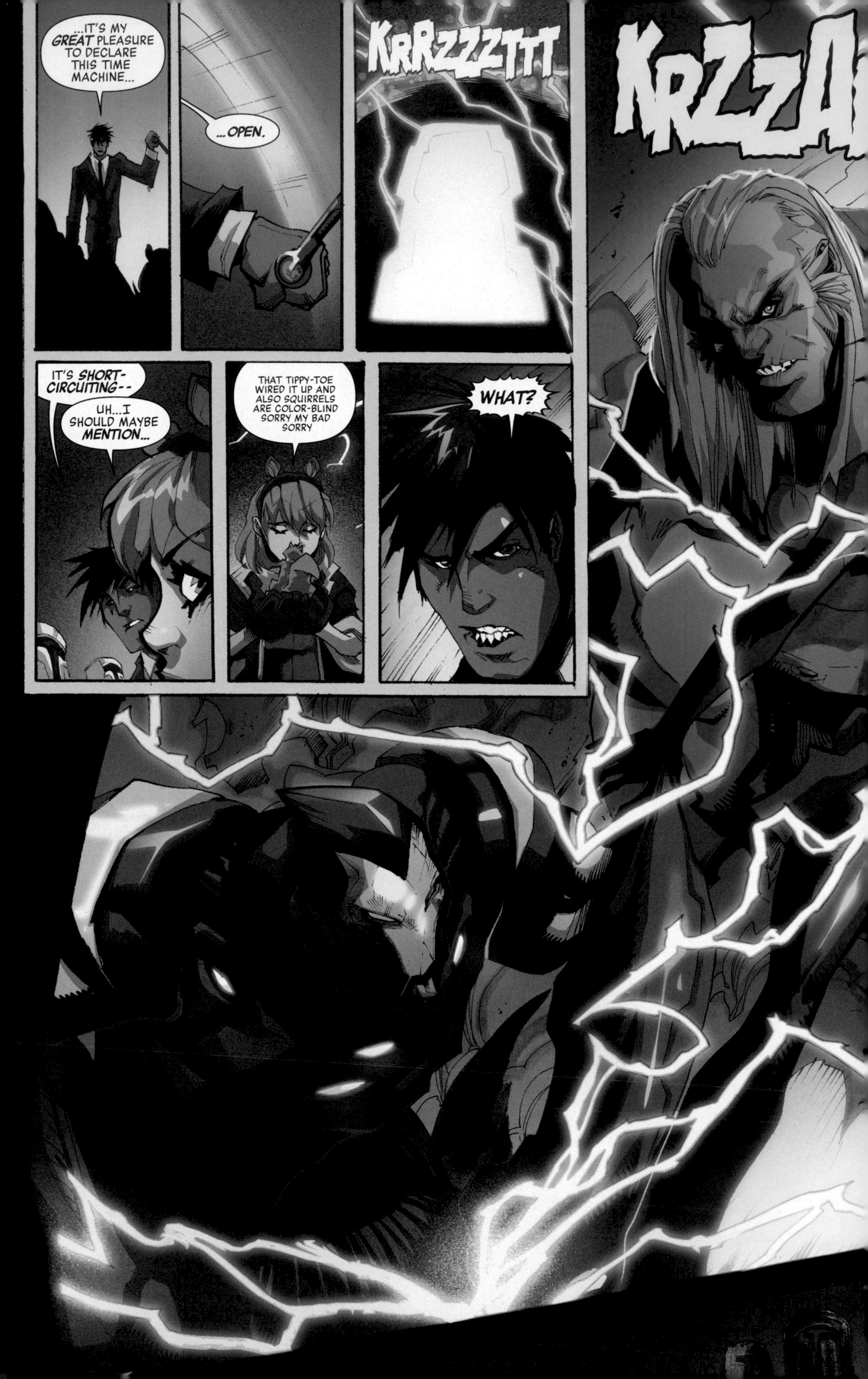
...IT'S MY GREAT PLEASURE TO DECLARE THIS TIME MACHINE...
...OPEN.
KRRZZZTTT
KRZZA
IT'S SHORT-CIRCUITING--
UH...I SHOULD MAYBE MENTION...
THAT TIPPY-TOE WIRED IT UP AND ALSO SQUIRRELS ARE COLOR-BLIND SORRY MY BAD SORRY
WHAT?

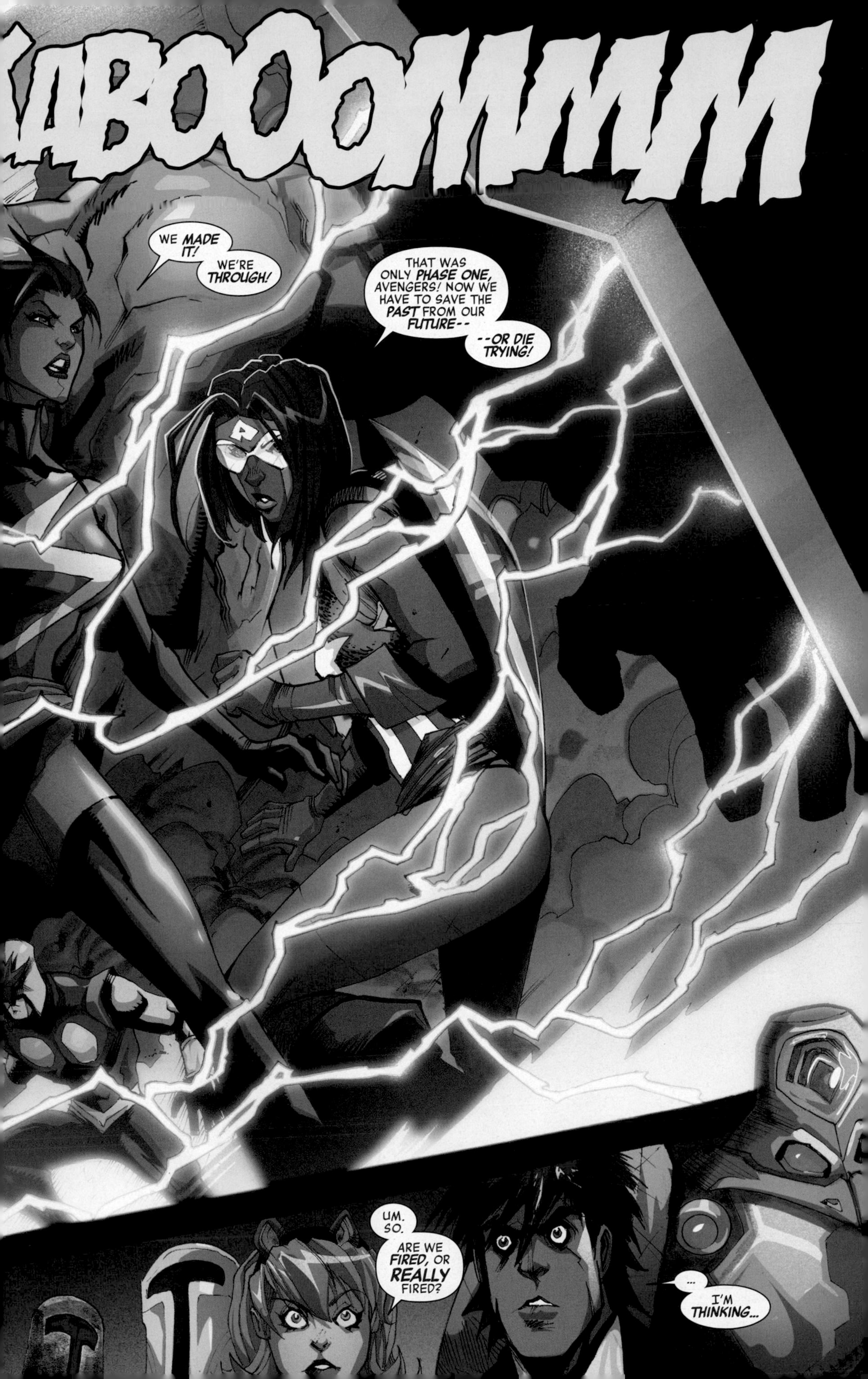

ABOOOMMM
WE MADE IT! WE'RE THROUGH!
THAT WAS ONLY PHASE ONE, AVENGERS! NOW WE HAVE TO SAVE THE PAST FROM OUR FUTURE--
--OR DIE TRYING!
UM. SO.
ARE WE FIRED, OR REALLY FIRED?
... I'M THINKING...

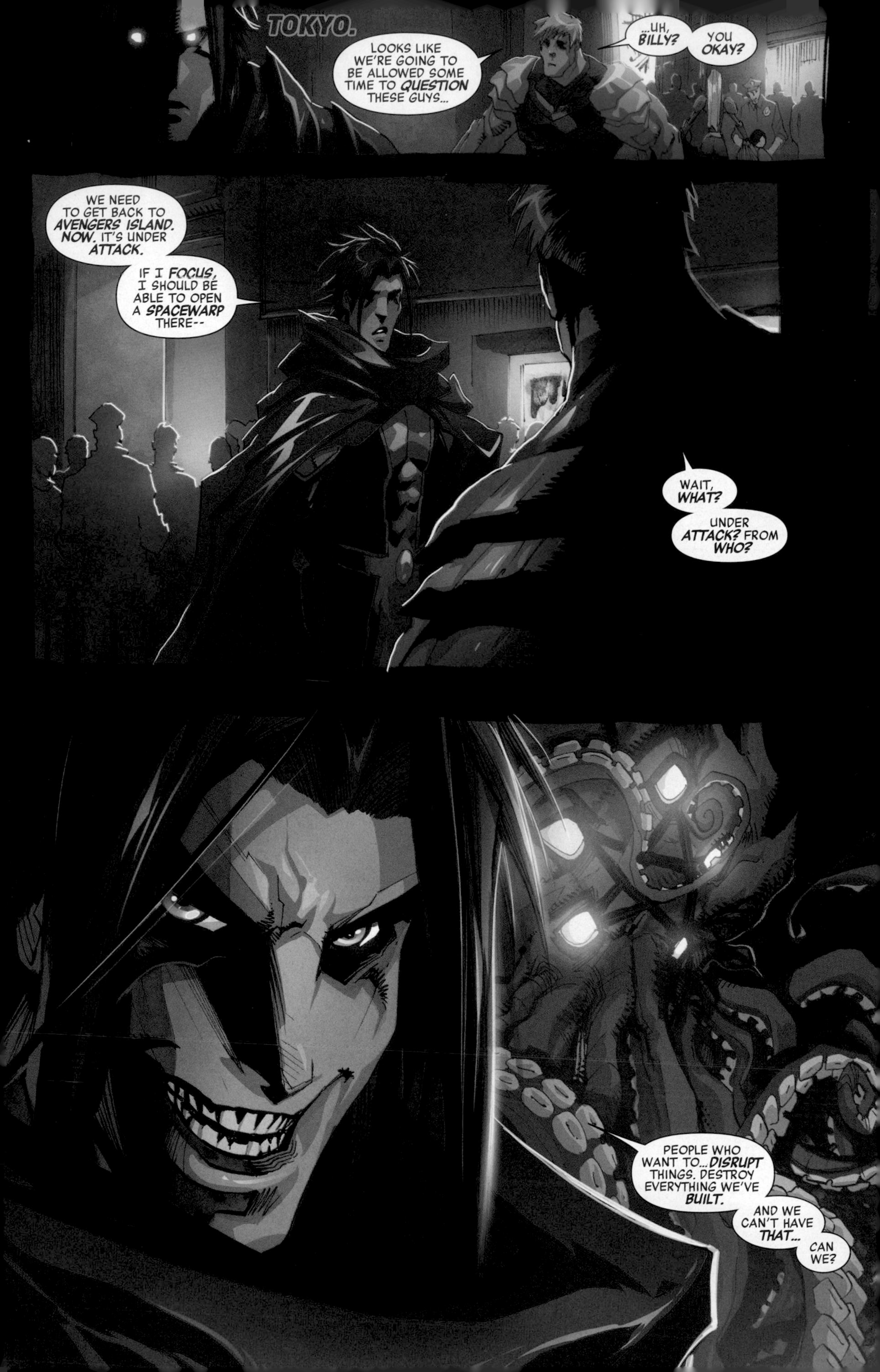
TOKYO.
LOOKS LIKE WE'RE GOING TO BE ALLOWED SOME TIME TO QUESTION THESE GUYS...
...UH, BILLY?
YOU OKAY?
WE NEED TO GET BACK TO AVENGERS ISLAND. NOW. IT'S UNDER ATTACK.
IF I FOCUS, I SHOULD BE ABLE TO OPEN A SPACEWARP THERE--
WAIT, WHAT?
UNDER ATTACK? FROM WHO?
PEOPLE WHO WANT TO... DISRUPT THINGS. DESTROY EVERYTHING WE'VE BUILT.
AND WE CAN'T HAVE THAT...
CAN WE?

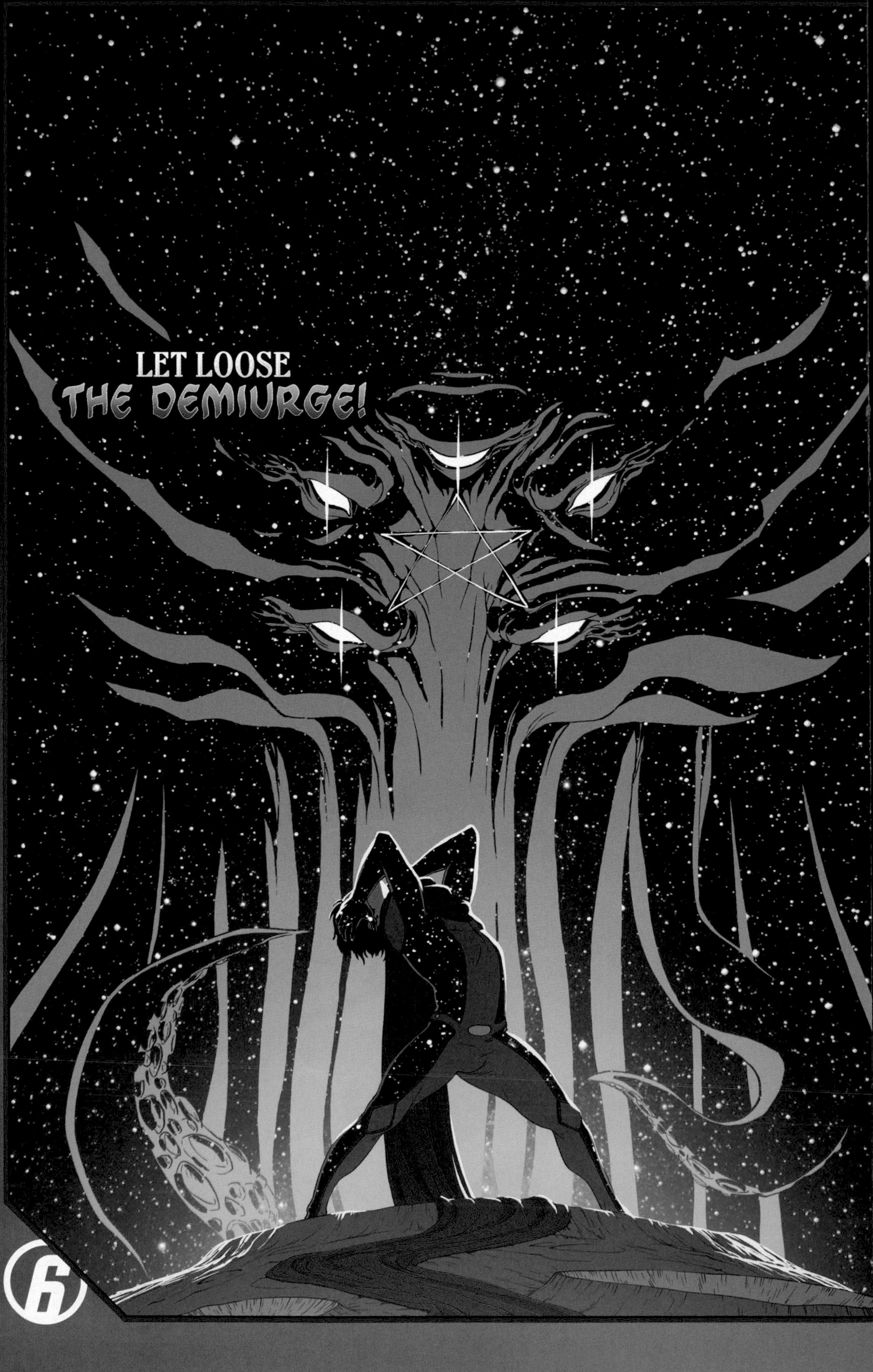
LET LOOSE
THE DEMIURGE!
6

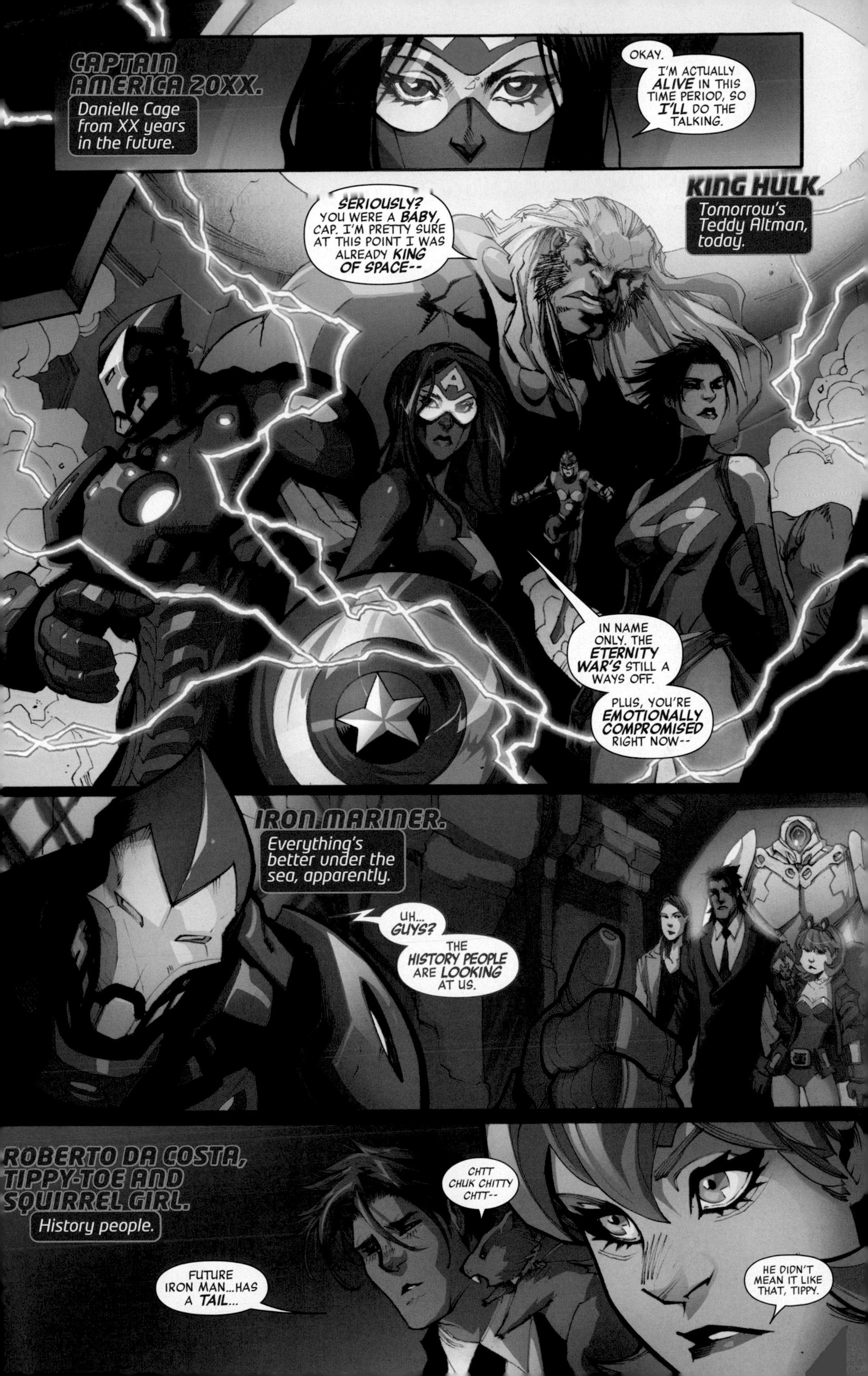
CAPTAIN AMERICA 20XX.
Danielle Cage from XX years in the future.
OKAY.
I'M ACTUALLY ALIVE IN THIS TIME PERIOD, SO I'LL DO THE TALKING.
KING HULK.
Tomorrow's Teddy Altman, today.
SERIOUSLY? YOU WERE A BABY, CAP. I'M PRETTY SURE AT THIS POINT I WAS ALREADY KING OF SPACE--
IN NAME ONLY. THE ETERNITY WAR'S STILL A WAYS OFF.
PLUS, YOU'RE EMOTIONALLY COMPROMISED RIGHT NOW--
IRON MARINER.
Everything's better under the sea, apparently.
UH... GUYS?
THE HISTORY PEOPLE ARE LOOKING AT US.
ROBERTO DA COSTA, TIPPY-TOE AND SQUIRREL GIRL.
History people.
CHTT CHUK CHITTY CHTT--
FUTURE IRON MAN...HAS A TAIL...
HE DIDN'T MEAN IT LIKE THAT, TIPPY.

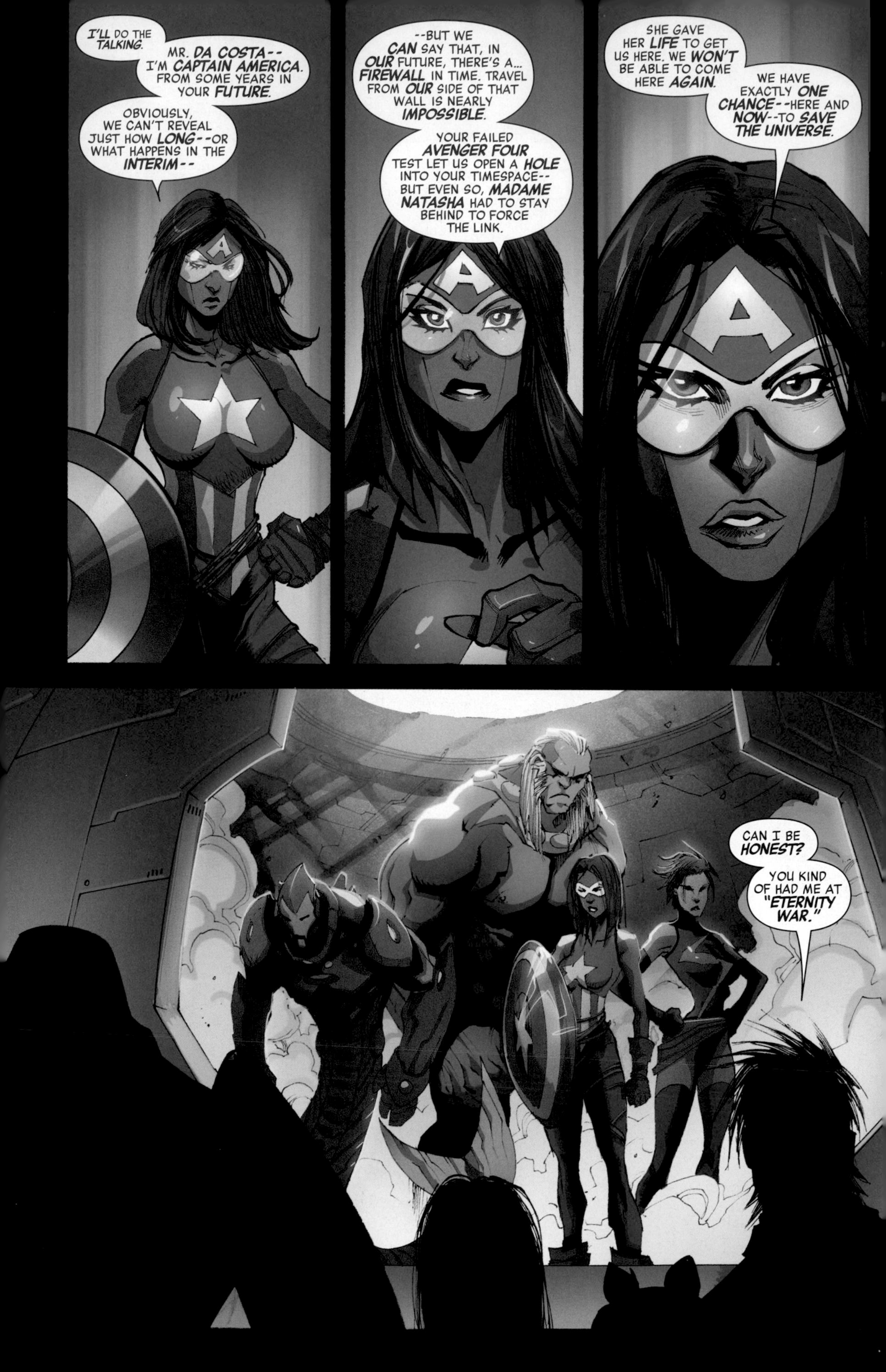
I'LL DO THE TALKING.
MR. DA COSTA-- I'M CAPTAIN AMERICA. FROM SOME YEARS IN YOUR FUTURE.
OBVIOUSLY, WE CAN'T REVEAL JUST HOW LONG--OR WHAT HAPPENS IN THE INTERIM--
--BUT WE CAN SAY THAT, IN OUR FUTURE, THERE'S A... FIREWALL IN TIME. TRAVEL FROM OUR SIDE OF THAT WALL IS NEARLY IMPOSSIBLE.
YOUR FAILED AVENGER FOUR TEST LET US OPEN A HOLE INTO YOUR TIMESPACE-- BUT EVEN SO, MADAME NATASHA HAD TO STAY BEHIND TO FORCE THE LINK.
SHE GAVE HER LIFE TO GET US HERE. WE WON'T BE ABLE TO COME HERE AGAIN.
WE HAVE EXACTLY ONE CHANCE--HERE AND NOW--TO SAVE THE UNIVERSE.
CAN I BE HONEST?
YOU KIND OF HAD ME AT "ETERNITY WAR."

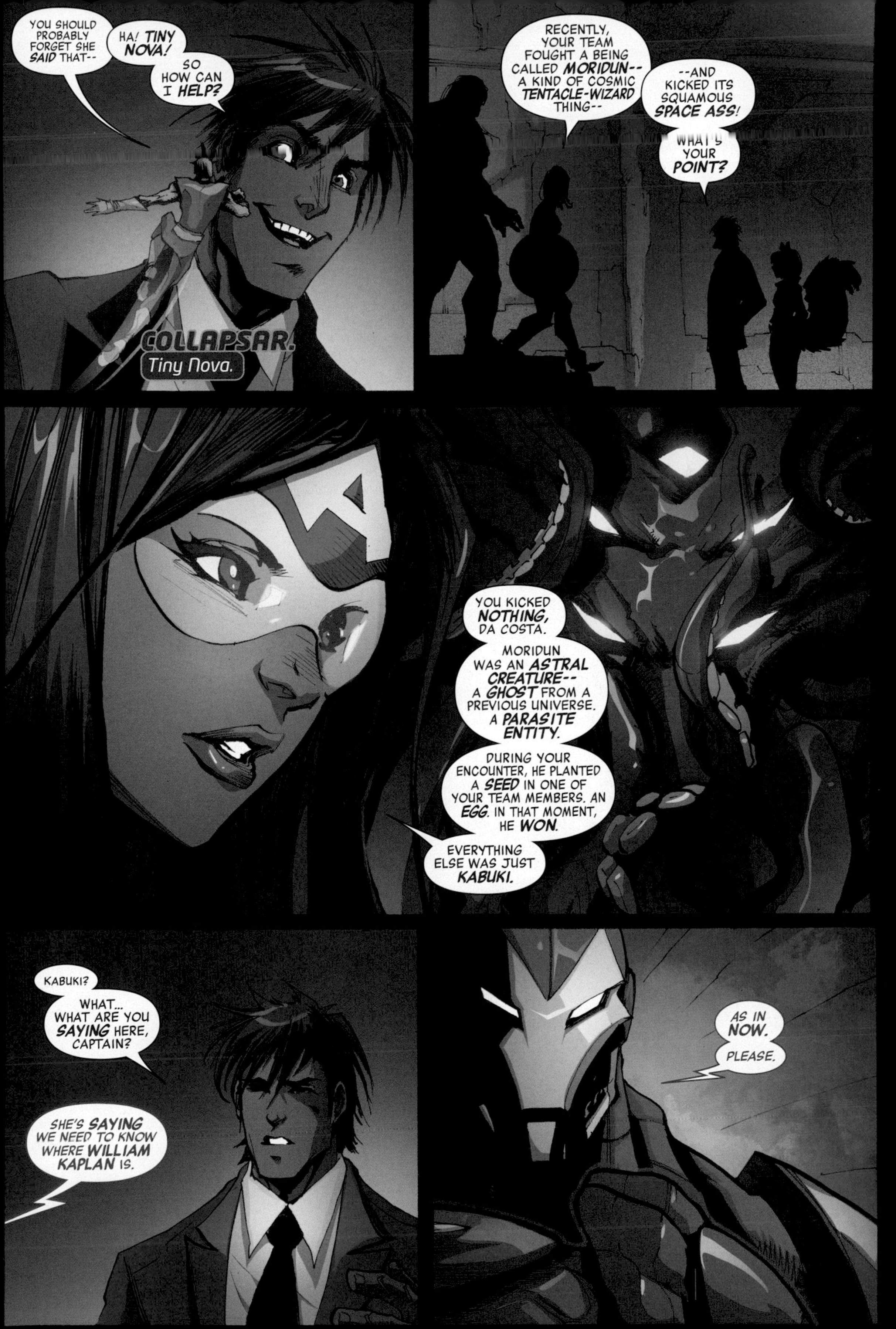
YOU SHOULD PROBABLY FORGET SHE SAID THAT--
HA! TINY NOVA!
SO HOW CAN I HELP?
COLLAPSAR.
Tiny Nova.
RECENTLY, YOUR TEAM FOUGHT A BEING CALLED MORIDUN-- A KIND OF COSMIC TENTACLE-WIZARD THING--
--AND KICKED ITS SQUAMOUS SPACE ASS!
WHAT'S YOUR POINT?
YOU KICKED NOTHING, DA COSTA.
MORIDUN WAS AN ASTRAL CREATURE-- A GHOST FROM A PREVIOUS UNIVERSE. A PARASITE ENTITY.
DURING YOUR ENCOUNTER, HE PLANTED A SEED IN ONE OF YOUR TEAM MEMBERS. AN EGG. IN THAT MOMENT, HE WON.
EVERYTHING ELSE WAS JUST KABUKI.
KABUKI?
WHAT... WHAT ARE YOU SAYING HERE, CAPTAIN?
SHE'S SAYING WE NEED TO KNOW WHERE WILLIAM KAPLAN IS.
AS IN NOW.
PLEASE.

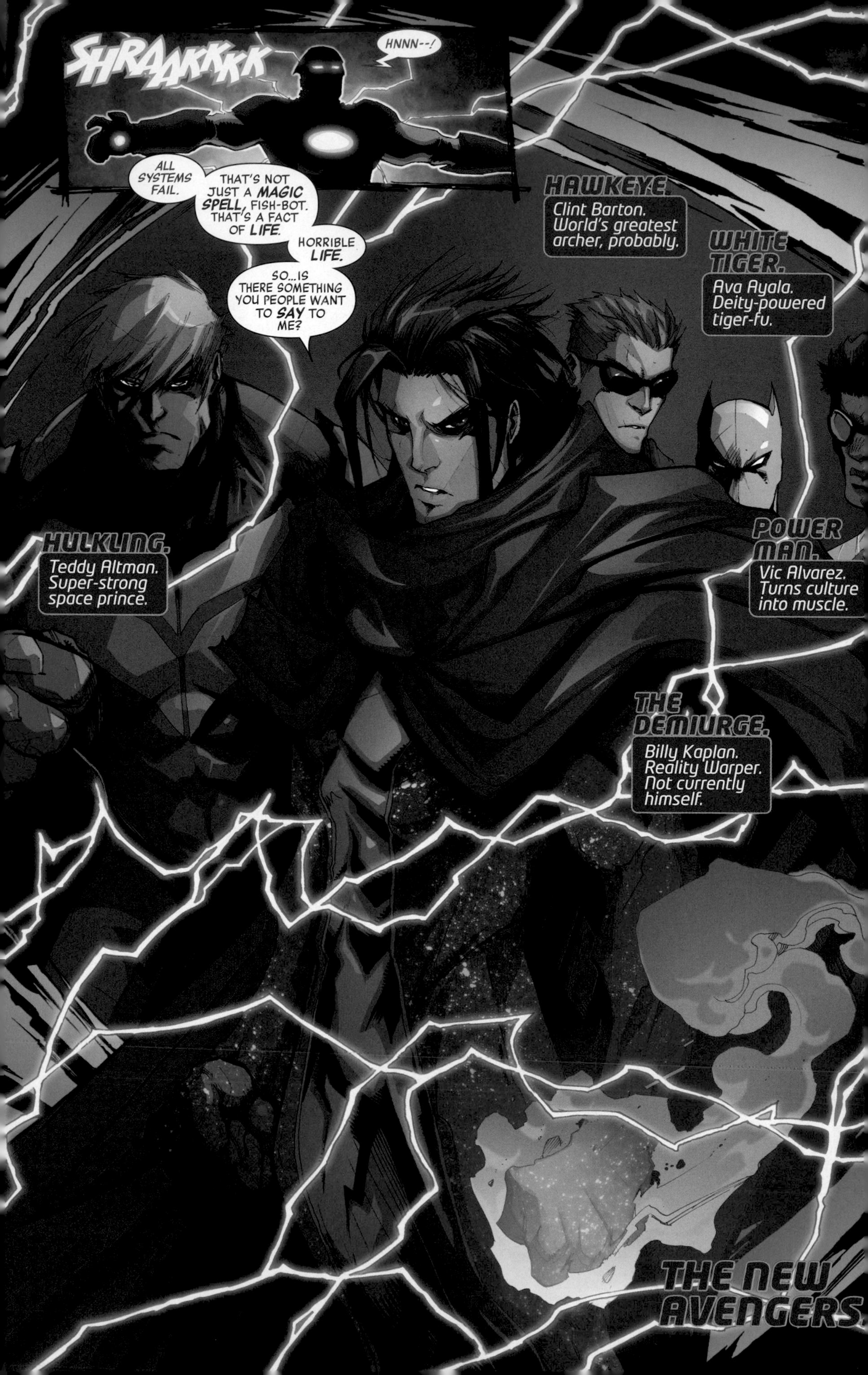

SHRAAKKKK
HNNN--!
ALL SYSTEMS FAIL.
THAT'S NOT JUST A MAGIC SPELL, FISH-BOT. THAT'S A FACT OF LIFE.
HORRIBLE LIFE.
SO...IS THERE SOMETHING YOU PEOPLE WANT TO SAY TO ME?
HAWKEYE.
Clint Barton. World's greatest archer, probably.
WHITE TIGER.
Ava Ayala. Deity-powered tiger-fu.
HULKLING.
Teddy Altman. Super-strong space prince.
POWER MAN.
Vic Alvarez. Turns culture into muscle.
THE DEMIURGE.
Billy Kaplan. Reality Warper. Not currently himself.
THE NEW AVENGERS.

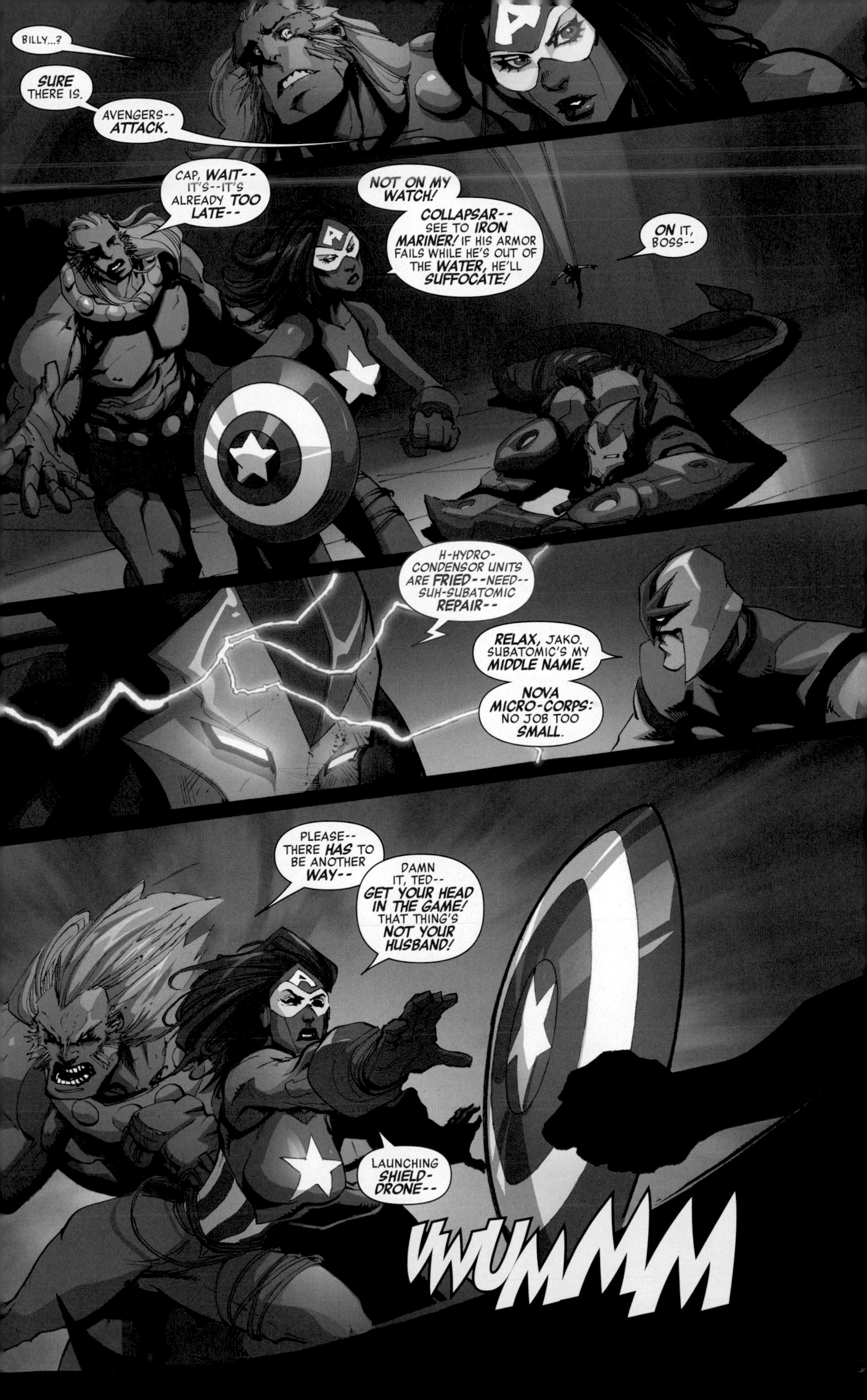

BILLY...?
SURE THERE IS.
AVENGERS-- ATTACK.
CAP, WAIT-- IT'S--IT'S ALREADY TOO LATE--
NOT ON MY WATCH!
COLLAPSAR-- SEE TO IRON MARINER! IF HIS ARMOR FAILS WHILE HE'S OUT OF THE WATER, HE'LL SUFFOCATE!
ON IT, BOSS--
H-HYDRO-CONDENSOR UNITS ARE FRIED--NEED-- SUH-SUBATOMIC REPAIR--
RELAX, JAKO. SUBATOMIC'S MY MIDDLE NAME.
NOVA MICRO-CORPS: NO JOB TOO SMALL.
PLEASE-- THERE HAS TO BE ANOTHER WAY--
DAMN IT, TED-- GET YOUR HEAD IN THE GAME! THAT THING'S NOT YOUR HUSBAND!
LAUNCHING SHIELD-DRONE--
VWUMMMM

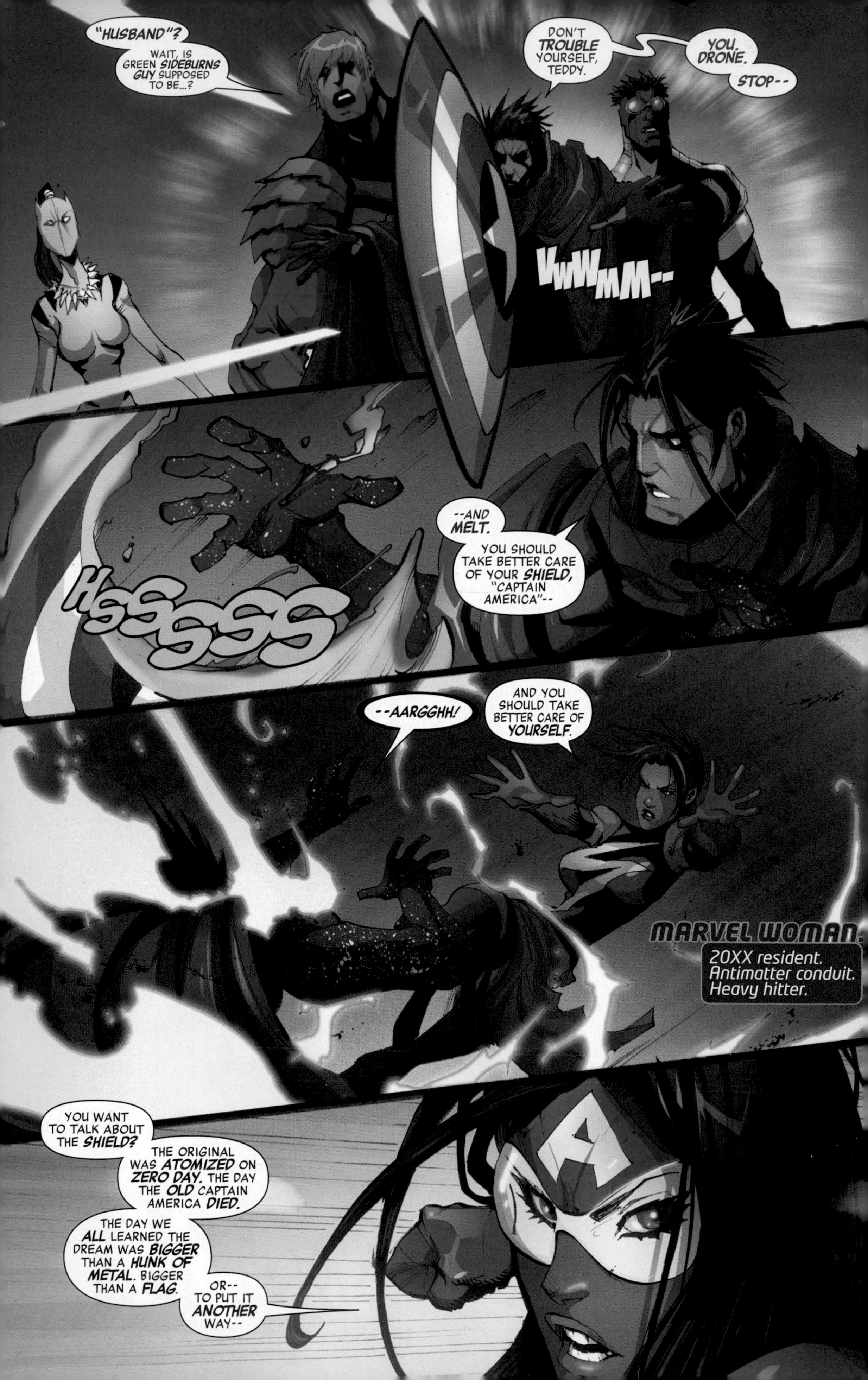
"HUSBAND"?
WAIT, IS GREEN SIDEBURNS GUY SUPPOSED TO BE...?
DON'T TROUBLE YOURSELF, TEDDY.
YOU. DRONE.
STOP--
VWWMM--
--AND MELT.
YOU SHOULD TAKE BETTER CARE OF YOUR SHIELD, "CAPTAIN AMERICA"--
HSSSSSS
--AARGGHH!
AND YOU SHOULD TAKE BETTER CARE OF YOURSELF.
MARVEL WOMAN.
20XX resident. Antimatter conduit. Heavy hitter.
YOU WANT TO TALK ABOUT THE SHIELD?
THE ORIGINAL WAS ATOMIZED ON ZERO DAY. THE DAY THE OLD CAPTAIN AMERICA DIED.
THE DAY WE ALL LEARNED THE DREAM WAS BIGGER THAN A HUNK OF METAL. BIGGER THAN A FLAG.
OR-- TO PUT IT ANOTHER WAY--

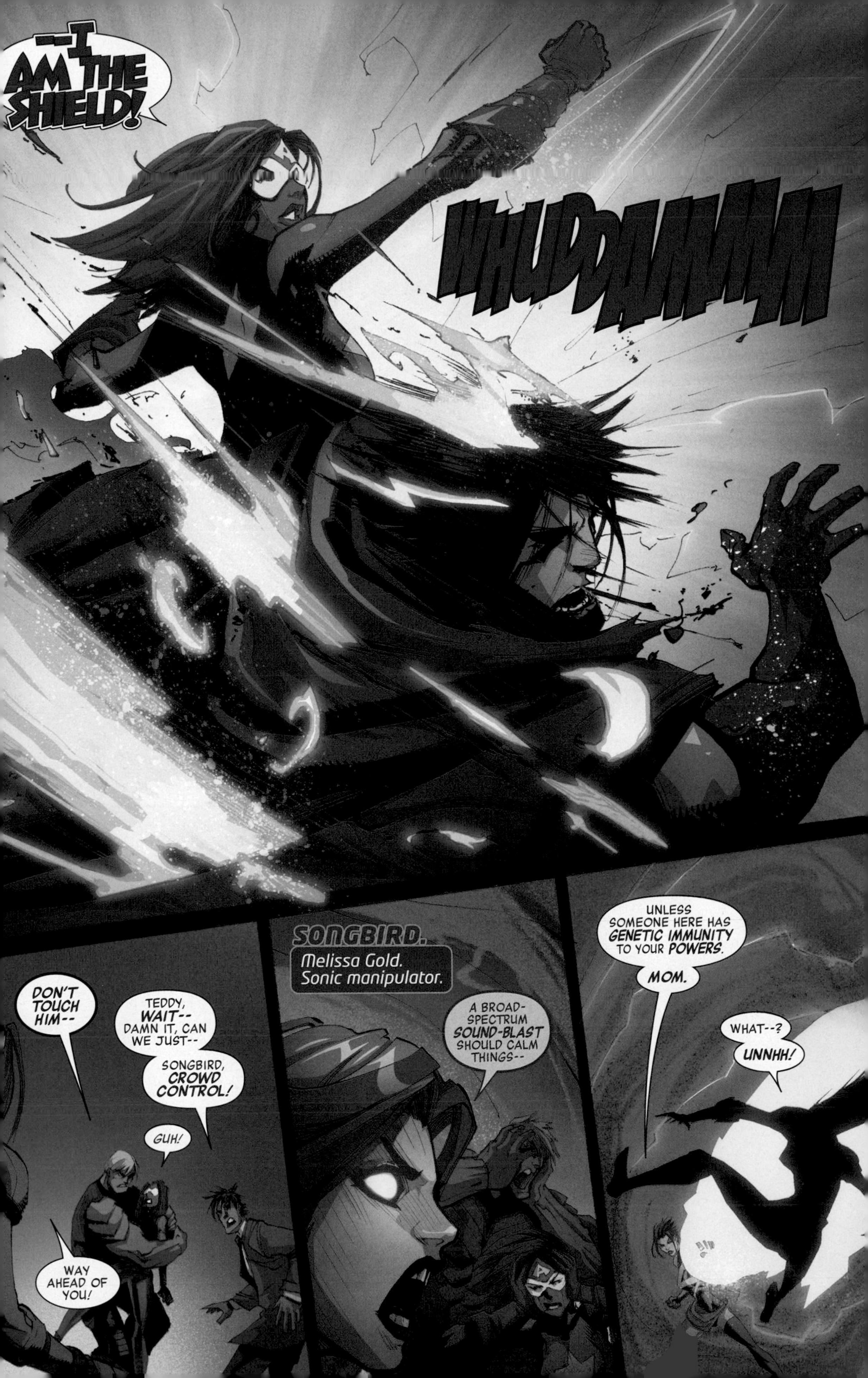

--I AM THE SHIELD!
WHUDDAMMM
DON'T TOUCH HIM--
TEDDY, WAIT-- DAMN IT, CAN WE JUST--
SONGBIRD, CROWD CONTROL!
GUH!
WAY AHEAD OF YOU!
SONGBIRD.
Melissa Gold. Sonic manipulator.
A BROAD-SPECTRUM SOUND-BLAST SHOULD CALM THINGS--
UNLESS SOMEONE HERE HAS GENETIC IMMUNITY TO YOUR POWERS.
MOM.
WHAT--?
UNNHH!

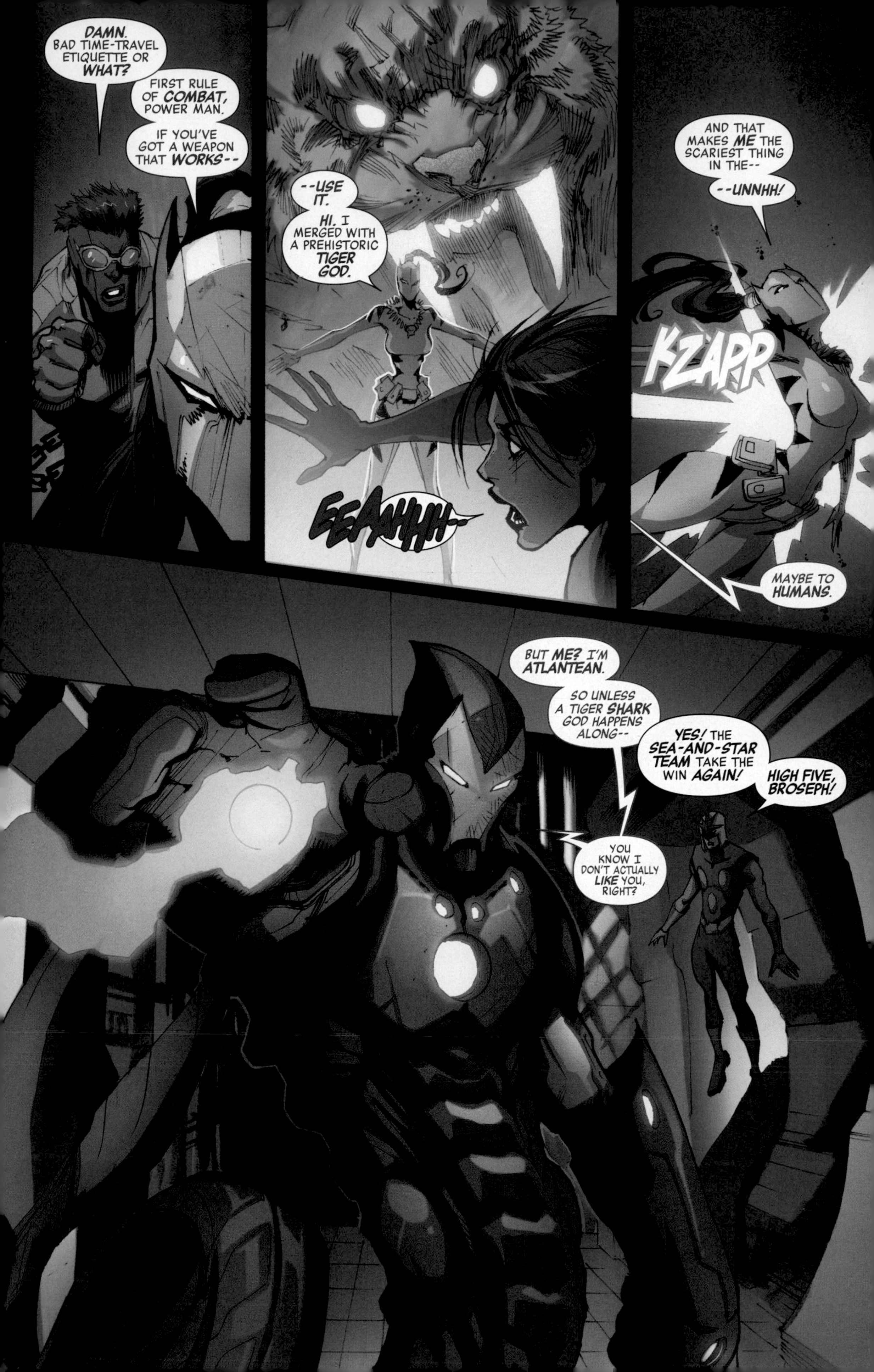
DAMN. BAD TIME-TRAVEL ETIQUETTE OR WHAT?
FIRST RULE OF COMBAT, POWER MAN.
IF YOU'VE GOT A WEAPON THAT WORKS--
--USE IT.
HI. I MERGED WITH A PREHISTORIC TIGER GOD.
EEAAHHH--
AND THAT MAKES ME THE SCARIEST THING IN THE--
--UNNHH!
KZAPP
MAYBE TO HUMANS.
BUT ME? I'M ATLANTEAN.
SO UNLESS A TIGER SHARK GOD HAPPENS ALONG--
YES! THE SEA-AND-STAR TEAM TAKE THE WIN AGAIN!
HIGH FIVE, BROSEPH!
YOU KNOW I DON'T ACTUALLY LIKE YOU, RIGHT?

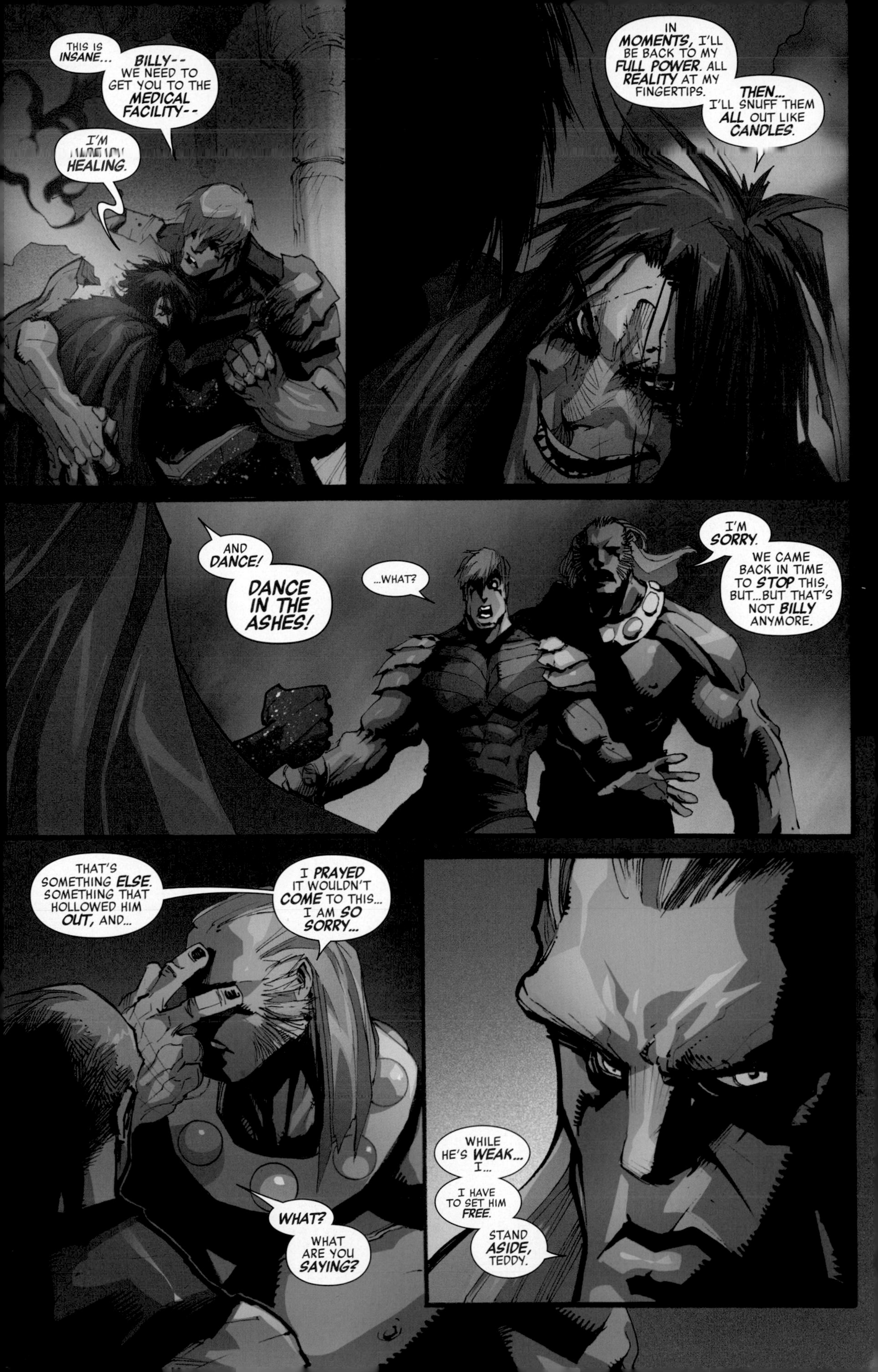
THIS IS INSANE... BILLY-- WE NEED TO GET YOU TO THE MEDICAL FACILITY--
I'M HEALING.
IN MOMENTS, I'LL BE BACK TO MY FULL POWER. ALL REALITY AT MY FINGERTIPS.
THEN... I'LL SNUFF THEM ALL OUT LIKE CANDLES.
AND DANCE!
DANCE IN THE ASHES!
...WHAT?
I'M SORRY.
WE CAME BACK IN TIME TO STOP THIS, BUT...BUT THAT'S NOT BILLY ANYMORE.
THAT'S SOMETHING ELSE. SOMETHING THAT HOLLOWED HIM OUT, AND...
I PRAYED IT WOULDN'T COME TO THIS... I AM SO SORRY...
WHAT?
WHAT ARE YOU SAYING?
WHILE HE'S WEAK... I...
I HAVE TO SET HIM FREE.
STAND ASIDE, TEDDY.

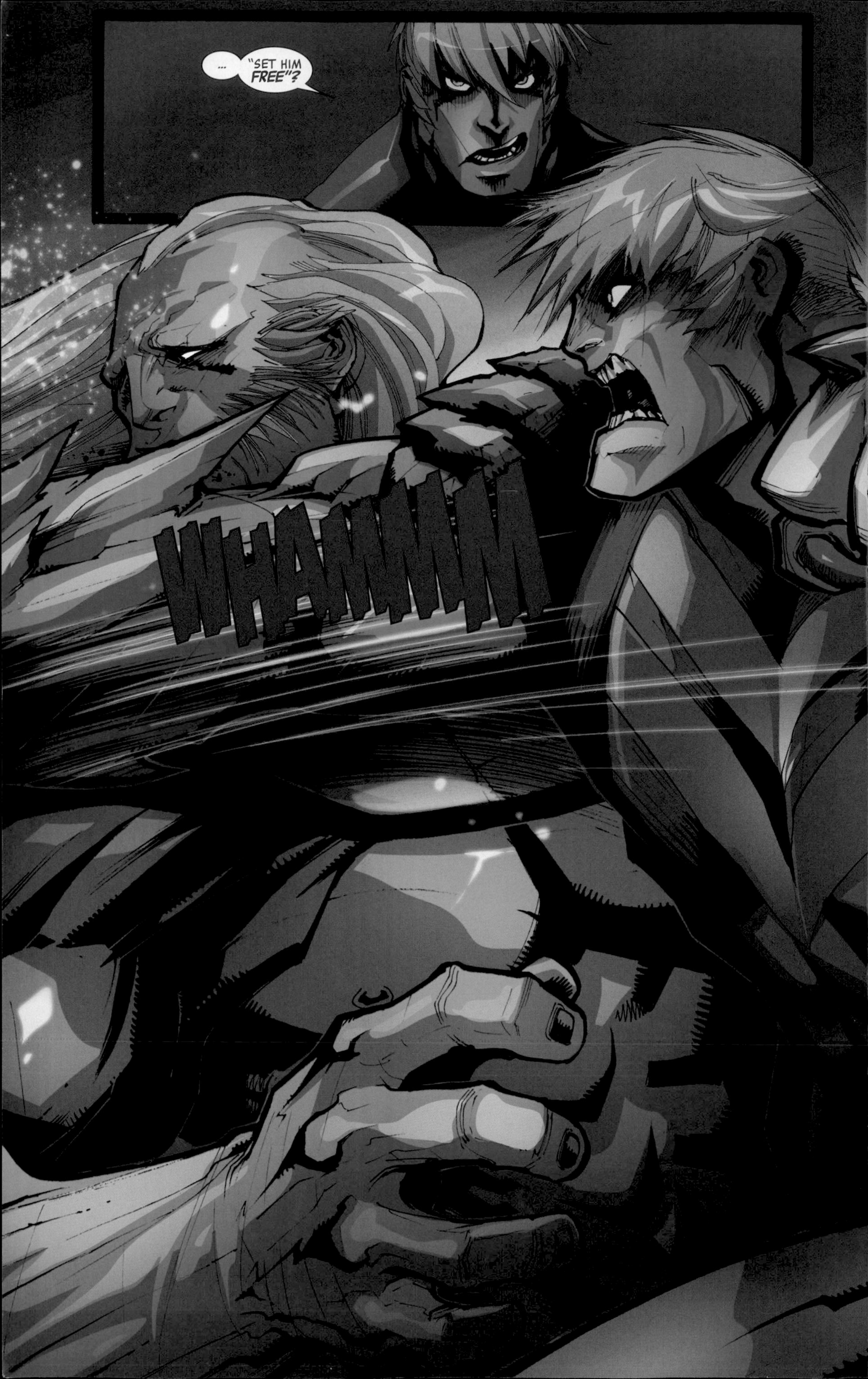
... "SET HIM FREE"?
WHAMMMM

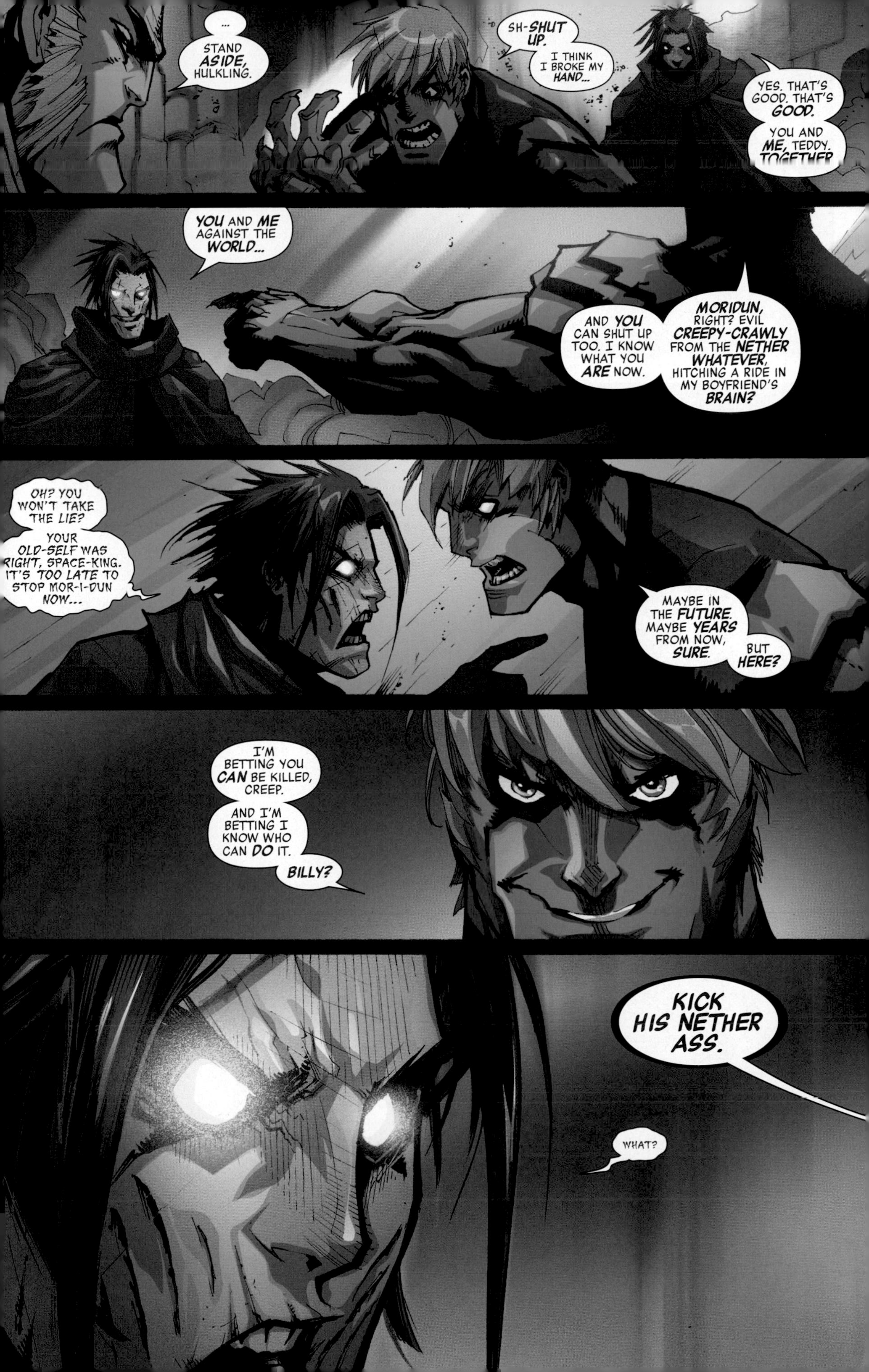
...
STAND ASIDE, HULKLING.
SH-SHUT UP.
I THINK I BROKE MY HAND...
YES. THAT'S GOOD. THAT'S GOOD.
YOU AND ME, TEDDY. TOGETHER
YOU AND ME AGAINST THE WORLD...
AND YOU CAN SHUT UP TOO. I KNOW WHAT YOU ARE NOW.
MORIDUN, RIGHT? EVIL CREEPY-CRAWLY FROM THE NETHER WHATEVER, HITCHING A RIDE IN MY BOYFRIEND'S BRAIN?
OH? YOU WON'T TAKE THE LIE?
YOUR OLD-SELF WAS RIGHT, SPACE-KING. IT'S TOO LATE TO STOP MOR-I-DUN NOW...
MAYBE IN THE FUTURE. MAYBE YEARS FROM NOW, SURE.
BUT HERE?
I'M BETTING YOU CAN BE KILLED, CREEP.
AND I'M BETTING I KNOW WHO CAN DO IT.
BILLY?
KICK HIS NETHER ASS.
WHAT?

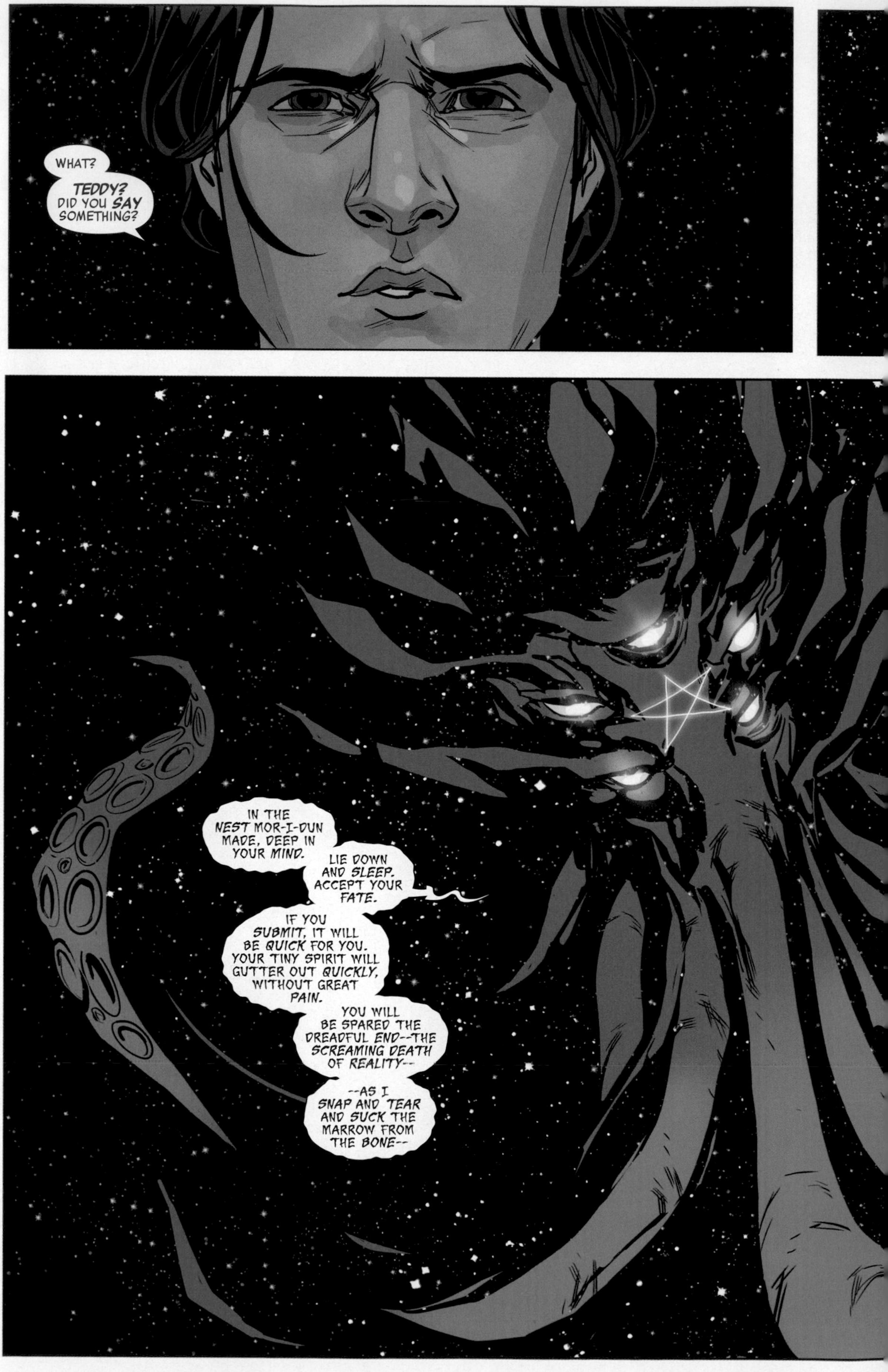
WHAT?
TEDDY? DID YOU SAY SOMETHING?
IN THE NEST MOR-I-DUN MADE, DEEP IN YOUR MIND.
LIE DOWN AND SLEEP. ACCEPT YOUR FATE.
IF YOU SUBMIT, IT WILL BE QUICK FOR YOU. YOUR TINY SPIRIT WILL GUTTER OUT QUICKLY, WITHOUT GREAT PAIN.
YOU WILL BE SPARED THE DREADFUL END--THE SCREAMING DEATH OF REALITY--
--AS I SNAP AND TEAR AND SUCK THE MARROW FROM THE BONE--

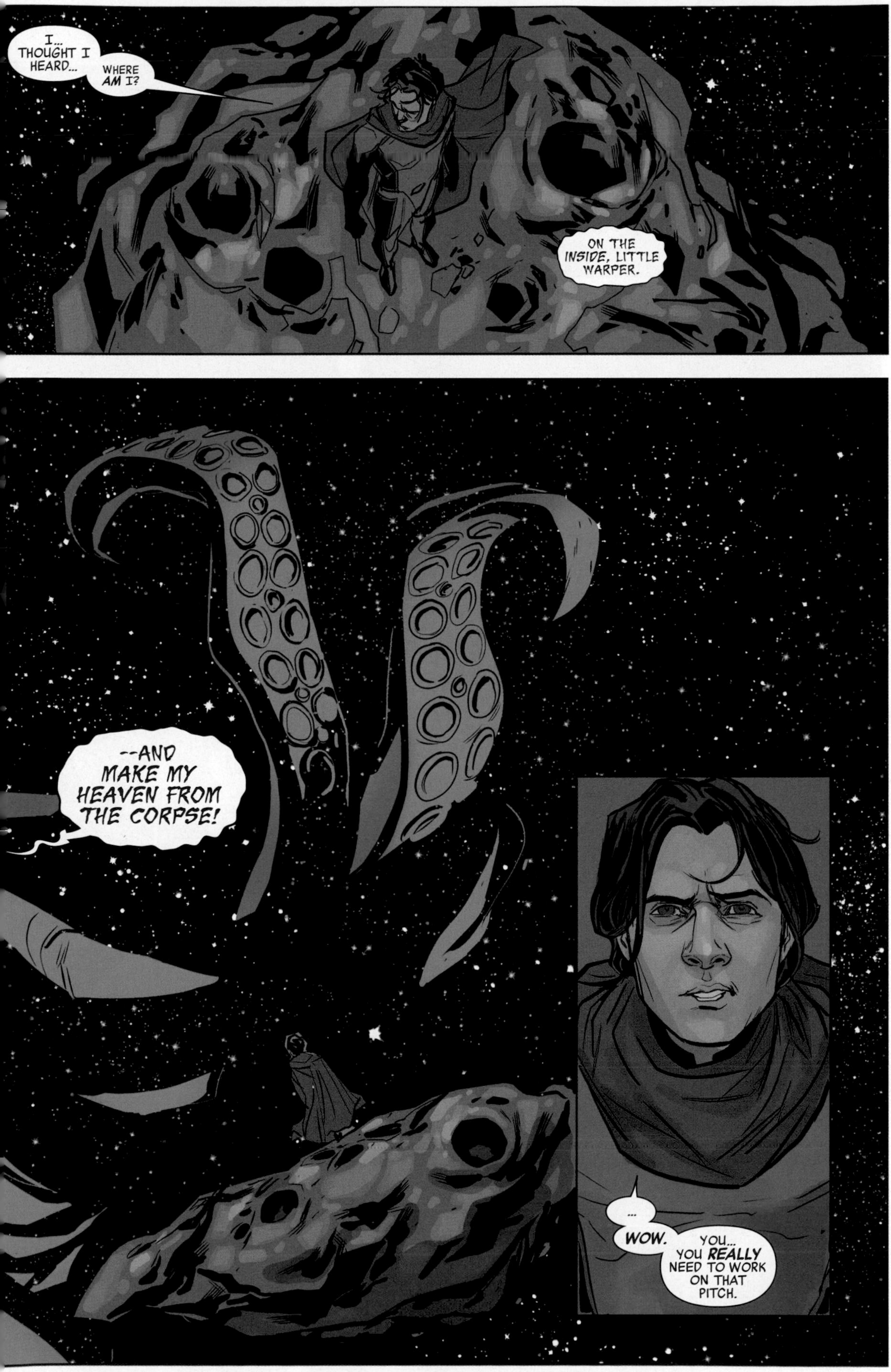
I... THOUGHT I HEARD...
WHERE AM I?
ON THE INSIDE, LITTLE WARPER.
--AND MAKE MY HEAVEN FROM THE CORPSE!
...
WOW.
YOU... YOU REALLY NEED TO WORK ON THAT PITCH.

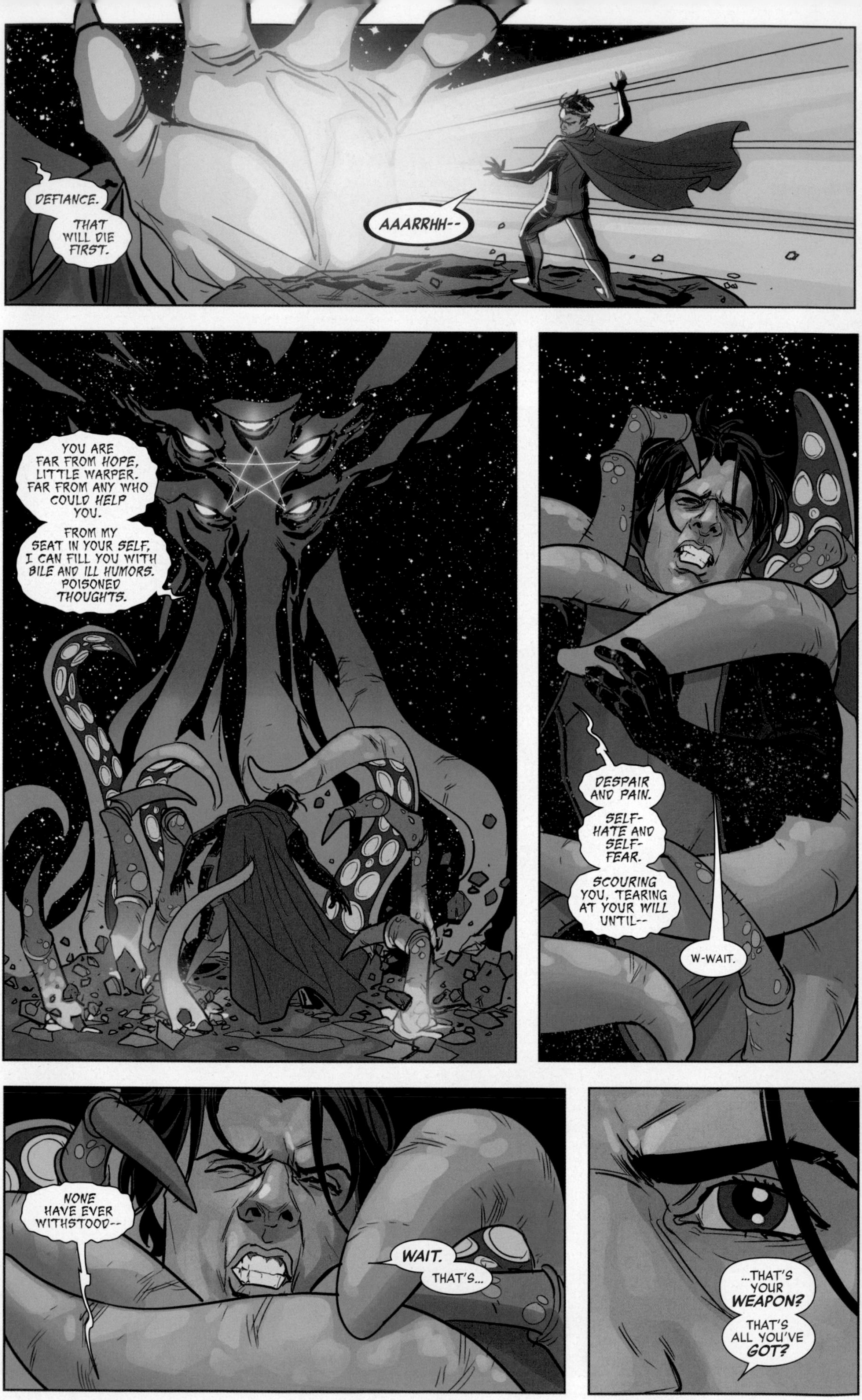
DEFIANCE.
THAT WILL DIE FIRST.
AAARRHH--
YOU ARE FAR FROM HOPE, LITTLE WARPER. FAR FROM ANY WHO COULD HELP YOU.
FROM MY SEAT IN YOUR SELF, I CAN FILL YOU WITH BILE AND ILL HUMORS. POISONED THOUGHTS.
DESPAIR AND PAIN.
SELF-HATE AND SELF-FEAR.
SCOURING YOU, TEARING AT YOUR WILL UNTIL--
W-WAIT.
NONE HAVE EVER WITHSTOOD--
WAIT.
THAT'S...
...THAT'S YOUR WEAPON?
THAT'S ALL YOU'VE GOT?

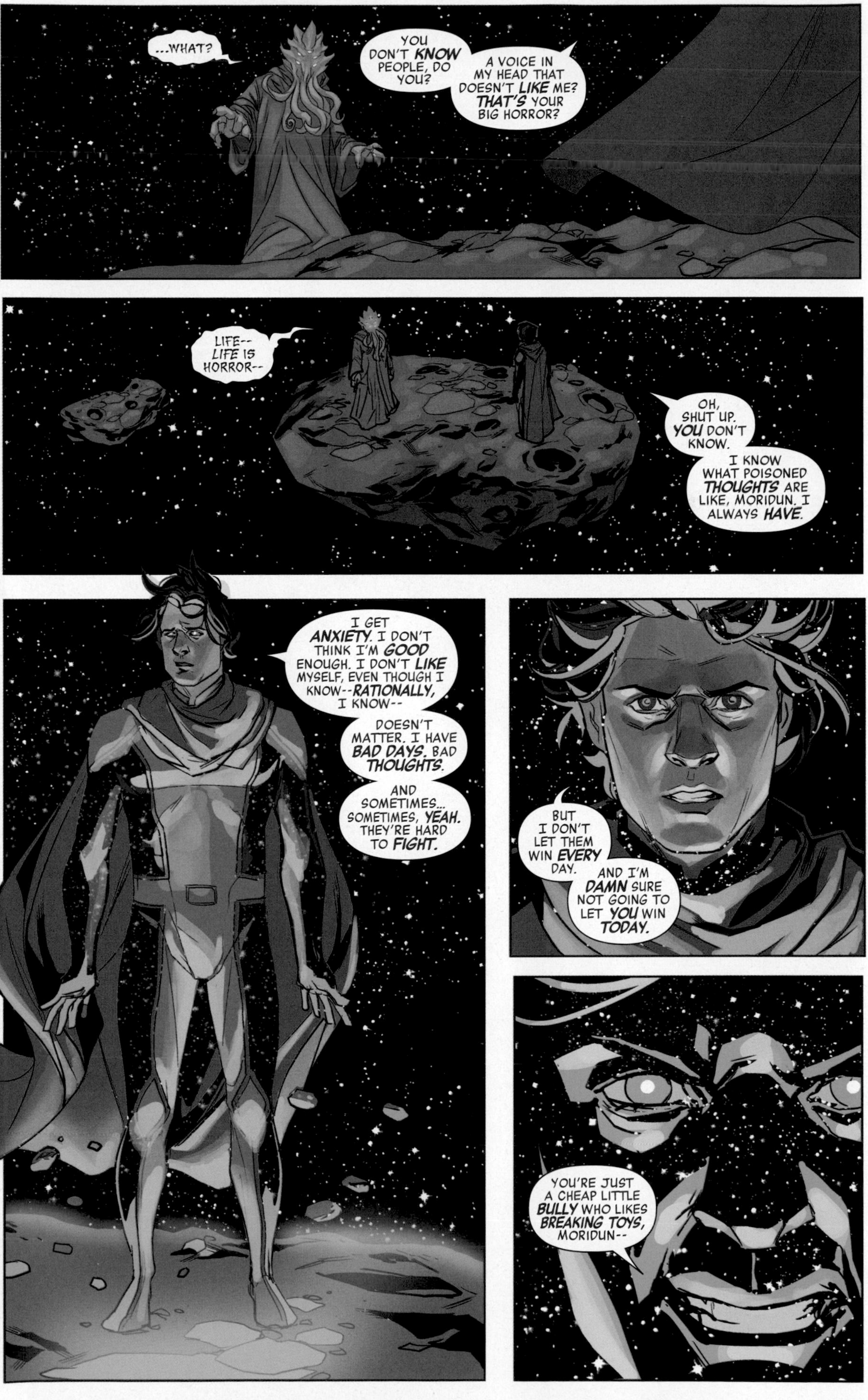
...WHAT?
YOU DON'T KNOW PEOPLE, DO YOU?
A VOICE IN MY HEAD THAT DOESN'T LIKE ME? THAT'S YOUR BIG HORROR?
LIFE-- LIFE IS HORROR--
OH, SHUT UP. YOU DON'T KNOW.
I KNOW WHAT POISONED THOUGHTS ARE LIKE, MORIDUN. I ALWAYS HAVE.
I GET ANXIETY. I DON'T THINK I'M GOOD ENOUGH. I DON'T LIKE MYSELF, EVEN THOUGH I KNOW--RATIONALLY, I KNOW--
DOESN'T MATTER. I HAVE BAD DAYS. BAD THOUGHTS.
AND SOMETIMES... SOMETIMES, YEAH. THEY'RE HARD TO FIGHT.
BUT I DON'T LET THEM WIN EVERY DAY.
AND I'M DAMN SURE NOT GOING TO LET YOU WIN TODAY.
YOU'RE JUST A CHEAP LITTLE BULLY WHO LIKES BREAKING TOYS, MORIDUN--

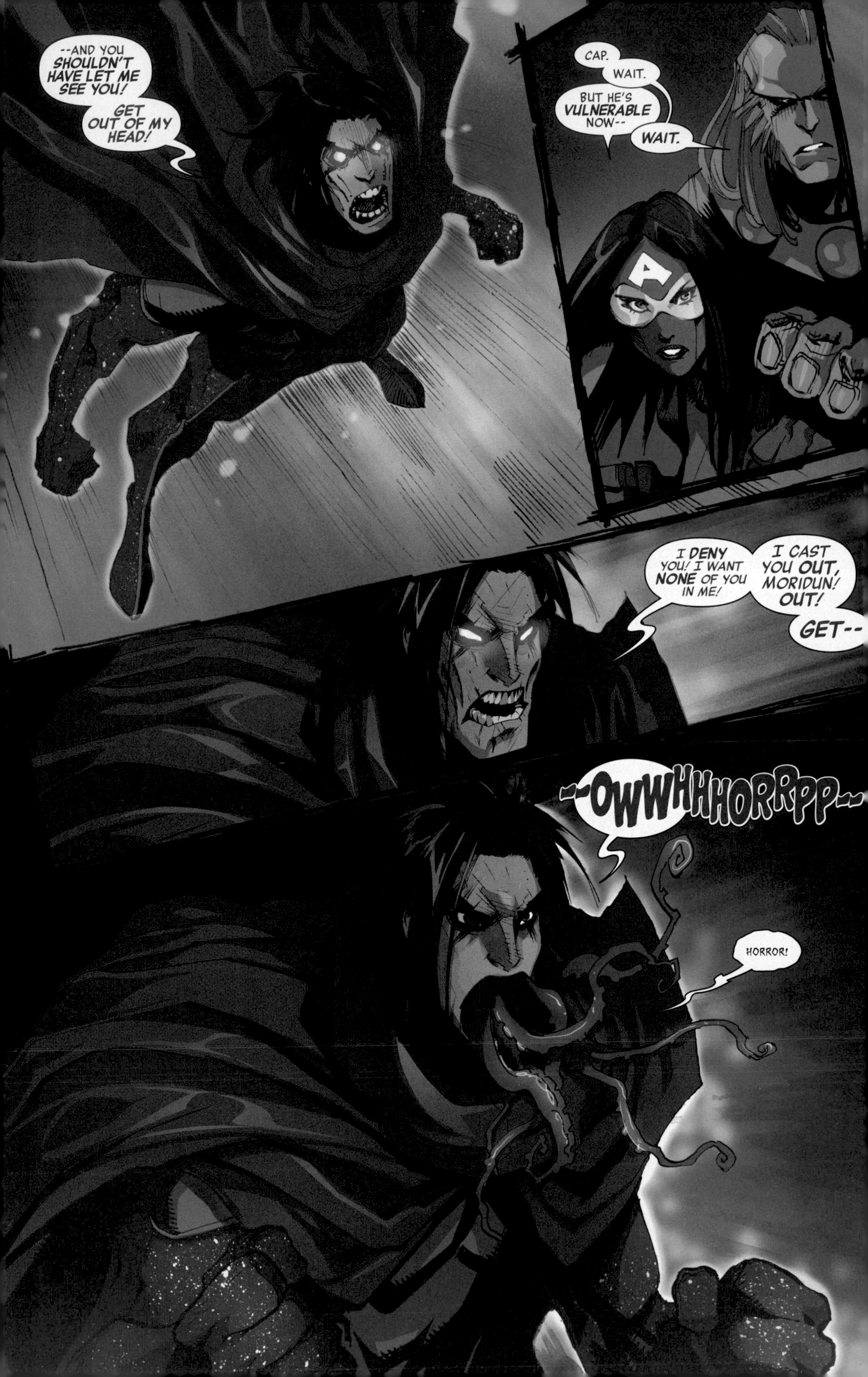
--AND YOU SHOULDN'T HAVE LET ME SEE YOU!
GET OUT OF MY HEAD!
CAP.
WAIT.
BUT HE'S VULNERABLE NOW--
WAIT.
I DENY YOU! I WANT NONE OF YOU IN ME!
I CAST YOU OUT, MORIDUN! OUT!
GET--
--OWWHHHORRPP--
HORROR!

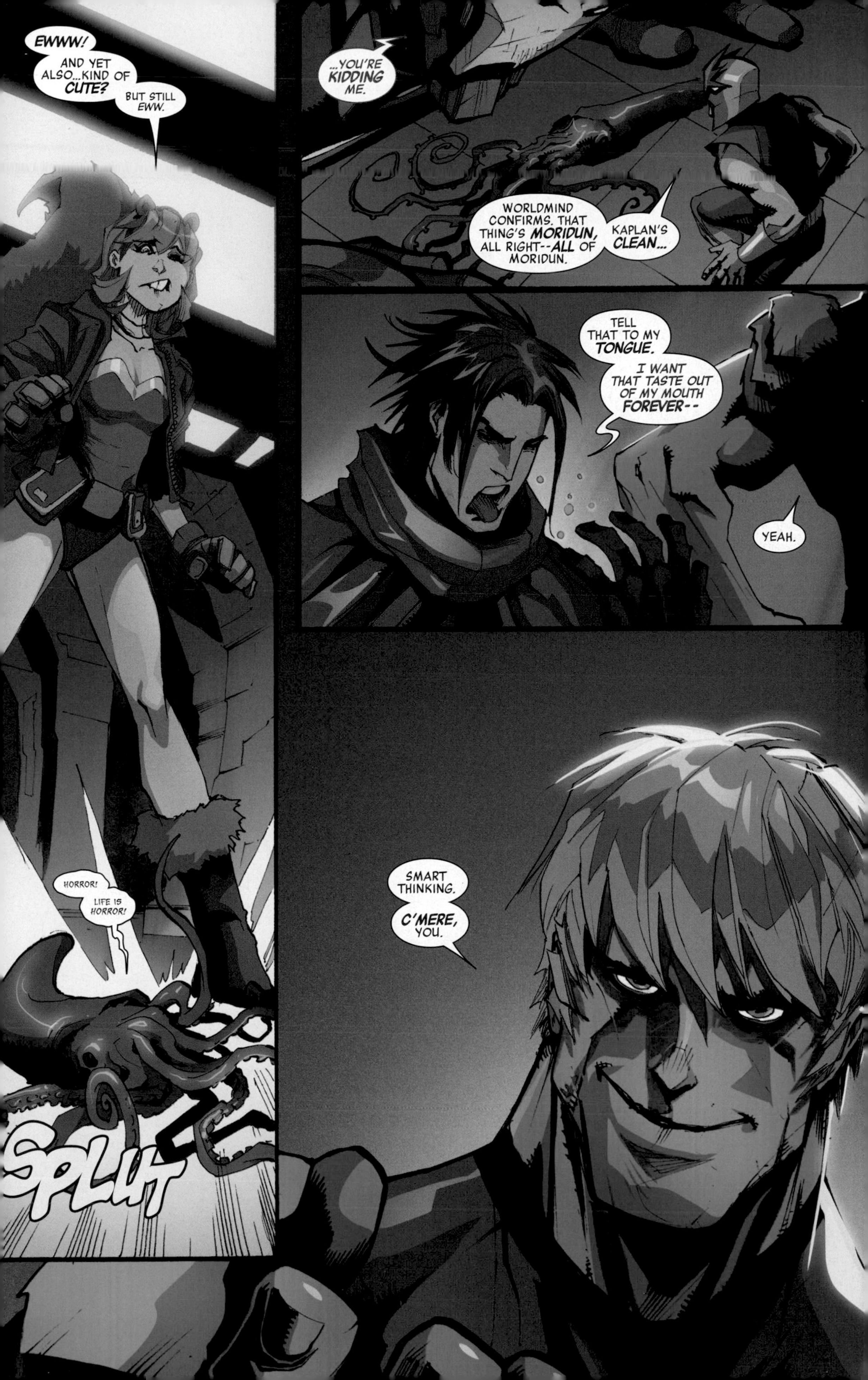
EWWW!
AND YET ALSO...KIND OF CUTE?
BUT STILL EWW.
HORROR!
LIFE IS HORROR!
SPLUT
...YOU'RE KIDDING ME.
WORLDMIND CONFIRMS. THAT THING'S MORIDUN, ALL RIGHT--ALL OF MORIDUN.
KAPLAN'S CLEAN...
TELL THAT TO MY TONGUE.
I WANT THAT TASTE OUT OF MY MOUTH FOREVER--
YEAH.
SMART THINKING.
C'MERE, YOU.

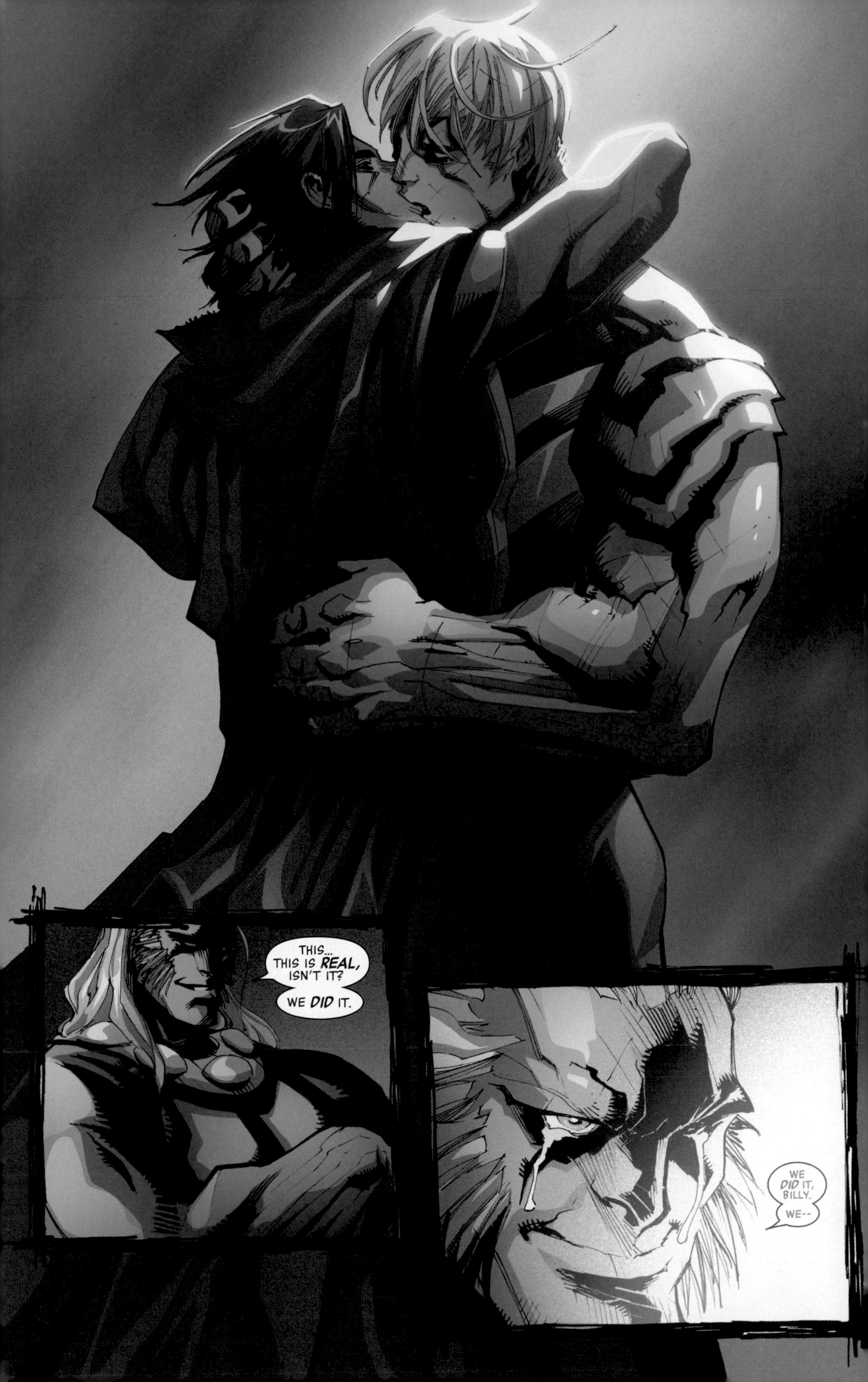
THIS... THIS IS REAL, ISN'T IT?
WE DID IT.
WE DID IT, BILLY.
WE--

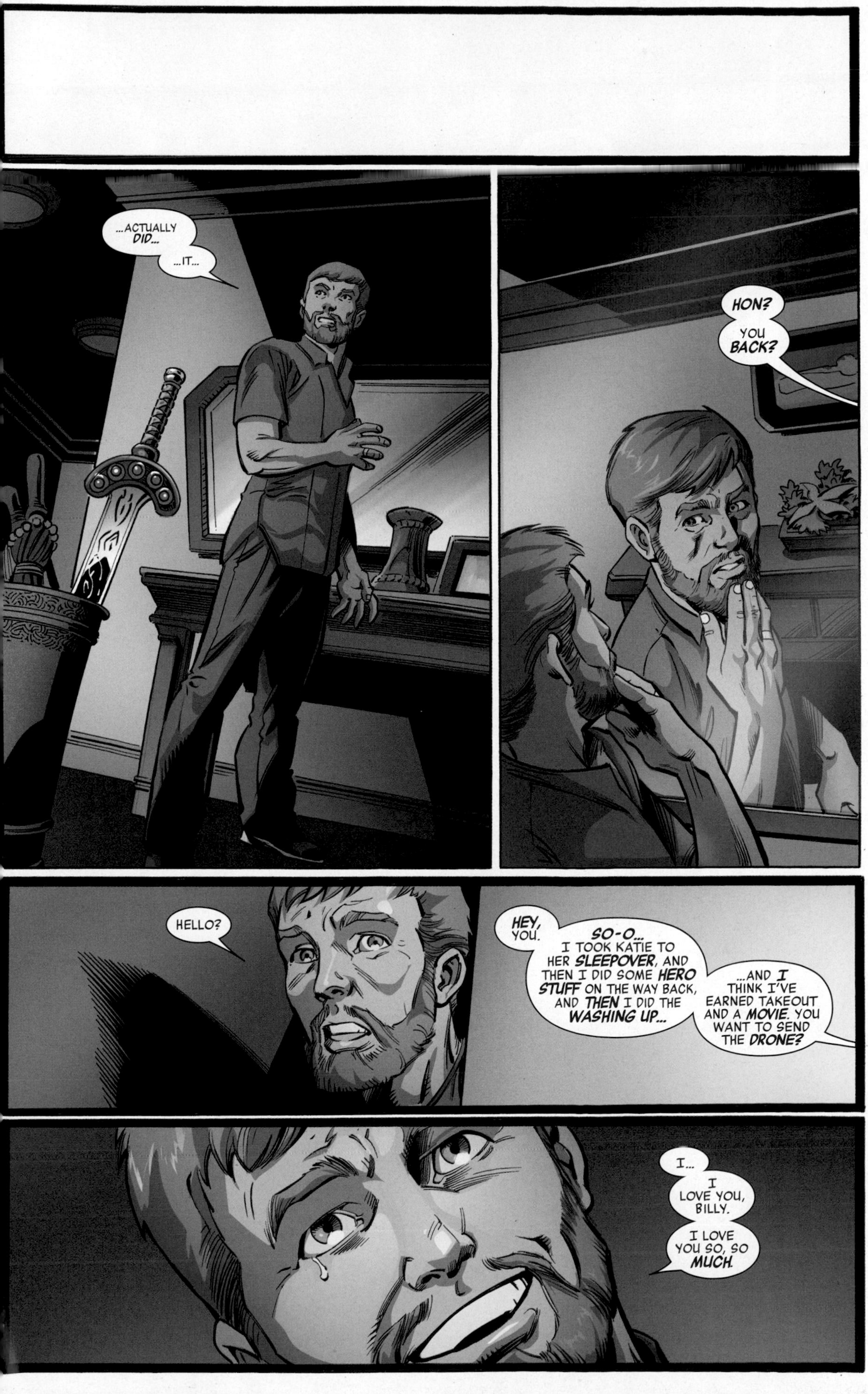
...ACTUALLY DID...
...IT...
HON?
YOU BACK?
HELLO?
HEY, YOU.
SO-O... I TOOK KATIE TO HER SLEEPOVER, AND THEN I DID SOME HERO STUFF ON THE WAY BACK, AND THEN I DID THE WASHING UP...
...AND I THINK I'VE EARNED TAKEOUT AND A MOVIE. YOU WANT TO SEND THE DRONE?
I...
I LOVE YOU, BILLY.
I LOVE YOU SO, SO MUCH.

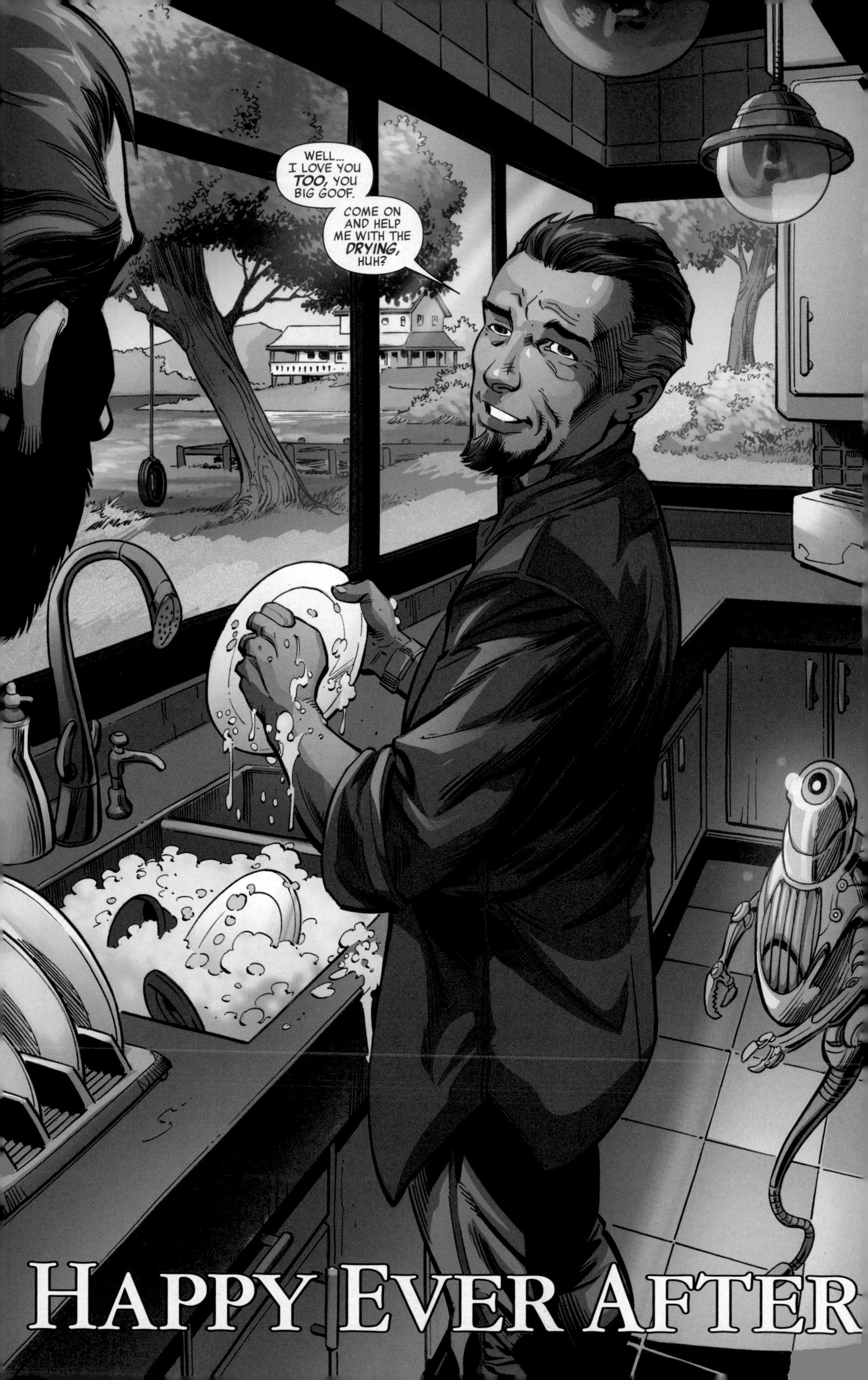
WELL... I LOVE YOU TOO, YOU BIG GOOF.
COME ON AND HELP ME WITH THE DRYING, HUH?
HAPPY EVER AFTER

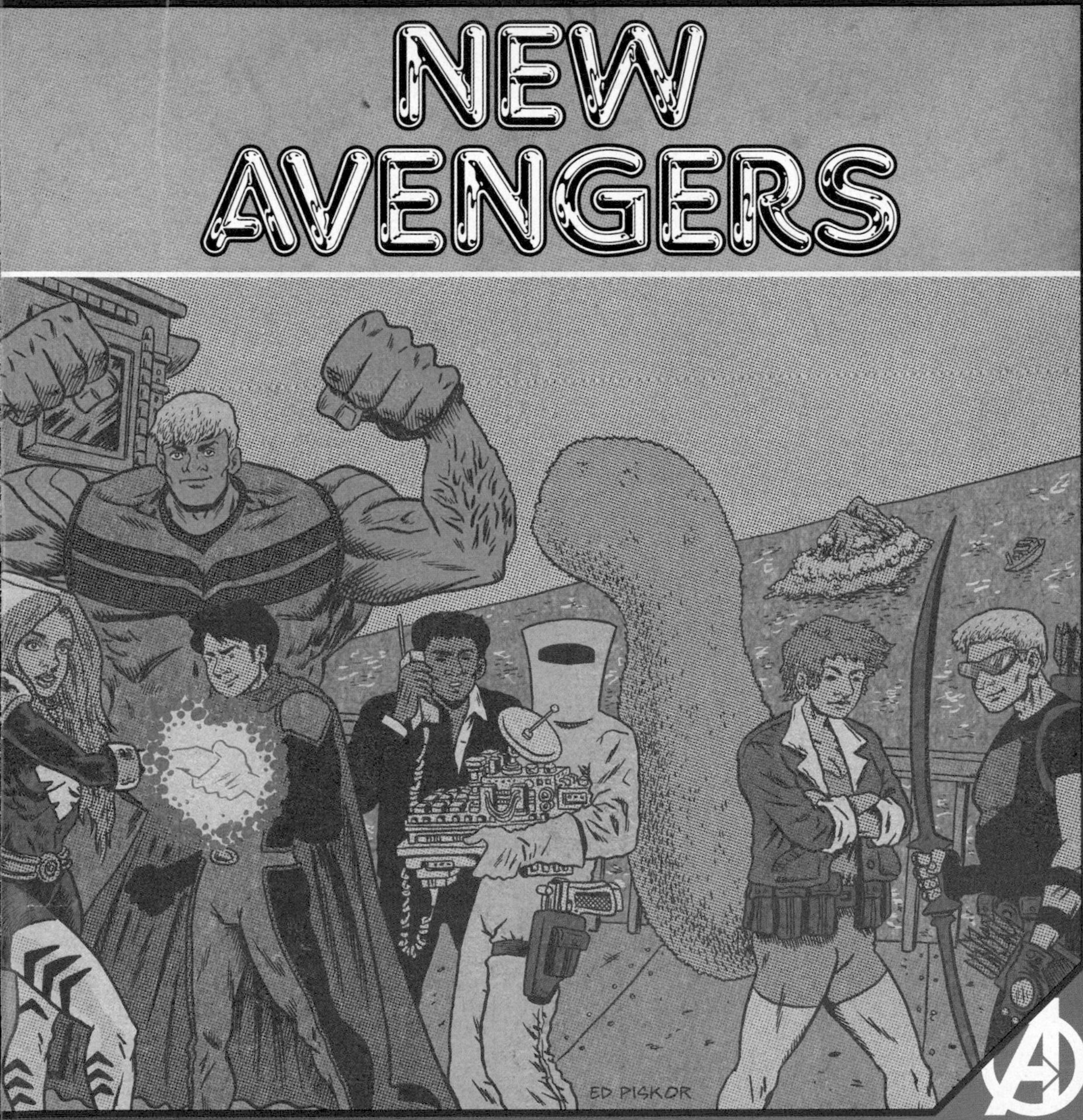
NEW
AVENGERS
ED PISKOR

#1 HIP-HOP VARIANT BY **ED PISKOR**